# The Sociology of Mennonites, Hutterites & Amish

A Bibliography with Annotations
Volume II 1977-1990

## Donovan E. Smucker

*Wilfrid Laurier University Press*

Canadian Cataloguing in Publication Data

Smucker, Donovan E., 1915-
  The sociology of Mennonites, Hutterites and Amish :
a bibliography with annotations volume II, 1977-1990

Vol. I (1977) published under title: The sociology
of Canadian Mennonites, Hutterites and Amish.
Includes index.
ISBN 0-88920-999-5 (v. 2)

1. Mennonites – Canada – Bibliography.   2. Mennonites –
United States – Bibliography.   3. Hutterite Brethren –
Canada – Bibliography.   4. Hutterite Brethren – United
States – Bibliography.   5. Amish – Canada – Bibliography.
6. Amish – United States –Bibliography.
I. Title.   II. Title: The sociology of Canadian
Mennonites, Hutterites and Amish.

Z7845.M4S59 1991      016.3056'87071      C90-095531-7

Copyright © 1991
Wilfrid Laurier University Press
Waterloo, Ontario, Canada
N2L 3C5


Cover design by Leslie Macredie

Printed in Canada

*The Sociology of Mennonites, Hutterites and Amish: A Bibliography with Annotations, Volume II,
1977-1990* has been produced from a manuscript supplied in electronic form by the
author.

*To*

*Christian Smucker I,*

*my great-great-great-great grandfather*

*who migrated from Montbéliard, France*

*to Reading, Pennsylvania in 1752*

*seeking freedom to live the Amish way*

*of life. His many descendants now live*

*in Ontario, Pennsylvania and Ohio.*

# Contents

# Preface and Acknowledgements

The publication of *The Sociology of Canadian Mennonites, Hutterites and Amish* by the Wilfrid Laurier University Press in 1977 reflected both a scholarly trend and, at the same time, met a real need. It reflected the enormous expansion of scholarly publications in social sciences dealing with the communal Hutterites, the semi-communal Amish and the highly varied Mennonites, plain and/or progressive. The book met a need, providing an annotated bibliography which printed descriptive and critical comments on nearly 800 items: books, graduate dissertations, articles and unpublished monographs. Now the person studying these three groups had real help in working through the large array of materials provided by the universities where the research was focused.

Canadian universities have dominated the research dealing with the Hutterites because the largest number of colonies are in Alberta, Manitoba and Saskatchewan, with smaller numbers just south of these provinces in South Dakota, Montana and North Dakota. American graduate schools are the leading researchers on the Amish communities because of the large number of Amish clusters in Ohio, Pennsylvania, Indiana, Illinois, and Kansas.

Studies of Mennonites take place in both nations. The Swiss Mennonites are dominant in the U.S.; the 1874 migrants from Russia are most numerous in the American Mid-West, but most of the 20,000 Mennonites who left the Soviet Union in 1924 after the Revolution came to Canada where they quickly became solid members of both urban and rural communities.

The 1977 book, now out of print, received many favourable reviews as a valuable new tool for sociologists. Meanwhile, another decade of vigorous research has taken place. Unlike the fragile and unstable hippie communes, the Hutterites are the oldest Western communal society in the world, showing remarkable ability to select by group decision any changes in their lifestyle — selective acculturation. Although assailed by creeping tourism, the Amish, too, are surviving very well, always moving to new communities, a step ahead of encroaching urbanism. The Amish Historical Library at Aylmer, Ontario now provides help to the outside scholars who need assistance in their research. The plain people, who are not Amish or Hutterite, have a horse and buggy group mainly in Canada called Old Order Mennonites, a somewhat more progressive version of the Amish with church buildings instead of house churches but the same restraint on technology and education. Now the progressive Mennonites are studying themselves as they live in many urban communities without assimilation. In 1988-1989 a huge new church member survey of the "progressives" was undertaken by their sociologists in the U.S. and Canada.

Thus, it is necessary to publish a second volume reflecting the ten years of research undertaken since the first volume.

The research was made possible by grants from the University of Waterloo research office, Conrad Grebel College, the Heritage Science division of the Canada Council. Canada provides excellent support for scholarly research.

Throughout the two years of work on this book I have had excellent research assistants: Carol Penner, Lucille Marr, Julian Fauth, and especially Debbie Fast. Their help was crucial. The typing of this complex manuscript was done by Rosemary Smith and Katie Hamm of the Conrad Grebel College, and Lenora Zacharias of Richmond, B.C.

Calvin Redekop, my colleague in Waterloo, also read the manuscript, contributed valuable advice all along the way, while writing several key notations.

My thanks to librarian Sam Steiner of Conrad Grebel, the University of Waterloo librarians, and the reference library of the University of British Columbia for helping to procure hundreds of items including many inter-library loans.

Because the focus of the research and the location of the researchers were bi-national in both the U.S. and Canada we have named the second volume, *The Sociology of Mennonites, Hutterites and Amish.*

For Volume II of this annotated bibliography, the editor has concentrated on the thirteen years from 1977 to 1990. Yet the reader will note some items published prior to 1977. These books, theses and articles were not available to us when the first volume was prepared. They have been added as exceptions to the 1977-1989 period in order to make this volume more valuable by making it more complete.

This book has been published with the help of a grant from the Social Science Federation of Canada, using funds provided by the Social Sciences and Humanities Research Council of Canada.

*June 1990*                                                      *Donovan E. Smucker*

# Introduction:
# The Sociology of Mennonites,
# Hutterites and Amish

This book provides an annotated survey and analysis of the sociological literature concerning three sectarian religious groups: the highly varied Mennonites, the communal Hutterites and the semi-communal anti-industrial Amish.

The publishing event of the eighties for students of religious life and thought was the great sixteen volume *Encyclopedia of Religion* edited by the late Mircea Eliade of the University of Chicago who utilized a multidimensional approach to religion. He assembled a remarkable international team from East and West, North and South using phenomenological comparative, sociological and psychological tools to examine the "great traditions" (Hinduism, Buddhism, Judaism, Christianity and Islam) and the "small traditions" in traditional African societies, Australian aboriginals, mesoAmericans and many others.

Robert Nisbet's article on the sociology of religion in Eliade noted that we have passed beyond the old controversies and that "the sociological interest in religion is as great today as it has ever been during the past two centuries." He saw "no reason to suppose that the close relation between religion and sociology, now close to two centuries old, will dissolve soon" (p. 391).

Near the end of this paper we will return to Eliade's monumental work to recognize the many ways in which it confirms the vigour of the research on sectarian religion, including the three studied in this book: Mennonites, Hutterites and Amish. Further attention will be drawn to the durability of the typology developed by Weber and Troeltsch, a typology expanded here and there, but definitely not abandoned. Finally, we will note the international nature of the research using the church-sect typology.

## Origins of Mennonites, Hutterites and Amish

The Mennonite and Hutterite groups emerged from the radical left wing of the sixteenth-century Reformation. The harsh response from the state churches forced them to change from sub-cultures to counter-cultures. Migration to the American colonies and Canada was an attractive alternative prior to the development of religious toleration in Europe.

The Amish defected from the Mennonites in the late seventeenth and early eighteenth century after 172 years. They wanted a tighter and tougher set of restraints against compromise and change. The freedom of North America permitted each group to follow its deepest sense of vocation and direction with a complex differing set of institutional patterns in religion, economics and culture. Consider, now, a brief summary of origins of each group.

The Anabaptist (re-baptizer) Mennonites originated in Switzerland in 1525, advocating separation of church and state, voluntary church membership based on free choice through adult baptism, rejection of military service and de-emphasis on sacramentalism. Persecution, including the death penalty, was the response of the established state churches. Holland was the first country to halt the persecution of Anabaptist-Mennonites. The hostility of the European Catholic and Protestant churches created the urge to migrate to the American colonies, leading to to the first migration in 1684. From these migrants in the American colonies came the first movement to Canada by covered wagons in 1805. Religious freedom in the U.S. and in Canada permitted the Mennonites to develop both conservative and progressive conferences. Later immigration established an ethnic division between the Swiss-South German groups and those of Dutch-Prussian background.

The Amish split from the Mennonites in Europe in 1697, with the earliest Amish migration to America taking place in 1727. In Canada, the Amish migrated directly from Germany in 1821. From that day to this, the Amish and Mennonites tend to live side by side in Pennsylvania, Indiana, Ohio and Ontario; the U.S. Amish outnumber the Canadian by thirty-three to one.

The Amish institutionalized austerity in every possible way by retaining the costume of the seventeenth-century German Black Forest, developing labour-intensive agriculture and, later, rejecting cars, tractors and electricity in house and barn, dropping out of school after the eighth grade, and boycotting all entitlements under Social Security. With individual ownership of land and home, they stand between the Mennonites and the Hutterites, linked by many networks of mutual aid in a semi-communal society with unlimited liability for the needs of the neighbour in the event of fire, sickness or natural disaster. Family *freundschafts* are tightly linked in house churches and the close proximity of kinship networks.

The Hutterian Brethren spread from Switzerland to Austria in 1527. Harsh repression led them to Moravia, where the nobles were more tolerant. There Jacob Hutter, in 1833, taught an understanding of Christian faith which included community of goods and services, and communal arrangements for the care and nurture of children, yet the retention of identity with the natural family. After a three-country odyssey, the Hutterites migrated from Russia to the Dakotas in 1874. During serious conflicts with American nationalism and militarism in World War I, many Hutterites moved to Canada. After the war, some returned but many remained, giving present-day Canada the largest number of Hutterite colonies.

Meanwhile, the progressive Hutterian Brethren, originally inspired by Aberhard Arnold of the Student Christian movement in Germany, have established five *Bruderhofs* in New York, Connecticut and Pennsylvania. They have a community of goods but permit advanced education and classical music. They have a publishing industry, including a journal called *The Plough*, available at Ulster Park, N.Y. 12487.

The Mennonites, Hutterites and Amish are sturdy dissenters and nonconformists more firmly established in North America than any other place in the world. The survival and even the expansion of the Hutterites make it a resilient, utopian, communal society — all this after 463 years! Other utopian communities of North America — now extinct — are dramatic proof of something very durable about the Hutterites.

John Hostetler has reminded us that the Amish are remarkably stable with no more defections than any voluntary association of substance in our society. The Mennonites are a leading peace church with a peace and service program which is a model of creativity and support, operating in fifty-five countries of the world with several thousand volunteers. A rich array of educational, cultural, health and economic institutions require advanced education.

Thus, seeing the origins four centuries ago for the Mennonites and Hutterites, and three centuries for the Amish, the question is *how* to study these three religious societies. It is good to report that several distinguished scholars showed genuine creativity in developing the church-sect typology.

## Weber and Troeltsch Come to America Bearing the Key to Sectarian Research

At the turn of the twentieth century, Max Weber and Ernst Troeltsch were colleagues, friends and neighbours at the University of Heidelberg. Both were the kind of towering academic figures in lecture hall and publishing house, which the Germans dearly loved. There were slight differences in fields with law, economics, politics and sociology for Weber; history, theology and sociology for Troeltsch.

Troeltsch's architectonic sweep in his 1,000-page two-volume classic, *The Social Teaching of the Christian Churches* (1911 in German, 1931 English translation by Olive Wyon) was acknowledge by Weber in the last footnote of his *Protestant Ethic and the Spirit of Capitalism* for "disposing of things I should have had to investigate in a way which I, not being a theologian could not have done; but partly in order to correct the isolation of this study and to place it in the whole of cultural development."[1]

The amazing development in the partnership of Weber and Troeltsch was their decision to travel to America together in 1905.[2] They had been invited to address "The Scientific World Congress" organized by Professor Hugo Munsterberg in connection with the World's Fair in St. Louis. After discovering the major German community in St. Louis, the two colleagues travelled at length through the southern and eastern states. Their lectures and visits planted in America the church-sect-mystic typology and Weber's highly original reading of the inner-worldly asceticism of the neo-Calvinist formulators of the Protestant ethic: piety, austerity, thrift, hard work, study and aggressive approach to the markets.

A characteristic definition of church and sect by Troeltsch is the following from the Social Teachings,

The *Church* is the holy institution and the institution of grace, endowed with the effect and result of the work of redemption. It can absorb the masses and adapt itself to the world, since, up to a certain point, it can neglect subjective holiness in exchange for the objective treasures of grace and redemption. The *Sect* is the free association of Christians who are stronger and more conscious of their faith. They join together as the truly reborn, separate themselves from the world, remain limited to a small circle, emphasize the law instead of grace, and in their ranks set up love as the Christian order of life with greater or lesser radicalism. All of this is regarded as the preparation for and the expectation of the coming Kingdom of God. *Mysticism* is the intensification and the subjectivization of the thoughts and ideas that have become solidified in cult and doctrine so that they are a purely personal and inner possession of the heart. Under its auspices only fluid and completely personally limited groups can assemble. What remains in them of cult, dogma, and connection with history tends to become so fluid that it disappears.[3]

Troeltsch provided an important place for the sects in the grand sweep of Christian culture. His visit to America made it even clearer that ascetic Protestantism in Puritanism and separatist Protestantism among the Mennonites were worthy of careful analysis.

(a) Troeltsch said that "the days of the pure church-type within our present civilization were numbered"[4] because the civil power no longer-could coerce religious unity.

(b) He also argued that "more and more the central life of the church-type is being permeated with the vital energies of the sect and mysticism."[5]

1. Max Weber, *Protestant Ethic and the Spirit of Capitalism* (London: George Allen and Unwin, 1974), p. 243.
2. Wilhelm Pauck, *Harnack and Troeltsch* (New York: Oxford, 1968), p. 71.
3. Ernst Troeltsch, *The Social Teaching of the Christian Church* (London: George Allen and Unwin, 1950), vol. 2, p. 993.
4. Ibid., p. 1107.
5. Ibid., p. 1108.

(c) Troeltsch saw the church, sect and mystical types as proximate neighbours, writing that "from the beginning these forms were foreshadowed, and all down the centuries to the present day, wherever religion is dominant, they still appear alongside of one another, while among themselves they are strangely and variously interwoven and interconnected."[6]

Suffering from public indifference and ignorance, the sects were rescued from irrelevance by Troeltsch and were given an important role as a small catalytic agent working next to the biggest church establishments.[7]

The place where Troeltsch complemented Weber was his analysis of neo-Calvinism in Puritanism, "Precisionism" in the Netherlands and Pietism on the Lower Rhine and Switzerland. The ethic of neo-Calvinism, he affirmed was fused with the ethic of bourgeois sect-type. The result of this fusion was the rise of a collective group of ascetic Protestantism. In Weber, this was called inner-worldly asceticism, a major causal factor in the rise of capitalism after the decline of the medieval Catholic synthesis.[8]

Weber's *Protestant Ethic* utilizes these concepts but with a much narrower focus on the rise of capitalism which gave the *calling* to business a new sanctity as worldly asceticism. Lady Poverty had been medieval Catholicism's model of piety but now money-making and piety were united in the godly businessman. Wesley said it: Make all you can. Save all you can. Give all you can.

But Weber's seminal work did not overlook the Mennonites or the Quakers. There are eight references to each of these sectarian groups in the *Protestant Ethics* There are ten citations from Troeltsch's *magnum opus*. Weber used the phrase the sectarians liked, "the believers church." One of Weber's final chapters was on the Baptist sects which he calls the second independent source of Protestant asceticism. He referred especially to the Mennonites, Quakers and, above all, the Baptists. Weber's high regard for the sects is seen in his likening them to the radicalism of St. Francis in rejecting sensual delights. Weber believes that the emphasis on the Holy Spirit was going to loosen up these rigorous Christians being tempted in the capitalist Garden by the apple of business. He does not seem to be aware of the Hutterites or the Amish separatism.

In any case, between Weber and Troeltsch the church-sect typology provided a key for research. As the progressive Mennonites became edu-

---

6. Ibid., p. 993.
7. The vigour of Troeltschian scholarship is quite remarkable. Bradley Edwin Starr wrote a Ph.D. dissertation at Claremont in 1987 on "Max Weber and Ernst Troeltsch on Religion, Theology and the Ethic of Responsibility"; Robert Rubanowice with a foreword by James Luther Adams, *Crisis in Conscience: The Thought of Ernst Troeltsch* (Florida State Press, 1982); and Pauck's *Harnack and Troeltsch* contains a chapter on Troeltsch and Max Weber. Toshimasa Yasuka, *Ernst Troeltsch: Systematic Theologian of Radical Historicality* (Atlanta: Scholars Press, 1986).
8. Roy Wallis edited a book of essays on *Sectarianism, Analyses of Religious and Non-Religious Sects* (New York: John Wiley, 1975) which follows the Weber-Troeltsch definition but focuses on new religions like Aetherius society, Krishna, Scientology, Maoists and DeLeonists, Recovery Inc. and Neurotics Nomine.

cated, professionalized and urbanized, Weber's inner-worldly asceticism[9] became a very rich part of the typology. Inevitably, scholars inside and outside the Mennonite Community began applying, revising and expanding this classic typology.

## Richard Niebuhr Starts with a Neo-Marxist Class Analysis and then Delineates an Elaboration of Weber and Troeltsch

In 1924, Richard Niebuhr wrote his doctoral dissertation at Yale on Troeltsch. Five years later the Yale Press published his neo-Marxist class analysis of the sects and denominations, titled, *The Social Sources of Denominationalism.* Here the sects are rooted in the revolt of the poor, the disenfranchised, the underprivileged who form religious conflict societies. The book was full of original research and excellent insights. But, after the complexity and scope of Troeltsch, Niebuhr needed to expand and enlarge on Troeltsch in a manner which went beyond the neo-Marxist class analysis.[10] The result was the masterpiece of his career—*Christ and Culture* (New York: Harper, 1951). Culture, Niebuhr says, is the total process of human activity. Or, culture is the artificial secondary environment imposed on the natural. The Bible labels culture as "the world."

There are five answers among Christians: (1) Christ against culture—the sectarian answer; (2) The Christ of culture—the liberal answer; (3) Christ above culture—the middle answer; (4) Christ and culture in paradox—the dualist answer; and (5) Christ the transformer of culture—the activist reformist answer.

Neibuhr called the sectarian answer "necessary" but "inadequate." Necessary, because culture frequently needs opposition and criticism. Inadequate, because it is irresponsible in the name of perfection.[11]

---

9. See Kenneth Davis, *Anabaptism and Asceticism* (Scottdale: Herald Press, 1974) for the linkage between Anabaptist leaders and their earlier Catholic, often monastic asceticism.
10. Werner Glock, *The Sociology of Religion: A Study of Christendom*, Vol. 2: *Sectarian Religion* (London: Routledge and Kegan Paul, 1967) is the first book using the Weber-Troeltsch typology in a volume wholly devoted to sectarian religion: *Origins, Nature, Variety and Decay* is a little-known major contribution (357 pp.). Also see Rodney Sawatsky, *Authority and Identity: The Dynamics of the General Conference Mennonite Church* (1987) for a rejection of Niebuhr's attempt to label sectarians as necessarily *against* culture because culture is ubiquitous, sin is omnipresent, the dynamics of missionary outreach and the heterogenicity of contemporary Mennonites.
11. From the Graduate Theological Union in Berkeley, Charles Scrivener has enlivened the debate on sectarian religion with his new book *The Transformation of Culture: Christian Social Ethics* (Scottdale: Herald Press, 1988). Scriven argues that the Anabaptists are the answer to Niebuhr by providing both a non-violent alternative society and a transformational example.

## Marxists in the Eastern Bloc Discover the Anabaptists as Crypto-Communists

Abraham Friesen of the University of California, Santa Barbara, spent two years in Europe studying the Marxist interpretation of the sectarian, radical Reformation of the Anabaptists. After surveying Engels and Zimmerman in the nineteenth century, he analyzed Ernst Bloch, East German Marxist scholar, who has been open to dialogue from all sides. Bloch wanted to claim a crypto-communist dimension of the left-wing Protestants known as Anabaptists. Lurking in the background was the Peasants war which had a strong populist ring to it and then in the left wing of the left wing were the hysterial apocalyptic followers of Thomas Muntzer who loathed religious and political aspects of the establishment.

Friesen's book was entitled *Reformation and Utopia: The Marxist Interpretation of the Reformation and Its Antecedents* (Wiesbaden, 1974).

While the Anabaptists were revolting against the militaristic and nationalistic territorial churches, Catholic and Protestant, Friesen found the Marxist conceptualization did not fit the facts. Friesen and Paul Peachey who did a doctoral dissertation in Zurich on the same social background of the sixteenth-century Anabaptists, summarized his research in *The Mennonite Encyclopedia* (Vol. 4, pp. 558-60) and concluded that the classical economic disinheritance theory must be set aside because of the genuine dominance of the religious quest among the Anabaptists for a totally new conception of a free, voluntary church which eventually would seek a free society.

But, at least, the Marxists saw that the caesaro-papism which sought a conservative theocratic state was not the only model which the Christian faith could support. There was also the Anabaptist vision which was in many ways a prophetic forerunner of the democratic pluralism, toleration and separation of church and state.

## Redekop Leads the Mennonite Sociologists in Revision of Troeltsch-Weber

Yinger helped when he labelled a more sophisticated version of the Mennonites and other sects as "established sects." Bryan Wilson of the United Kingdom developed a new typology of sects: conversionist, introversionist, adventist, and gnostic. The Park and Burgess Chicago school suggested that there is a sect cycle, from pure beginnings to gradual assimilation.

It remained for Calvin W. Redekop, the Chicago-trained senior Mennonite sociologist at Conrad Grebel College, University of Waterloo, to argue in the *Journal for the Scientific Study of Religion* that the early Reformation studies analyzed radical sects operating in a hostile environment, whereas recent studies dealt with nonradical sects in a tolerant environment (Ontario, for example, permits the Old Order people to have parochial schools taught by uncertified teachers).

Redekop concludes that sect development involves a dialectical process between sect and host society. "To use a word," Redekop declared, "to refer to a religious group requires a specification as to where it is in history. One should know the history of a particular sect before it can be meaningfully placed within a classification scheme."[12]

Thus, historical context is needed with the sociological analytic when using the church-sect typology. Meanwhile, the Mennonite sociologists have an excellent record: John Hostetler studying Amish and Hutterites; Redekop with a large output of publications covering Paraguay, Mexico, U.S. and Canada; Leo Driedger with many important articles; Leland Harder and Howard Kaufman who guided the largest empirical study ever made of North American Mennonites; J. Winfield Fretz who was the second American Mennonite sociologist after the pioneering study of the sect cycle by Edmund Kaufman in 1937 at Chicago. Fretz followed Kaufman in a doctoral study ten years later in 1941. In 1989, he climaxed a long career by a definitive, comprehensive study of the sixteen Mennonite, Amish and Hutterite communities in Waterloo County, Ontario.

## The Eliade Encyclopedia Confirms the Vigour
## and Range of Sectarian Research

Michael Hill of Victoria University in New Zealand wrote the six-page article on sects which builds on Weber and Troeltsch. He quotes with approval Bryan Wilson's definition of the sect:

Typically a sect may be identified by the following characteristics: it is a voluntary association; membership is by proof to sect authorities of some claim to personal merit — such as knowledge of doctrine, affirmation of a conversion experience, or recommendation of members in good standing; exclusiveness is emphasized, and expulsion exercised against those who contravene doctrinal, moral or organizational precepts; its self-conception is of an elect, a gathered remnant, possessing special enlightenment; personal perfection is the expected standard of aspiration, in whatever terms this is judged; it accepts, at least as an ideal, the priesthood of all believers; there is a high level of lay participation; there is opportunity for the member spontaneously to express his commitment; the sect is hostile or indifferent to the secular society and to the state.[13]

Hill makes much of the different sub-types of sects, drawing upon Becker, Yinger, Niebuhr, Wilson, Wach and Beckford. On this basis the Amish and Hutterites would be introversionists and the progressive Mennonites "an established sect." Hill is also aware that churches can have sectarian enclaves *within* the church.

There is a vigorous debate concerning the term "cult." Hill is inclined to retain the term as sects which make a sharper break from the dominant

12. Calvin Redekop, "A New Look at Sect Development," *Journal for the Scientific Study of Religion*, 13:3 (Sept. 1974).
13. Mircea Eliade, *The Encyclopedia of Religion* (New York: Macmillan, 1987), Vol. 13, p.157.

religious tradition. James Beckford of the University of Durham urges the reader to abandon the term "cult" for "new religions," warning us that the variety of new religions defies the selection of a single all-purpose term.

Winthrop S. Hudson of North Carolina, Chapel Hill, wrote with conviction against confusing the term "denomination" with "sect." Sect is exclusive; denomination is inclusive showing mutual respect and recognition.

Along with the struggle for definitional clarity and theoretical formulations to assist comparisons and classification, the Eliade tome reveals the attention paid by leading scholars to the Mennonites, Hutterites and Amish. There are five notices of Mennonites, seven comments on the Amish and three on the Hutterites, with a key article by William M. Kephart of the University of Pennsylvania. The eight pieces on sects are excellent; the thirty-three citations and analyses of Max Weber top the list. Second are the fourteen references to Ernst Troeltsch.

Cornelius J. Dyck's essay on Mennonites concedes the presence of a church-world dualism from the beginning but notes relief and service activities in fifty-five countries as "legitimizing the social significance and usefulness of a traditionally pacifist and persecuted people." Hence the dualism is highly qualified.

In what will be the definite encyclopedia of religion for many years, part of the international community of scholars is focusing on sectarian research, with some version of the Weber-Troeltsch typology, along with enormous array of issues, subjects, types and patterns of religion, including those of the Mennonites, Amish and Hutterites.

It is well to add a final asset of Eliade's sixteen volumes: every article is followed by a superb bibliography, permitting comparison and follow-up.

## Conclusion

Under the microscopic scrutiny of scholars and field observers, under the theoretical framework provided by Troeltsch, Weber and their followers like Niebuhr, Wilson, Yinger, Redekop, Park and Burgess, the Mennonite and Amish and Hutterite situations look like this:

(1) The Amish have demonstrated the most effective resistance of any group in North America to the main trends in our society. On school attendance, they have defied government authority and then won their case before the U.S. Supreme Court. In wartime, they maintained an impressive resistance to military service. They have kept mechanization at bay. Above all, their unique costume, buggies, folkways and rural practices have created a symbolic interaction of the highest order. To be Amish is to be colourfully, visibly, and appealingly non-conformist. Alas, this is so true that hordes of tourists swoop down on the Amish in Lancaster, Pennsylvania; Nappanee, Indiana; and to a lesser extent Elmira-Waterloo, Ontario.

Thomas Foster of Ohio State, Mansfield, sees some external threats to their existence:[14] partial accommodation to work in small factories in small towns; carpentry work taking them off the farm; cottage industry employment; and resistance to government mandates in health care and schools. Finally, there is the rising cost and growing scarcity of farmland and the continuing high birth rate.

Yet the Amish have shown remarkable strength under strain and stress and they have outstanding leaders like Joseph Stoll and David Luthy, a graduate of Notre Dame and a converted Amish member who has brought outstanding skills in writing, publishing and archival collections to the group. Stoll and Luthy both live in rural Aylmer, Ontario.

(2) The Hutterites have expanded in North America from three colonies in 1874 to 300 colonies and 30,000 members today (250 colonies in Canada). They are the oldest, most durable, most successful communal utopian society in North America. They are not technologically conservative as are the Amish.

Their secret is controlled, selective acculturation. Social change takes place but it is managed by a corporate decision. They twice have lost the communal pattern of ownership and then recovered it. They have altered their farming from mixed to one or two main crops plus chickens, hogs and cattle. They have a very high birth rate, yet make enough profit from their collective farms to finance expensive new technology and the vans used for their own transportation.

Fundamentalist Christians have made some inroads among their groups and their most trusted friends among the Mennonites have counselled them to have a more spirited worship service to lessen the vulnerability to charismatic Protestants on the outside.

Yet there is no doubt that the Hutterites have a creative, workable social system resembling the Central European nucleated village, sound patterns of conflict resolution, a tested pattern of colonization for new communities, a family system which mixes collective nurture of children with real but limited living in the family apartment at night, conservationist agriculture and a cautious but genuine reaching out to the larger world as in the *Festival* multicultural program in Manitoba.

Meanwhile, there are a growing number of genetic and mental health studies of the Hutterites as the most inbred group in North America. Harvard, Johns Hopkins and Wisconsin universities are leaders in Hutterite genetic research.

Visitors to the colonies are always amazed at the mix of agri-business — large scale, mechanized farming — and the uniquely communitarian, patriarchal society connected with it — a paradox indeed.

(3) The Mennonite predicament is the most complex of the three. There are educated, professionalized, affluent Mennonites, conservative Mennonites who still wear plain clothes, restrain education but drive cars

---

14. See his articles on pages 163-64.

and tractors, and use electricity, and there are Old Order Mennonites who differ from the Amish only by the absence of beards and the use of plain, austere church buildings instead of the Amish house church. Transportation is by horse and buggy.

Particularly in Canada, the progressive Mennonites are now dominantly urban and have operated in the free market, with the Protestant ethic leading to large incomes. If one multiplies the number of Mennonites in Canada by the per capita income of $13,350, total Mennonite income is $1,295,000,000 per year. The 323,000 members in the U.S. multiplied by a per capita income of $13,850 gives a total income of $3,427,000,000 per year. The latest research indicates that North American Mennonites contribute 6.6 of their income to all causes sponsored by the church. The total giving in both countries thus is $292,000,000 per year.[15]

This kind of wealth and philanthropy among sectarians invites the formulations of Max Weber and R. H. Tawney concerning the Protestant ethic. Consequently, the Mennonite scholars held a major conference on Mennonites and economic life at the University of Waterloo in the spring of 1990. The relation between the billions in income and millions in giving very likely indicates that Weber's intra-mundane asceticism has replaced the separatist, anti-mundane asceticism of the Amish and conservative Mennonites. The Hutterites require further analysis because they have affluent colonies yet impecunious individuals.

(4) Scholars of religion like Mircea Eliade, Joachim Wach, Emile Durkheim, and C. Van der Leeuw work on such a vast scale studying all religions, in all cultures, in all eras of history that the specific issues posed by our three Christian sectarians may be obscured. On the fly-leaf of Wach's *Sociology of Religion* (Chicago, 1944) is a quote from Ephesians 3:9, "And to make all men see what is the fellowship of the mystery." The sociological scholars are lessening the mystery.

---

15. These figures calculated with assistance from Howard Raid, Professor of Economics, Bluffton College, Ohio.

# I. Bibliographies and Encyclopedias

ANDERSON, ALAN B.

*Ethnic Communities in Saskatchewan: Bibliographic Sources*
Saskatoon Multicultural Council, 1986

This bibliographic report lists over 1000 entries, including books, community histories, research reports and monographs, graduate theses, bibliographies, government documents, archival files, journal articles and special issues, chapters, conference proceedings, and media sources, pertaining (in whole or in part) to ethnic communities within the Province of Saskatchewan. There are 200 Mennonite and Hutterite entries.

BIBBY, REGINALD W.

*Fragmented Gods: The Poverty and Potential of Religion*
Toronto: Irwin, 1987

Ken Westhues of the University of Waterloo sociology department has labelled this book as "the most comprehensive, most factual, most readable, most important book yet published on religion in Canada." Bibby of Lethbridge (Alberta) University is a master of survey research, grounded in solid theology, knowledgeable in history and capable of personal anecdotes.

Basically Bibby is rather negative about the hollow character of Canadian religion which he calls "religion à la carte." The mainline religionists have, in his opinion, capitulated to the culture. But Westhues has pointed out that Bibby is unconvincing when he tries to provide answers for the illness of Canadian religion.

Bibby places the Mennonites with conservative Protestants without taking into account the radical ethical witness of Mennonites against war, statism, and insensitivity to human suffering. On the whole he is not a trustworthy guide to Mennonites, Amish or Hutterites.

The eleven-page bibliography is a very important guide to research in Canada. His look at all the survey data is the best available.

DRIEDGER, LEO

*The Ethnic Factor. Identity in Diversity*
Toronto: McGraw-Hill Ryerson, 1989

Leo Driedger has written thirty articles and four books on ethnicity starting with his University of Chicago master's thesis in 1955 on the Old Colony Mennonites of Saskatchewan. *The Ethnic Factor* climaxes his career in what is likely to be the definitive work on ethnicity with special reference to Canada as a pluralist society. There is a fine balance here between a basic knowledge of theory in the first two chapters and subsequent parts with an encyclopedic grasp of the empirical context and current research. From William McNeill's Toronto lecture Driedger borrows the term polyethnicity, normal in civilized societies, with one ethnically unitary state exceptional in theory and rarely approached in practice. Since the publication of Driedger's book the polyethnic state of the Soviet Union has experienced the intransigence of the ethnic and regional minorities within its borders. The resurgence of French nationalism in Quebec brings the same set of social forces into Canadian life.

Driedger is aware of ethnic solidarity within a heterogenous society, a trend consistent with Weber's multidimensional and comparative analysis. He is realistic in conceding the presence of socio-economic and racial stratification qualifying pretensions of pure equality. Despite social distance, stereotypes, prejudice and discrimination the author believes that the majority of Canadians want to affirm the United Nations and Canadian charters of rights and freedoms in the quest for a pluralist society.

The second edition of this excellent book only needs to grapple with data coming from the current European paradox of national freedom and ethnic rights.

DYCK, CORNELIUS J. and DENNIS D. MARTIN (EDS.)
*The Mennonite Encyclopedia*
5 vols. Hillsboro, Kans.: Mennonite Brethren Publishing House;
Scottdale, Pa.: Herald Press; Newton, Kans.: Mennonite Publications
Office. Vols. 1-4, 1955-59; 2nd ed., 1969-73; Vol. 5, 1990

For thirty years, this massive encyclopedia provided terse, accurate, scholarly summary articles on an amazing variety of topics related to Mennonites, Amish and Hutterites, including a fine array of sociological summaries on wide ranging topics from mutual aid to Hutterite colonies.

The date of publication is 1990 for a completely new fifth volume which will update articles with new information, add topics inadvertently left out of the first four volumes and, in all cases, cite the latest and best bibliography on hundreds of topics. It is a major publishing event which has had the participation of almost every established scholar researching Mennonites.

Six hundred writers contributed 1,400 articles to the new fifth volume, bringing the total number of written pieces in the complete set to 7,000, spread across the 5,000 pages. The editorial management of this new volume was handled by the Institute of Mennonite Studies, the research arm of the Associated Mennonite Biblical Seminaries in Elkhart, Indiana.

ELIADE, MIRCEA
*The Encyclopedia of Religion*
16 vols. New York: Macmillan, 1987

Monumental is the word for this sixteen-volume encyclopedia edited by the late Mircea Eliade, who held professorships in Europe and America. The introductory essays by Eliade, Claude Conyers and Joseph Kitagawa provide the best recent introductions to contemporary multidimensional, international scholarship dealing with religion in its many manifestations. On more specific topics, Michael Hill on Sects, Winston Davis on Sociology and Religion, Seymour Cain on the Study of Religion, Robert Nisbet on Sociology and James Beckford on New Religions are first class.

On the three sectarian groups featured in this book, Cornelius J. Dyck's survey of the Mennonites is superior because he is a Mennonite scholar with comprehensive knowledge of the sixteen varieties of Mennonites; William M. Kephart on the Hutterian Brethren writes a briefer essay. References to the Amish are marginal and disappointing.

All of the articles in the Eliade volumes append helpful bibliographies.

EPP, FRANK, RODNEY J. SAWATSKY and JOHN RYAN
*The Canadian Encyclopedia*
2nd ed. Edmonton: Hurtig Publishers, 1988

Frank H. Epp and Rodney J. Sawatsky of Conrad Grebel College, University of Waterloo, have written the best brief analysis now available of Canadian Mennonites. Early in their survey, they point out that the Mennonites who came to Canada with one of the German dialects were both a religious and an ethnic group. They trace the four waves of migration from the first in the late eighteenth century, to the latest group of 20,000 in the 1920s fleeing the Russian war and revolution. Epp and Sawatsky write with a sure hand about the two types of Mennonites: the Old Orders and the progressives who call their structures "conferences." The central difference is between those who believe that "lives of discipleship in separated communities is the essence of Christian living, and the progressives who insist that penetration of, adaptation to and involvement in the world is essential to the Christian message." The new members of Mennonite churches include French, Chinese, Indian and Anglo-Saxon. Eighty percent of Mennonite marriages in 1981 were mixed.

The authors point out that approximately 10 percent of Mennonite children and young people are in private church schools. Regarding politics, there has been a reversal; a number of Mennonites are now in elected office and many more are active civil servants and public school teachers. Epp and Sawatsky are basically optimistic that strong family life, dynamic youth programs and creative congregations minimize the losses "to the larger secular community."

The authors might well have labelled this obviously durable form of progressive Mennonite culture an "established sect" or a denomination, the latter no longer fully sectarian.

John Ryan contributes a superior essay on the Hutterites, pointing out their rigorous insistence on communal living, starting in Czechoslovakia (Moravia) in 1528. Along with communal living, they stressed non-violence and opposition to war, and adult baptism. Because of persecution, they moved from Czechoslovakia to Hungary, Romania, Tsarist Russia, the U.S. and finally Canada. In 1987, the total Hutterite population was 30,000, 66 percent of whom lived in Manitoba, Alberta and Saskatchewan, while the remainder were in the United States.

They live in rural colonies of about thirteen families, with an average population of eighty-five. Despite the collective nurture of children, each nuclear family has a private apartment in a row house. After the eighth grade 50 percent of the students proceed to grade ten by correspondence courses; and some take special diploma courses in veterinary science or teaching.

The colony is managed by an executive council which is elected by baptized males twenty years and older. Women hold managerial positions in kitchen, kindergarten, purchasing and vegetable production.

Ryan is impressed with their ability to retain their basic beliefs while adopting features of modern life necessary to their economic and social well being. In an interdisciplinary encyclopedia, it would have strengthened Ryan's essay to place the Hutterites in the continuum of utopian and communal societies; and to probe more intensively why the Hutterites span the centuries where other communalists have brief existence.

The Mennonite and Hutterite articles are nevertheless a genuine contribution of the *Canadian Encyclopedia*.

FRIESEN, BERT
*Where We Stand: An Index of Peace and Social Concerns Statements by the Mennonites and Brethren in Christ in Canada (1787-1982)*
Mennonite Central Committee, Winnipeg, Manitoba and Akron, Pa., 1986

For nearly 200 years Mennonites have made formal declarations about their convictions concerning peace and social concerns. It is a valuable record of the church's best thinking on many key issues. This well-researched and well-documented index covers a period of 193 years, from 1787 to 1982. The "peace" content ranges from a biblical understanding on non-resistance to ways of doing alternative service. The "social concerns" content includes topics such as clothing and dress, life insurance, television and relief.

While the purpose of this index is not openly stated, it is clearly a valuable tool for those doing research and study in Mennonite peace and social concerns issues.

FRIESEN, MARK D.
*Mennonite Life Index*
1981-1985

This illustrated journal of Mennonite life has published scores of articles of real merit with photographic illustrations. It also has contained an accurate annual list of theses and dissertations dealing with Mennonite, Amish and Hutterite leaders, communities and social experiences.

GIESBRECHT, HERBERT
*The Mennonite Brethren Church: A Bibliographic Guide*
Board of Christian Literature, General Conference of Mennonite Brethren Churches, Fresno, Calif., 1983

Mennonite Brethren are Russian Mennonites who combine evangelical fervour with an activist stance toward the economic and political institutions of Canada and the U.S. Their scholars have been researching and publishing with special vigour in recent years.

HOSTETLER, JOHN A. and NANCY L. GAINES
*A Bibliography of The Old Order Amish: Sources Available in English*
Philadelphia, Pa.: Communal Studies Center, Temple University, 1984

The definitive list of books, articles, and monographs on the Old Order Amish by the senior researcher in this field serving as co-editor with Nancy Gaines. The Communal Studies Center at Temple University has been a productive ancillary institution to stimulate research dealing with the Old Order people. John Hostetler has unique credentials in addition to advanced degrees in sociology. He was reared in an Amish family and then chose to leave that way of life for secondary and higher education.

JANZEN, WILLIAM
*The Limits of Liberty in Canada: The Experience of The Mennonites, Hutterites and Doukhobors*
Toronto: University of Toronto Press, 1990

This is a revision of Janzen's doctoral dissertation at Carleton University, Ottawa, in 1981. Janzen is director of the Mennonite Central Committee office in the Canadian capital where he represents the concerns of the church on many issues.

It is an important and original study revealing how the civil and religious rights of these three minorities developed in the context of history and society leading to ambiguity and freedom. At times one or another of the three groups rejected government compromise, as in the case of the Doukhobors' negation of Alternative Service and the Hutterite objection to a tax agreement.

Janzen asserts that his study also reveals the flexibility of the Canadian political system, illustrated by Ontario Mennonites in World War I receiving "leave without pay" in lieu of genuine alternative-service status. He concludes that despite unsympathetic attitudes toward the consciences of Mennonites, Hutterites and Doukhobors there was mutual accommodation which provided a significant measure of liberty for the minorities. Repressive societies would appear to be societies with intransigent actions against minorities not open to negotiation. Democratic societies are political entities capable of interaction and compromise between principles and context.

KRAHN, CORNELIUS
*The Mennonites, A Brief Guide to Information*
Newton, Kans.: Faith and Life Press, 1976

A useful thirty-two-page compendium of information about Mennonites, including history, beliefs, geographical spread, witness, service and mission. Included are 200 book references, lists of libraries and bookstores for basic research, and bibliographies and educational institutions.

MEAGHER, PAUL KEVIN, THOMAS C. O'BRIEN and
SISTER CONSUELO MARIA AHERNE
*Encyclopedic Dictionary of Religion*
Washington, D.C.: Corpus Publishing, 1979

A leading Catholic encyclopedia with three articles on Mennonites and one on Menno Simons (1496-1561), the Dutch priest who left the Catholic church to form a dissenting group of Anabaptists and later received the distinction of providing the name for the Mennonites.

The Mennonite article by T. C. O'Brien provides a reliable historical summary of the origins in Europe and the migration to North America. The many divisions are noted as is the emphasis on personal holiness rather than trinitarian and soteriological doctrines.

The sociological dimension of the complex Mennonite and Amish communities was not adequately utilized.

MELTON, J. GORDON
*The Encyclopedia of American Religions: Religious Creeds*
Detroit: Gale Research, 1987

Presenting more than 450 creedal or theological texts, this is a comprehensive survey based on a limited doctrinal methodology covering both Christian churches and hundreds of Jewish, Islamic, Buddhist, Hindu and other traditions with followings in the U.S. and Canada. In addition, there are historical notes and comments of assistance to researchers.

Printing the most authoritative and representative theological statements without adequate historical or sociological context limits the usefulness of this large undertaking. Melton's taxonomic gifts are innovative because he divided the religious groups of North America into twenty "families." Under these rubrics, he then recorded the names and creeds of religious groups with similar outlooks. The Mennonites are listed under the label of the *European Free Church Family* along with the other two historic peace churches: the Quakers and the Church of the Brethren. Two old Anabaptist-Mennonite theological statements are recorded: Schleitheim (1527) and Dordrecht (1632).

The Baptists, Congregationalists, Disciples and Unitarians would object to any Mennonite or Peace Church monopoly of the term or category of *Free Church*. All of the foregoing churches rejected rule by Bishops or rule by Presbyteries as they affirmed separation of church and state by which Free Churches could flourish.

Melton also muddled the Mennonite listing by placing the Amish under the German Mennonites (Amish emerged from Switzerland) and incorrectly classified General Conference Mennonites as solely Russian when, in fact, they represent a union of Swiss and Russian Mennonites.

Although the device of listing twenty religious families is useful, the creedal framework is lacking in historical and sociological depth.

MEYERS, TOM and HENRY REGEHR (EDS.)
*Newsletter of the Association of Mennonite Sociologists*
Waterloo, Ont.: Conrad Grebel College, February, 1989

Published by eighty Mennonite anthropologists and sociologists, this issue focused on a 1988 conference dealing with Church Profile II, an empirical study of North American Mennonites. It is a follow-up on the 1972 Church survey of five Mennonite and Brethren in Christ denominations reported in Kauffman and Harder, *Anabaptists Four Centuries Later* (Herald Press, 1972). The new design seeks to maximize the comparability between the two data sets.

In this conference, the scholars wrestled with the persistence of Mennonite sacralization in the face of powerful secularization. There was genuine debate on the best theory of social change with Donald Kraybill viewing modernization as the overarching concept along with secularization, individuation and assimilation. There was agreement that Bellah's individualism as expressed in *Habits of the Heart* is an unacceptable diagnosis since Mennonite individualism is tested by religious communalism.

Editor Henry Regehr argued for supplementation of questionnaire research with process research which taps real life experiences.

O'DEA, THOMAS F.
*International Encyclopedia of Social Science*
New York: Macmillan and Free Press of Collins Macmillan, 1968

There are no major articles on Mennonites, Amish and Hutterites in the venerable encyclopedia. However, the one relevant article of merit is O'Dea's summary of current literature dealing with sects and cults. O'Dea's research on the Mormons and Catholic sectarianism gives him a special perspective for this essay but he reveals a knowledge of the three sectarian groups featured in this bibliography.

OOSTERMAN, GORDON
*Minority Groups in Anglo-America: An Introduction and Bibliography of Selected Materials*
Grand Rapids, Mich.: National Union of Christian Schools, 1970

A paper, the result of a resolution of the Association of Christian School administrators, on minorities in the United States and Canada. The groups considered are of racial and religious distinction. Major emphasis is on Blacks, North American Indians, Spanish Americans, Orientals, Jews, and Amish. Topics dealt with include the rationale for teaching about minorities, specific materials for grades K-12, resource materials for teachers, and a list of organizations which are specifically concerned with minorities.

In Canada at least, this bibliography comes on a wave of interest in multiculturalism — sparked by government sponsorship — which has encouraged greater education for the public in the area of minorities among us.

PERICHO, PRISCILLA
*Interfaith Relations in Children's Books: A Bibliography*
New York: Friendship Press, 1976

A comprehensive survey of ways in which books for children deal with racial, cultural, national, and religious minorities. In the latter category, Pericho deals with Mennonites and Amish.

REDEKOP, CALVIN
*A Bibliography of Mennonites in Waterloo County*
Waterloo, Ont.: Conrad Grebel College, 1987

A comprehensive list, edited by a leading Mennonite sociologist, of over 100 books and articles, dealing with all varieties of Mennonites in Waterloo County. It is copyrighted and available through the college. It confirms the large amount of research taking place among the rich mosaic of Mennonite life in the county located 60 miles from Toronto.

REDEKOP, CALVIN and LEO DRIEDGER
"Sociology of Mennonites: State of the Art and Science."
*Journal of Mennonite Studies*, 1, 1 (1983)

This is a thirty-page bibliographic survey and essay by the two senior Mennonite sociologists of Canada who were trained in the States. In short compass it is the finest survey available. The survey concludes with six suggestions for future research with focus on community, ethnicity and religion, the role of economic factors, urbanization, the larger intellectual quest and the Anabaptist-Mennonite view of history.

The *Journal of Mennonite Studies*, Vol. 1, No.1, can be ordered from the *Journal*'s offices, University of Winnipeg, Winnipeg, Manitoba, R3B 2E9 ($8.00).

REIMER, MARGARET LOEWEN
*One Quilt, Many Pieces: A Concise Reference Guide to Mennonite Groups in Canada*
Waterloo, Ont.: Mennonite Publishing Service, 1983

*One Quilt, Many Pieces* is an apt description of the contents of this compact but valuable booklet. It summarizes the history, faith and cultural distinctives that characterize the many and varied groups in Canada (twenty-seven in all) claiming common Anabaptist-Mennonite roots and still identifying themselves with that tradition.

RILEY, MARVIN P.
*The Hutterite Brethren: An Annotated Bibliography with Special Reference to South Dakota Hutterite Colonies*
South Dakota: Agricultural Experiment Station, South Dakota State University, 1965

This pioneer bibliography goes beyond the South Dakota context with references from other areas in the United States along with Canada and nations overseas. The items include field studies and surveys of culture, intergroup relations, social organization, agriculture, and mental and physical health.

For additional Hutterite bibliographies, see John A. Hostetler, *Hutterite Society* (Baltimore: Johns Hopkins University Press, 1977); and Karl A. Peter, *The Dynamics of Hutterite Society: An Analytical Approach* (Edmonton: The University of Alberta Press, 1987).

RYAN, JOHN
*The Agricultural Economy of Manitoba Hutterite Colonies*
Toronto: McClelland and Stewart, 1977

> Material first presented in a Ph.D. dissertation entitled "The Agricultural Operations of Manitoba Hutterites" (McGill University, 1972). This definitive study of Hutterite agriculture is complete with many maps, charts and photographs. Ryan bases his study on a detailed census of Hutterite agricultural operation, and has produced a book which is most valuable to scholars of Hutterite economic life.
>
> While this publication (1977) has not revised and updated the data (originally collected 1968-1971), the author has included an epilogue that discusses events and changes in the intervening years.

SMUCKER, DONOVAN E. (ED.)
*The Sociology of Canadian Mennonites, Hutterites and Amish: A Bibliography with Annotations*
Waterloo, Ont.: Wilfrid Laurier University Press, 1977. Vol. 1

> This pioneering annotated bibliography of over 800 items covers books, articles, theses and unpublished monographs utilizing a sociological orientation in studying the three groups, from the post-war years until 1977.
>
> The editor, Donovan E. Smucker, writes a critical survey of the many types of Mennonites, the sturdy communal Hutterites, and the semi-communal Amish.
>
> Volume 2, the present book published in 1991, updates the first volume following a decade of extensive research all across North America.

SWARTLEY, WILLARD and CORNELIUS DYCK (EDS.)
*Annotated Bibliography of Mennonite Writings on War and Peace 1930-1980*
Elkhart, Ind.: Institute of Mennonite Studies, 1987

> Annotated bibliographical entries on every book, article and poem written about war and peace by Mennonites in the English language for fifty years from 1930 to 1980. Also includes writings by non-Mennonites edited by Mennonite publishers. A few significant works since 1980 are included. The entries are organized according to topic, ranging from one-sentence to two-paragraph summaries.

# II. Mennonites

# A. Books and Pamphlets

BIRD, MICHAEL and TERRY KOBAYASHI
*A Splendid Harvest: Germanic Folk and Decorative Arts in Canada*
Toronto: Van Nostrand Reinhold, 1981

> *A Splendid Harvest* takes its place as part of a large selection of illustrated books dealing with the folk art and craft of Mennonites and Amish. While the authors include the Germanic folk art of Lutherans and Catholics, the major emphasis is on the Amish and Mennonites. Mennonites traditionally have resisted being identified in terms of their material possessions and accomplishments; "Mennonite," however, refers not only to a faith, but to a way of life. Material things are necessarily part of that lifestyle. Much praise is given for the folk art — such as quilts, furniture, and fraktur — of these people: one reviewer refers to those "whose devotion to simplicity and whose family cohesiveness operate to produce and to preserve functional and beautiful material expressions of life" (John F. Schmidt, *ML* 39, 3: 28).
>
> The book includes brief historical accounts, as well as many photographs and drawings.
>
> For related studies (a few of many), see Marilyn Lithgow, *Quiltmaking & Quiltmakers* (Funk & Wagnalls, 1974); Laura Siegel Gilberg and Barbara Ballinger Buchholz, *Needlepoint Designs from Amish Quilts* (Charles Scribner's Sons, 1977); and Lynda Musson Mykor and Patricia D. Musson, *Mennonite Furniture* (Toronto: James Lorimer, 1977).

BOYNTON, LINDA LOUISE
*The Plain People: An Ethnography of the Holdeman Mennonites*
Salem, Wis.: Sheffield Publishing, 1986

> Originally a thesis done at California State University, this ethnography explores the political, economic, social and materialistic customs which reinforce the religion of the Holdeman Mennonites and maintain consistent practices. There is almost unanimous agreement within the sect that the regulation of their total physical and spiritual lives is necessary for the unity and continuity of their spiritual culture.
>
> These social regulations operate through the use of cultural boundary markers, which serve as symbols for the maintenance of their group consciousness and social unity (p vii). Boynton examines this by looking at various areas of Holdeman Mennonite life: religious and beliefs system; family life, role of women; dress, adornment and its symbolic use; the education system; and the code of ethics.
>
> The Holdeman Mennonites perpetuate and enforce the use of many cultural boundary markers, due to their intense commitment to their religious value system. Thus in many ways they remain separated from the larger American society.
>
> For a related study, see Marilyn Assheton-Smith and Kelleen Toohey, "School-Centered Community Conflict: The Holdeman

Mennonite Case in Alberta," *Alberta Journal of Educational Research*, 25, 2 (June 1979): 77-88.

BREDNICH, ROLF WILHELM
*Mennonite Folklife and Folklore: A Preliminary Report*
Canadian Centre for Folk Culture Studies, Paper No. 22, National
Museum of Man Mercury Series, Ottawa, 1977

This study is part of the Mercury Series, produced by the National Museum of Man. The author proposes to study the folkculture of the Mennonites in Western Canada, which he says has been largely neglected in favour of historical and religious aspects. The Hague-Osler-Rosthern region north of Saskatoon is the focus of the paper. The report comprises a brief historical sketch of Mennonites and their settlement in the area, and deals with ethnic identity, material culture and the oral traditions of the settlers.

Brednich identifies the most significant result of the study as being that "Mennonite religion has functioned as a stabilizing element in Mennonite folklife . . . under the influence of religious norms and customs there developed a large number of traditional patterns of behaviour and attitudes which demonstrates that there still exists a 'Mennonite folklore' in its own right" (p. ii).

BURKHOLDER, J. LAWRENCE
*The Problem of Social Responsibility from the Perspective of the Mennonite Church*
Elkhart, Ind.: Institute of Mennonite Studies, 1989

This is a re-issue of the 1958 Princeton doctoral dissertation which embraced Niebuhrian ambiguity and social realism too heavily for the Mennonite scholars of that time. The author's social realism developed in China and India, 1944-49, when he shifted from Mennonite relief work to the United Nations (UNRRA) where multiple, contradictory demands were regular parts of the daily task. Later at Princeton, Professor Paul Lehman tutored Burkholder in a theology and ethic of power.

Thirty-one years later a leading Mennonite research organization has published this controversial Ph.D. thesis as a book. One senses that the Mennonites are changing. Burkholder has not fully solved the problem of pacifism and the Mennonite bias toward perfectionism and sectarian enclaves. It is, however, an example of a study written thirty years ahead of its time, and a rugged encounter with the real world and the pervasive power of evil.

DENLINGER, A. MARTHA
*Real People: Amish and Mennonites in Lancaster County, Pennsylvania*
Kitchener, Ont.: Herald Press, 1981

This book was compiled to answer the questions of tourists regarding the Amish and Mennonites in Lancaster County, Pennsylvania; the author collected these questions in the course of her work at the Mennonite Information Center. The material included is regional in scope and personal in nature, as the author herself is Mennonite. In a clear and informative way, Denlinger discusses every aspect of Amish and Mennonite life, including home and family, economics, education, religious life, and the impact of tourism.

While this fifth printing is somewhat outdated — particularly in terms of photographs — it remains an informed and helpful introduction to these groups living in Lancaster County.

DRIEDGER, LEO (ED.)
*The Canadian Ethnic Mosaic — A Quest for Identity*
Toronto:  McClelland and Stewart, 1978

A collection of articles dealing with various perspectives on the diversity of Canadian ethnic identity. These are listed under the headings Ethnic Pluralism, Ethnic Migration and Immigration Policy, Psychological Development of the Ethnic Child, The Native Quest for Identity, and Ethnic Minorities. Of particular interest to this bibliography are Leo Driedger's "Ethnic Identity in the Canadian Mosaic" (pp. 9-22), and "Problems of Mennonite Identity: A Historical Study," by Frank H. Epp (pp. 281-94).

DRIEDGER, LEO, (ED.)
*Ethnic Canada: Identities and Inequalities*
Toronto:  Copp Clark Pitman, 1987

Almost a decade after Driedger's first important anthology of articles, *The Canadian Ethnic Mosaic* (1978), he has edited a second collection characterized by much greater interest in theoretical frameworks without overlooking specific cases. Twenty-one of the best essays available are brought together in this definitive collection concerning the mosaic of ethnic collectivities set in regional patterns and historical eras of Canada.

Marx and Durkheim were not preoccupied with ethnicity, but Max Weber is very relevant to ethnic studies through race, *Volk*, tribe, nationalism and social circles. Driedger also utilizes Raymond Breton on symbolic order, Jean Burnet on the Canadian multicultural and bilingual framework, and many other theorists. Driedger's introduction is a rich survey of the theoretical basis for utilization of empirical data.

The editor's own chapter provides a fresh sophisticated framework to set forth the bargaining model, the oppositional model and Wellman's discussion of "lost," "saved" and "liberated" communities. He then launches into an analysis of the small Mennonite community in Warman, Saskatchewan, which in 1980 surprised everyone by waging a vigorous campaign of opposition to a proposed hexafluoride refinery in the community. Twenty-two hearings during twelve days pitted the formidable Eldorado Nuclear company against the rural coalition of three kinds of Mennonites along with smaller groups of Catholics, Doukhobors, Orthodox and Lutherans, a general ethnic mosaic.

In one of the most impressive analyses ever made of conflict in a small rural community, Driedger concludes that the "saved" (Wellman's model) leaders of the Warman Mennonite community combined strong traditional community ties and extensive liberated networks to successfully fight the proposed nuclear invasion. David triumphed over Goliath.

With this book Driedger has provided an excellent guide to the most stimulating literature dealing with ethnicity.

DRIEDGER, LEO
*The Mennonite Quest: Identities in Conflict*
Lewiston, N.Y.: Edwin Mellen Press, 1987

Leo Driedger's long career as a researcher of Mennonite identity climaxes in this book reflecting his comparative sociological studies of Mennonites and other ethno-religious groups and the special impact of urbanization and democratic pluralism.

DRIEDGER, LEO and LELAND HARDER (EDS.)
*Anabaptist-Mennonite Identities in Ferment*
Occasional Papers No. 14. Elkhart, Ind.: Institute of Mennonite Studies, 1990

Five sociologists and two theologians presented papers at Elkhart, Indiana in 1988 to find new ways of conceptualizing a second North American social survey of Mennonite and Brethren in Christ church members.

There was no debate on using an empirical research method heavily relying on questionnaires. Conceptually, Calvin Redekop in his paper on "Sectarianism and the Sect Cycle" noted the difference between nonradical sects in tolerant societies and radical sects operating in a hostile environment. He concluded by affirming the need for a dialectical process between sect and host society. This presupposes that one knows where a particular sect is in the historical process before making the analysis.

This is the second time (1975 and 1990) that massive empirical data has been gathered on North American Mennonites using the methodologies of Glock and Lenski and the approach of the National Opinion Research Centre in Chicago. Mennonite sociologists have joined the mainstream of research in the sociology of religion while sharpening their own assumptions in social theory.

H. Kauffman and Driedger are writing the major scholarly volume based on this data. For a preliminary, brief summary of findings see Appendix A in this volume.

DYCK, CORNELIUS J. (ED.)
*Something Meaningful for God*
Scottdale, Pa., and Kitchener, Ont.: Herald Press, 1981

This book contains seventeen biographies of persons who have played a central role in the Mennonite Central Committee (MCC). The women and men featured give us a sampling of the variety of people and activities involved with the MCC: Nasri Zananiri, a Palestinian Arab; Henry A. Fast, a General Conference Mennonite church leader; Irene Bishop, a Mennonite farm girl; P. C. Hiebert, Mennonite Brethren leader; Edna Ruth Byler, initiator of the Self-Help program; Susie Rutt, a woman called to "work" when most women remained at home; Elfrieda Dyck, active in aiding Russian Mennonite refugees to reach a new home in Paraguay; Cornelius Wall and C. A. Defehr, Russian Mennonite emigrants who also wished to serve; J. J. Thiessen, witness to God's miracle as he aided Russian refugees to emigrate to North America; John and Clara Schmidt, called to work with the problem of leprosy in Paraguay; Pyarelal Malagar, a native-born Mennonite of India; Harry and Olga Martens, as they fulfilled their vision of giving one-tenth of their time in service; C. N. Hostetler, Jr., Brethren in Christ churchman; and Norman Wingert, known to his fellow Brethren in Christ as Mr. MCC.

The major flaw in the book is an unevenness in the quality of the biographies. Some are written with academic precision while others are disappointing.

EPP, FRANK H.
*Mennonites in Canada*
*1920-1940: A People's Struggle for Survival*. Vol. 2
Toronto: Macmillan of Canada, 1982

With his projected three-volume history of Canadian Mennonite history, the late Professor Frank Epp of Conrad Grebel College, Waterloo, changed the face of historiography by concentrating on the unique and complex history of Canadian Mennonites, extrapolated from a fuzzy synthesis with U.S. church history.

This second volume covers 1920-40, and proved to be Epp's last scholarly contribution before his death in 1986.

It is focused on waves of migration, principally from Russia, in the largest movement of Mennonites in their history. The intransigent Old Colony Mennonites moved from Manitoba to Mexico and Paraguay because of rejection of mandatory English in their schools on the prairies.

Always encyclopedic, the author often clings to micro-history when the larger strokes were needed. But this is a *magnum opus* indispensable for the understanding of the complex array of Canadian Mennonites.

Bibliography and footnotes are massive.

EPP, FRANK H.
*Mennonite Peoplehood: A Plea for New Initiatives*
Waterloo, Ont.: Conrad Press, 1977

This rather polemical book was written by Frank Epp to protest against the ecclesiastical domination of Canadian Mennonites by the older and larger conferences in the U.S. Before the institutions and agencies of the two nations can work together they must organize separately and then plan to meet together on a regular basis. This is the organizational prerequisite for genuine sharing of policies, plans, programs and ministries.

Behind this tract for the times is the maturation of Canadian Mennonites through large waves of educated members ready for equality.

Professor Epp was a living example of this with an M.A. and Ph.D. from the University of Minnesota.

In the decade since this book was written the bi-national organization proposed by the author has taken place.

EPP, FRANK H. (ED.)
*Partners in Service: The Story of Mennonite Central Committee Canada*
Winnipeg: Mennonite Central Committee, 1983

This book was prepared as a twentieth anniversary publication of the Mennonite Central Committee Canada, in an attempt to reflect on the past and to plan for the future. The book's foreword refers to this work as Epp's expression of gratitude to God and his people, who became partners with God and each other in service. The publication is also an invitation to reinforce the partnership, to make it stronger for the larger tasks that lie ahead. It is attractively laid out chronologically, with corresponding black and white photographs.

EPP-TIESSEN, ESTHER
*Altona: The Story of a Prairie Town*
Altona, Man.: D. W. Friesen and Sons, 1982

Described in the preface (by Dr. Gerald Friesen of the University of Manitoba) as a "fine local history," this account of Altona's story combines a feeling for the community with scholarly research. Esther Epp-Tiessen has succeeded in telling the story of Altona's first century with balance and tact. Like every work of history, this volume has selected significant and representative information to depict the larger story. Its virtue is that we learn so much about this Russian Mennonite community of nineteenth-century immigrants and appreciate so clearly its origin and distinctiveness. Unique features of Altona are a Mennonite-owned printing company with a national market, and the large number of scholars born in this vital small town.

FLINT, JOANNE
*The Mennonite Canadians*
Toronto: Van Nostrand Reinhold, 1980

This colourful and descriptive booklet is a well-balanced, informative survey of the two major Mennonite groups in Canada—those of Swiss background, and the Russian Mennonite immigrants of the late nineteenth and early twentieth centuries. The book, geared to elementary-school students, is quite accurate historically as well as in its present-day description. While Flint may at times paint an overly idyllic picture of Mennonite life in Canada, this may perhaps be excused in consideration of her young audience.

FRETZ, J. WINFIELD
*The Waterloo Mennonites: A Community in Paradox*
Waterloo, Ont.: Wilfrid Laurier University Press, 1989

This is the climactic book of a scholar who has been studying Mennonites sociologically for fifty years with twenty-five of those years specifically focused on the Waterloo County, Ontario, context. In addition to this singularity of specialization Fretz grew up among both plain and progressive Mennonites of Eastern Pennsylvania.

In methodology, Fretz combines the scientific sociology of the Chicago school with an anthropologist's passion for direct experience with the people he is studying—hence, his myriad visits to the farms, homes, schools and churches of the Old Order people in Waterloo county. And yet, he maintains the Chicago commitment to gathering statistical data, and his book includes over 40 statistical tables.

In social theory, the author relies on Tonnies' Gemeinschaft-Gessellschaft typology, Troeltsch's church and sect distinction and Durkheim's emphasis on the ubiquity of belief, ritual and symbol in all religions. The major theoretical construct is the Gemeinschaft-Gessellschaft emphasis of Tonnies because it permits him to analyze both Old Orders and progressives.

Like the Lynds in *Middletown* or John Seeley in *Crestview Heights*, Fretz, too, delimited his research to a small area and then made a microscopic analysis of it.

One detects in this remarkable book an intense admiration for the Old Order people. They are Protestant monastics who have defied many features of modern society in a heroic attack on acculturation. Fretz succeeds so well in describing their virtues in family life, farming, mutual aid, social change, non-violence and independence of government that he makes a puzzle of himself and the progressive Mennonites with whom he is firmly affiliated. Are the progressive Mennonites lapsed Old Orders? Or are they Christians who have embraced modernity in order to serve human need more fully and more effectively?

This is an important book without a serious rival at this time.

FRIESEN, JOHN W.
*People, Culture and Learning*
Calgary, Alta.: Detselig Enterprises, 1977

This book is an attempt to combine theory and practice in relation to a significant factor in education—the phenomenon of culture. Friesen cites the prominent idea among educators that the "whole child" must be educated—including personal, social and cultural background, as well as family context. Friesen examines many aspects of what he terms "intercultural education." His Russian Mennonite background informs this research.

Neither organization nor style is adequate, but the book does provide valuable insight into this particular educational theory and practice.

FRIESEN, JOHN W.
*When Cultures Clash: Case Studies in Multiculturalism*
Calgary, Alta.: Detselig Enterprises, 1985

In five cases of multiculturalism in Canada, Friesen walks on the tightrope between assimilation and integration. The Hutterites and Mennonites are included in the set of cases without opening up any new data or fresh theory, but Friesen does provide a fine summary of the seven most commonly made attacks on the Hutterite life style: land expansion, population growth, payment of taxes, community destruction, freedom and individualism, military exemption and education. The thirteen-page summary of Mennonite characteristics is useful but not original.

HAMM, PETER M.
*Continuity and Change Among the Canadian Mennonite Brethren*
Waterloo, Ont.: Wilfrid Laurier University Press, 1987

This study of the manner in which the Mennonite Brethren have survived and changed over the length of their existence uses social science theory and methodology. Hamm believes that the best way to understand their life and its change is to understand the Brethren as having faced two opposing processes: namely sacralization, and secularization.

The theory of secularization, very widely developed in sociology, is seen as the dynamic pulling the Brethren away from their original commitments, while the sacralization process, defined as the perpetuation and entrenchment of the norms and values, is seen as the countervailing process which contains and controls the secularizing process. Evidences of secularization and sacralization in the Mennonite Brethren are convincingly presented based mainly on the empirical study of North American Mennonites done by Kauffman and Harder in *Anabaptist Four Centuries Later*, but supplemented by research done by other scholars. Sacralization factors consist of delineating boundaries, enhancing cohesion, facilitating socialization, and reinforcing integration. Factors of secularization include education, urbanization, occupational changes, economic ascendency and assimilation.

Hamm concludes from his study that the dialectic of secularization and sacralization has produced the present identity of the Mennonite Brethren, and that the body has withstood the process rather well. Hamm believes that the continuity of the sectarian identity will persist because the sacralization process has kept pace with secularization.

An extensive bibliography concludes the text. This is one of the first thorough analyses of a Mennonite group using the Kauffman-Harder study as a source base line, and hence is paradigmatic for further study of other groups. It is also first in utilizing the sacralization-secularization schema in the analysis. It will provide insights for other studies and certainly helps understand the Mennonite Brethren. The author tends to be overly optimistic about the Mennonite Brethrens' ability to retain their identity; further his analysis of the sectarian, sacralization and secularization concepts are somewhat contrived, overtly eclectic and syncretistic. Almost every sociological theory and theorist is used, and at points the integration of the various concepts is difficult to follow or accept. But apart from these weaknesses, it is an important sociological treatment of a Mennonite group.

HOSTETLER, JOHN A.
*Mennonite Life*
Kitchener, Ont.: Herald Press, 1983

This colourful and well-written booklet is one of three by John A. Hostetler; the other two deal with Amish and Hutterite life. Hostetler, a prominent sociologist of Amish background, deals in a clear and concise way with the complex Mennonite social reality. He takes on the task of explaining the many different sub-groups of Mennonites, as well as simplifying the many-faceted stories of origins and history, and succeeds very well. The material presented is brief but informative, written in an academic style. The addition of colourful and artistic photographs completes an attractive and valuable learning resource. The congruence of this type of format and a level somewhat beyond secondary school leaves some doubt, however, as to the intended purpose of this booklet. (See also: Hostetler, *Amish Life,* and *Hutterite Life.*)

HOSTETLER, JOHN A. and others
*Cultural Transmission and Instrumental Adaptation to Social Change: Lancaster Mennonite High School in Transition*
Philadelphia, Pa.: Temple University, and Washington, D.C.: National Centre for Educational Research and Development, 1974

This study of a Mennonite community and a sample of its students in both a Mennonite and a public high school examines the educational process. Researching the ethnography of the Mennonite school, patterns of cognition, the function of informal networks and ethnic identity in the transmission of culture, this study gathered information by participant observation, formal and informal interviews, and various measures of ethnicity and cognitive perception. The impact of the Mennonite school on student attitudes is found to be most influential in the areas of normative, preferred or accepted activities. The school appears to have minimal impact on student attitudes toward ethnicity, orthodoxy, and self-concept.

For related studies, see Donald B. Kraybill, "Religious and Ethnic Socialization in a Mennonite High School," *MQR*, 51, 4 (October 1977): 329-51, and Bernie Wiebe and Calvin W. Vraa, "Religious Values of Students in Religious and Public High Schools," *Psychological Reports* (June 1976): 709-10.

JONES, DONNA R.
*Western Kansas Country Schools. Country School Legacy: Humanities on the Frontier*
Washington, D.C.: National Endowment for the Humanities, and Silt, Colo.: Mountain Plains Library Association, 1982

Oral histories provide background information for five essays which address the development of country schools in western Kansas during the late 1880s. They deal with topics such as the rural community, curriculum of these schools, and instructional materials. The last paper portrays the public and parochial public country school as one of the major elements in western Kansas that helped immigrants learn American customs, history, language, and patriotism. Among the ethnic groups discussed are: American Indians, Volga-Germans, Blacks, French, Swedes, Mennonites, and Czechoslovakians.

JUDGE, SARA E.
*Eastern & Central Kansas Country Schools. Country School Legacy: Humanities on the Frontier*
Washington, D.C.: National Endowment for the Humanities, and Silt, Colo.: Mountain Plains Library Association, 1982

Country schools in eastern and central Kansas are explored from six different aspects: country schools as historic sites; teachers; reading, writing, arithmetic, and recitation; country schools as community centres; and country schools today. Establishment of these schools is traced from sod or wood structures erected by local families to stone structures built to state-prescribed specifications. Although the majority of early settlers were already "Americans" when they reached Kansas, the schools are shown to have had considerable impact on American Indians and German Mennonite immigrants from Russia.

JUHNKE, JAMES C.
*A People of Two Kingdoms*
Newton, Kans.: Faith and Life Press, 1975

Juhnke examines the process of Mennonite acculturation on the basis of the political behaviour of the Kansas Mennonites, from the 1870s, when many Mennonites migrated from Russia to America to escape Russian militarism, to the mid-twentieth century. He notes that although the American government gave the migrants no guarantee of military exemption, greater American political freedom began to break down the traditional church-state dualism the Mennonites had adopted in Europe. However, if Mennonite voter turnout as compared to the American norm is an indication of the rate of acculturation, that process was a slow one: Juhnke points out that Mennonite voting remained below the American norm well beyond the Second World War. Nor was a clear pattern of acculturation discernible in Mennonite office-holding. On the other hand, one would expect an as yet little acculturated ethnic group to vote overwhelmingly for one political party, rather than spread its allegiances more evenly as the process of acculturation continued. In contrast to such groups as the Kansas Swedes, the Mennonite vote was initially divided between political parties much like the American norm, but around 1940 a renewed effort to preserve Mennonite identity and yet be "good America citizens" resulted in an overwhelmingly Republican Mennonite vote. Juhnke explains this ambivalence in Mennonite political behaviour by pointing out the continuing tension between the Mennonite ideology and American nationalism. This tension was largely ignored during the Spanish-American War, but the First World War brought home to the Mennonites the conflict between a desire to be good citizens and a pacifist creed and German background renewing their distrust of the state. In an attempt to resolve this continuing conflict between nationalism and the Mennonite faith, Juhnke argues, the Mennonites developed alternative service programs and engaged in important world-wide relief service. He concludes that Mennonite acculturation is as yet incomplete: the Mennonites remain a "people of two kingdoms."

KLIPPENSTEIN, LAWRENCE
*David Klassen and the Mennonites: We Built Canada*
Agincourt, Ont.: The Book Society of Canada, 1982

Part of a series dealing with key personalities who led various movements and migrations in and to Canada. It provides a vivid picture, profusely illustrated, of David Klassen, a Russian Mennonite pioneer of the 1874 migration. Arriving in Canada, settling in pioneer communities, battling the elements, starting a new life and a picture of the current scene are in this booklet. Designed for schools, it is a colourful addition to the literature about the Prairie Mennonites during the past century.

KLIPPENSTEIN, LAWRENCE (ED.)
*That There Be Peace: Mennonites in Canada and World War II*
Winnipeg: Manitoba Conscientious Objector Reunion Committee, 1979

This excellent book contains personal accounts by several Mennonite pacifists of their experiences during the Second World War. A host of photographs and other illustrations supplement descriptions of life in Conscientious Objector forest camps, of care services in hospitals, of one man's experience as a medic in the army and of another man's going to prison for his convictions. Mennonite Conscientious Objectors, on the whole, willingly performed alternative service that would not violate their beliefs, and the government adhered to the letter of the Order-in-Council that granted exemption from combat duty to Mennonites. Nevertheless, the Objectors were subjected to a good deal of hostility from the non-Mennonite population, because their German descent and their refusal to fight in the Second World War made them suspect. The book includes chapters on the Conscientious Objectors' self-image as presented in *The Beacon*, a forestry-camp paper, and of the image of them presented by the public press.

The book opens with a historical introduction to Mennonite pacifism, from Conrad Grebel's and Menno Simons' early stand on nonresistance to the migration of Mennonites to Russia to avoid Prussian militarism. In Russia, they were granted many privileges, including military exemption, but these privileges seemed to be threatened in the 1870s, prompting further migration to Canada. Canada guaranteed military exemption to the Mennonites, but both the First and the Second World War brought great pressure on them. Different Mennonite groups could not agree on what kind of alternative service they were prepared to perform, and the government made distinctions between Mennonite groups that had come to Canada at various times. Nevertheless, on the whole, their objector status was respected, despite talk of deportation, and the majority of ex-COs found their stand on nonresistance to have been a worthwhile, enriching experience in retrospect. The book illustrates well the courageous example set by those who were non-cooperative with conscription. It is descriptive rather than critical.

KRAYBILL, DONALD B. and PHYLLIS PELLMAN GOOD (EDS.)
*Perils of Professionalism: Essays on Christian Faith and Professionalism*
Kitchener, Ont.: Herald Press, 1982

The editors of *Perils of Professionalism* propose to examine the relationship between Christian faith and professionalism, about which surprisingly little has been written. Not an academic enterprise, the book is rather a collection of articles and stories written by professionals, telling of their own experiences. The focus is on the Mennonite experience of professionalism; many are "first-generation professionals" who deal with dilemmas unknown within their agrarian background. Writers deal with such questions, for example, as the relationship of professionalism to marriage and family, church response and/or support, the conflict of demands involved, and a possible theology for professionals. For example, Carl Bowman asks the question, "If ethical concerns can't be integrated with technical training, might they be sacrificed for income, prestige and domestic stability?"

For a related study, see *Professionalism: Faith, Ethics, and Christian Identity*, a publication of the 1978 Professionalism Conference, Philadelphia, Pennsylvania, March 1978.

KRAYBILL, DONALD M.
*Ethnic Education: The Impact of Mennonite Schooling*
San Francisco, Calif.: R. and E. Research Associates, 1977

The purpose of this study is to integrate the available data on Mennonite education; it makes use of five recent studies done in this area, and interprets them from a sociological perspective. Criticism of the public school system has increased, parallel to a surge of interest and concern for ethnicity. Thus, a study of Mennonite schools—as one "ethnic school"—is quite timely. The study includes historical background, and covers many aspects of the Mennonite educational system.

For related studies, see Shirin and Edward Schluderman, *Beliefs and Practices in Mennonite and Catholic Schools, JMS*, VIII (1990); and Bruce E. Hunsberger, "A Reconsideration of Parochial Schools: The Case of Mennonites and Roman Catholics," *MQR*, 51, 2 (April 1977): 140-51.

KREIDER, ROBERT and RACHEL WALTNER GOOSEN
*Hungry, Thirsty, Stranger: The Mennonite Central Committee Experience*
Scottdale, Pa. and Kitchener, Ont.: Herald Press, 1988

Against the background of trying to serve human need in the turbulent context of modern history, this book reveals a pattern of response by the Mennonite Central Committee which utilizes a case approach to policy. Granted that love and justice are the basic ethical presuppositions, the Mennonite food, health, education and development workers discovered an older ethical tradition called casuistry. For example, in Vietnam the Mennonite workers faced the monumental task of disengaging from the American occupation and the South Vietnamese war effort, while locating non-military needs and serving the needs of the civilian population. One relief worker, Max Ediger, an American, wrote on his return that he would have refused a Vietnam assignment if he had known in advance the ethical dilemmas. Kreider and Goosen record many situations in other nations where the *ad hoc* responses were more successful.

The case method recorded in this book may seem too pragmatic for a Biblical-theological people like the Mennonites. One answer to this critique is that the Mennonite Central Committee is an international coalition of 17 North American Amish, Mennonite and Brethren in Christ churches working in 50 countries of North America, Europe, Africa, the Far and Middle East, Latin America and the Caribbean. A coalition working in faraway places may have more freedom to work case by case than it would in environments adjacent to their American and Canadian constituencies.

KYLE, RICHARD G.
*From Sect to Denomination: Church Types and Their Implications for Mennonite Brethren History*
Hillsboro, Kans.: Center for Mennonite Brethren Studies, 1985

In this book, Richard Kyle, professor of history and religious studies at Tabor College, proposes to examine Mennonite Brethren history from the perspective of classical ecclesiastical types, using concepts of the sociology of religion. These "types" are identified: sect, established sect, denomination, and church. The central focus of Kyle's book is the shift from the largely sectarian nature of the Mennonite Brethren Church in Russia to an increasingly denominational structure in North America. He identifies evangelical bodies in North America as having great influence on the balance between pietistic and Anabaptist elements in present Mennonite Brethren churches.

As one reviewer (J. H. Kauffman, *MQR*, 61, 2 [1986]: 236-38) notes, Kyle does not recognize in his analysis the variation among Mennonite Brethren church members with respect to their sectarian beliefs and practices; for example, some congregations no longer identify their congregations with the word "Mennonite."

The book does, nonetheless, offer a valuable contribution to the study of Mennonite Brethren history, and encourages further pursuit of this endeavour.

LEDERACH, PAUL and JOHN H. RUDY
*Stewardship of the Gospel: A Business Person's Perspective: Essays*
Winnipeg: Mennonite Economic Development Associates, 1982

The content of this booklet is an edited version of presentations given at the joint convention of Mennonite Industry and Business Associates (MIBA) and Mennonite Economic Development Associates (MEDA) in Lancaster, Pennsylvania, November 10-13, 1981. These two organizations raise ethical questions posed by the owners and managers of small and middle-sized businesses. This is not the world of the big corporation.

LOEWEN, HARRY (ED.)
*Mennonite Images: Historical, Cultural and Literary Essays Dealing*

*with Mennonite Issues*
Winnipeg: Hyperion Press, 1980

This collection of twenty essays is in large part an outgrowth of the recently established chair of Mennonite Studies at the University of Winnipeg; all were originally represented as papers or given in lecture form. The essays fall into three categories: historical tensions, cultural identity, and literary images. They cover a great diversity of format and content, ranging from a photo essay to a literary critique to historical analysis. As Ted Regehr states in his review of the book, "it is a landmark, not only because of what it says about Mennonite Studies, but because it shows how the methods and insights of the liberal arts can be applied to Mennonite topics" (*MQR*, 56, 3 [July 1982]: 293).

While not all of the essays are of consistently good quality, the collection is nonetheless a positive contribution to Mennonite scholarship in the areas of history, culture and literature.

LOEWEN, HARRY
*Why I Am a Mennonite. Essays on Mennonite Identity*
Scottdale, Pa. and Kitchener, Ont.: Herald Press, 1988

Thirty autobiographical essays by Mennonite professionals could have been personal credos but turned out to be what Gordon Kaufman, Harvard theologian, called descriptions of pilgrimages. The autobiographies are case studies in the development of Mennonite intellectuals from the United States, Canada and Europe, primarily birthright Mennonites who had to test their outlook on life and faith by rugged historical and academic encounters. Kaufman, for example, faced the resilient non-pacifist criticism of his peace position at Yale Divinity School under Richard Niebuhr.

John Howard Yoder wrote the final essay calling for liberation from whatever enslaves us as the true goal of Mennonite faith and life.

Because Old Order Plain People are in the Mennonite family, the editor should have included chapters by some of them, since there are writers among them.

See also Loewen's *Vision and Realities*, edited with Al Reimer (Winnipeg: Hyperion Press, 1985).

LONGACRE, DORIS JANZEN
*Living More With Less*
Kitchener, Ont.: Herald Press, 1980

Far from being a dry and legalistic catalogue of ways to "cut back," this book is an inspiring and usable collection of personal stories interwoven with practical suggestions and insightful commentary. Doris Janzen Longacre came to this book with a desire to initiate others into a pilgrimage toward simplicity, and to "help unconvinced people see that their lives actually *do* affect the lives of the poor." She achieves this by exploring many aspects of our life in the world, as is evidenced by the far-reaching scope of the chapter headings: Do Justice; Learn from the World Community; Nurture People; Cherish the Natural Order; and Nonconform Freely. One is not left feeling overwhelmed with the need to drastically change lifestyle, however; Doris Longacre brings together the personal stories of ordinary people all over the world, each of whom is working toward a simpler lifestyle in his or her own way. And as one reviewer has observed, there is an "exhilarating new freedom" in the process.

MARTIN, MAURICE and MIRIAM MAUST (EDS.)
*Mennonites in Ontario: A Mennonite Bicentennial Portrait 1786-1986*
Kitchener, Ont.: Mennonite Bicentennial Commission, 1986

The *Mennonites of Ontario* is a privately published bicentennial book which views the whole spectrum of Mennonites, from Old Order to progressives, through photographs and essays. The editors asked the people to contribute the pictures for the final selection.

Miriam Maust's preface stresses the centrality of agriculture, the pro-British sentiments of Ontario Mennonites during the Revolutionary War era and the freedom of conscience in Ontario for the Mennonites during the last two hundred years.

There are nine essays written by Frank Epp, Maurice Martin, Ken Bechtel, Ferne Burkhardt, Margaret Reimer, Gord Hunsberger, John Bender, Sue Steiner and Harvey Sider. The essays are usually two pages in length, presenting in brief form excellent analyses of the Ontario Mennonites but they are basically descriptive and appreciative rather than critical.

The picture book is a special method of interpretation. Unconnected essays may not be the best way to interpret a whole region when the focus is on the photograph. Moreover, the editors made a questionable decision in not identifying people, places, and dates of the photographs.

Meanwhile, the reader can enjoy some uninterpreted colour photographs often from Old Order experience: collecting maple syrup, boys fishing, a broken-down buggy, 60 buggies at church, making hay, picking fruit, feeding the calf, ploughing, a roadside vegetable stand, a barn-raising, making buggy wheels, a one-room school, and a wonderful photo of an auctioneer selling a quilt at the Mennonite sale in New Hamburg.

Old Order people receive excessive attention because their activities and costumes are so photogenic. But the treatment of the two vigorous but youthful Mennonite schools (Conrad Grebel College and Rockway Mennonite Collegiate high school); the merger of the three main progressive conferences; the impressive ministry of the MCC; the editing of *The Mennonite Reporter* in Waterloo; the range and vigour of the many congregations and conferences in Ontario; the majestic heights of the great Mennonite choirs; the 600 young Mennonites attending institutions of post-secondary education and finally, the rise of the non-ethnic Chinese, Mong, native and Spanish congregations—these developments were inadequately covered by the photographic media.

METZLER, JAMES E. (ED.)
*Laurelville Symposium, '78*
Laurelville, Pa.: Laurelville Mennonite Church Center, 1978

The Mennonite penchant for study conferences to aid in policy formation is well illustrated by this stimulating array of papers by social scientists, theologians, ethicists, Biblical scholars, scientists and ministers. Sixteen serious papers probe the state of current social, political, economic, ecclesiastical and ethical crises and trends. From the first paper by Calvin Redekop, who sets forth a crisp description of macro trends, to the final paper by Arnold Cressman, the reader discovers that the Mennonite scholars are no longer naive, innocent or ill-informed about the nature of the culture in which they are living. A sophisticated descriptive understanding of our predicament is not the same as a manifesto for action to answer the ills of our time. But the watchers, listeners, monitors, observers, and analysts recorded here totally destroy the myth that Mennonites of the educated type are living in isolated enclaves oblivious to the world.

MOL, HANS
*Faith and Fragility, Religion and Identity in Canada*
Burlington, Ont.: Trinity Press, 1985

In this systematic sociological overview of religion in Canada, Professor Mol of McMaster University utilizes the critical-identity frame of reference for the study of religion. It treats society as a "jostling configuration of cooperating and contending units of social organizations" labelled as identities. Religion either reinforces these identities, reconciles them, or redresses imbalances.

There is a brief chapter on the Mennonites and Hutterites which recounts considerable history, ending with the striking phrase of *Täuferkrankheit* (Anabaptist illness), the vulnerability to schism and splits. But the author predicts a durable and resilient future despite this frequent collapse of unity. The survey of Hutterites is superior to the discussion of Mennonites but neither provide any new theory or data.

NEUFELD, VERNON H. (ED.)
*If We Can Love: The Mennonite Mental Health Story*
Newton, Kans.: Faith and Life Press, 1983

This book is a collection of essays dealing with the Mennonite Mental Health Service (MMHS). Its precedents and origin are described in E. M. Ediger's chapter, "Roots." During World War II, many Mennonite conscientious objectors served in mental hospitals, and MMHS resulted from increased awareness among Mennonites of the inadequate care given to mentally ill persons in the large, impersonal state hospitals. Vernon Neufeld, in "Mennonite Mental Health Services," describes the establishment of a mental health care program by MCC in 1947 and the subsequent development of MMHS as the individual centres struggled for greater autonomy, and as the role of non-Mennonite professional psychiatric staff needed to be defined. Gradually, MCC delegated more control to the individual centres, who came to MMHS as a forum for discussion, a body providing direction and a co-ordinating organ, on the basis of a greater partnership between the Mennonite church and the centres. This process, and the role of MMHS, is discussed by Alfred Neufeldt in "MMHS in Perspective." In addition to the four original centres, other institutions not originally founded by MCC have joined the MMHS framework, and MMHS has begun to establish international links. The book includes chapters dealing with each individual centre, as well as evaluative chapters on the program by both participants and non-participating experts. The aim, to give compassionate and professional mental health care from a Mennonite religious standpoint, is illustrated, and the organizational structures in their development are described. The book is of interest as a study of Mennonite interaction with the larger society as well as of the organization of the program. It does not probe the impact of non-judgemental, non-directive counselling on a people with a rigorous — even perfectionist — ethic.

OHE, WERNER VON DER (ED.)
*Kulturanthropologie: Beiträge Zum Neubegin einer Disziplin*
Festgabe für Emerich K. Francis zum 80 Geburtstag
(Sozialwissenschaftliche Abhandlungen der Görres-Gesellshaft Band 15),
Berlin: Duncker & Humbolt, 1987

The first sociological study of the large western Canadian Russian Mennonite communities was made 45 years ago by the German sociologist, E. K. Francis. After teaching and research in North America he returned to Ludwig-Maximilians-Universitat, Munich, where he wrote twenty articles, supervised thirty doctoral dissertations and completed five books.

The *festgabe* published in his honour has been edited by a colleague, Werner van der Ohe. The only English article in the book was written by Leo Driedger of the University of Manitoba: "The Pluralist Ethnic Option: Francis' Contribution to Multiculturalism." It is Driedger's opinion that Francis was a sociological pioneer working in Canada just as the field began to flower. He made an in-depth study presenting a pluralist ethnic option focused on face to face ethnological research. The monumental *Interethnic Relations* climaxed a brilliant career in 1976.

It is not an exaggeration to say that Francis was the first great pioneer in research among the Russian Mennonites in Canada yet with an awareness of European backgrounds both in social theory and the context of agriculture, community life, and ethnic relations out of which the Mennonites came.

PATTERSON, NANCY-LOU
*Swiss-German and Dutch-German Mennonite Traditional Art in the Waterloo Region, Ontario*
Canadian Centre for Folk Culture Studies, Paper No. 27, National
Museum of Man Mercury Series, Ottawa, 1979

In this study, the contemporary arts in the folk tradition of Swiss German Mennonites, those who moved from Switzerland to the Rhenish Palatinate to Pennsylvania to Southern Ontario, are compared with those of Dutch German Mennonites, those who moved from the Netherlands to Prussia to Russia to Ontario. The first tradition dates in Ontario from the early nineteenth century and the second from the late nineteenth and early twentieth centuries. There are distinct ethnic variations in the work of these two groups both in the past and today; these differences are based on folk/vernacular style, "Pennsylvania German," formal and traditional styles.

Patterson examines the folk arts of these two groups within the context of Waterloo County, Ontario. Other works by Nancy-Lou Patterson include *The Language of Paradise* (London, Ont.: London Regional Art Gallery, 1985) and *Wreath and Bough: Decorative Arts of Amish-Mennonite Settlers in Waterloo County* (Waterloo, Ont.: Ontario German Folklife Society, 1983).

PETKAU, IRENE FRIESEN
*The Story of the Conference of Mennonites in Canada*
Winnipeg: History Archives Committee of the Conference of Mennonites in Canada, 1978

This book is a unique "collage" of photographs, charts, quotations and description, tracing the development of the conference of Mennonites in Canada. The book is valuable as a resource, and as an accessible and colourful glimpse of this Christian community. Mennonites use the word "conference" in place of the term denomination.

REDEKOP, CALVIN
*Mennonite Society: Amish, Mennonite, Hutterite*
Baltimore: Johns Hopkins University Press, 1988

This volume presents a historical background for the North American Mennonite family, followed by six chapters of descriptive material on the Mennonite beliefs, religious structure, social organization, personality, intellectual life and community, using sociological concepts and categories. The third section consists of analysis of the five major institutions, namely the family, education, economics, politics, and missions; analytical material is presented indicating the functions of the institutions and the major conflicts each faces.

The fourth section consists of discussions of the schismatics in Mennonite life, the external and internal threats to Mennonite cohesion and survival, and a treatise on the Mennonites as a utopian movement which was not fully able to achieve its objectives. An appendix presents a typological analysis of the Mennonite saga, proposing three major periods through which Mennonitism has gone, with the latter diverging into three major strands — traditionalist-conservative, acculturationist, and utopian restitutionist. A bibliographic survey presenting the best sources of Mennonite research from an historical, sociological, and theological point of view concludes the book.

This book fills a serious need for a single volume that tells the Mennonite story from a particular perspective or orientation. This is a difficult task and the book may be too technical for some readers and not theoretical enough for others. Its basic thesis, namely that the Mennonite society in its varied forms is the result of the dynamic interaction of the inner thrust with societal resistance and influences, may be too "deterministic" for those who hold that Mennonitism was, and continues to be, the expression of a theological awakening within a corrupt church. But for those who believe that religious movements are related to and influenced by social conditions, this book is a welcome contribution. It is the key book among the six volumes Redekop has written and edited.

REDEKOP, CALVIN
*Strangers Become Neighbours: Mennonite Indigenous Relations in the Paraguayan Chaco*
Scottdale, Pa.: Herald Press, 1980

A senior Mennonite sociologist has written an important book which supplements the earlier studies of Winfield Fretz on Paraguay in 1953 and 1980. Redekop employs comparative sociology and anthropology in his analysis of Russian Mennonite refugees of the 1920s and 1940s who moved to the remote interior of Paraguay. There they found themselves neighbours to several tribes of Indians living a precarious existence in the context of sparse resources of food, education, health services and income. These parallel settlements started interacting: food-gathering Indians met food-producing Mennonites; native languages encountered low German; animism faced Christian community; illiteracy engaged education.

U.S. anthropologists pronounced all this as cultural imperialism. Redekop views it as sharing among two permanent societies which created a new cultural synthesis permitting the Indians to survive. In any case, the classic status of Mennonites as an oppressed, dissenting minority was exchanged for that of a majority trying to share resources with the native minority. The strangers became neighbours. An original work with a bold thesis.

REDEKOP, CALVIN and URIE A. BENDER
*Who am I? What am I? Searching for Meaning in Your Work*
Grand Rapids, Mich.: Academie Book, 1988

Given the obsession with work on the part of Mennonites, Amish and Hutterites, it is not surprising that Mennonite scholars have finally published a book on work.

It is an unusual book with several methodologies, asking questions from a Christian perspective and using insights from the social sciences for most of the answers. The book has seven case studies or excurses, one of which is written by a Mennonite college woman professor titled, "Why I went to work when I was already working."

The sociological writing is excellent, underscoring the high cost in unemployment of new technologies, the differentiation of work from family, kinship and community, the job as status symbol and work as a commodity.

The authors believe that meaning can be restored to work by the Judeo-Christian perspective which rejects hierarchies, judges work by results, and stresses the primacy of moral norms in the evaluation of work. The book reveals the eclectic way in which theology, ethics, sociology and literature are utilized by Mennonite scholars. The pluralism of methodologies and concepts needed a sharper focus and a less fragmented approach. Oddly enough, the word Mennonite doesn't appear in the index.

REDEKOP, CALVIN W. and SAMUEL J. STEINER
*Mennonite Identity: Historical and Contemporary Perspectives*
Lanham, Md.: University Press of America, 1988

Of the making of study conferences on Mennonite sociology, there is no end. But this is the best of the lot. The topic of identity cuts across many disciplines. The Biblical, historical, philosophical, psychological, artistic and sociological sections of the conference, May 28-31, 1986, at Conrad Grebel College, University of Waterloo, provided genuine interaction among the disciplines.

The debate among three sociologists — Donald B. Kraybill of Elizabethtown College (Lancaster County, Pa.), Calvin W. Redekop of Conrad Grebel College, Waterloo, and Alan B. Anderson of the University of Saskatchewan — provides a sharp insight into the central sociological question.

Kraybill argues that ethnicity among the Mennonites is an important but transformed key which has moved from separation of dress, language and land to separate institutional structures and ideological particularism. Redekop sees the Anabaptist Mennonite phenomenon as a religiously motivated utopian movement. Yet as a utopian movement it was constantly confronted with "ethnicizing" tendencies. But the Mennonites never fully accepted this "ethnicizing" because of religious ideology.

After a brilliant critique and summary of Kraybill and Redekop, Anderson comes forth with a new combination word: Mennonites are *ethno-religious* peoples. "They are not simply an ethnic group, nor are they simply a religious group. . . . The challenge for academics, then, in studying Mennonite identity is to avoid overgeneralization and appreciate its complexity."

Kraybill's complex chart (p. 161) on traditional and modern ethnicity, Winfield Fretz's famous typology of "conservative, moderate and progressive" in his *Mennonites of Ontario* (1974) and the encyclopedic membership lists in *Mennonite World Handbook* (1978, 1984, and 1990) of nearly 100 separate conferences in every continent support Anderson's warning against oversimplification. But *Mennonite Identity*, nonetheless, is an important new contribution to the sociological theory and praxis among the increasingly varied Mennonites.

REDEKOP, JOHN H.
*A People Apart: Ethnicity and the Mennonite Brethren*
Winnipeg and Hillsboro, Kans.: Kindred Press, 1987

The name Mennonite, derived from Menno Simons of the sixteenth-century Netherlands, is used by nearly twenty different versions of the Anabaptist (the original name) Mennonite groups throughout the world. The Mennonite Brethren originated in Russia under the influence of Baptist evangelists. As the denomination reached out in North

America, the name Mennonite was closely linked with ethnicity, a linkage less acceptable as this rather evangelistic church began to receive
non-ethnics into the church. After surveying 600 members of the
church, John H. Redekop, Canadian political scientist, proposes changing the name of his conference to *Evangelical Anabaptist*, while dropping
the older denominational name Mennonite Brethren.

Twenty copies of his book were given advanced circulation, letting
"the genie out of the bottle," to quote the author. A church-wide
debate is now underway on this interesting proposal. Perhaps the most
negative argument against the new name is that every denomination (a
North American device) is in some sense ethnic, thus creating an
inherent ethnic predicament, regardless of name. Meanwhile, the Mennonite Brethren have voted against a change of name.

SAWATSKY, RODNEY
*Authority and Identity: The Dynamics of the General Conference Men-
nonite Church*
North Newton, Kans.: Bethel College, 1987

This is the most cogent analysis now available of the leading progressive Mennonite denomination of North America as it struggles to
retain its tension with society while reaching out to serve and aid this
same society. Immigrants from South Germany, France, Volynia, Gala-
cia, the Ukraine, Prussia, and Poland joined the original founders who
were Swiss German.

Chapter II is titled "Sociology: Essentials and Nonessentials." Very
quickly, Sawatsky discovers analysts like H.S. Bender and George
Brunk III who are optimistic about the adaptive power of the Mennonites, and J. H. Yoder and Theron Schlabach who see the insidious
impact of interaction culturally. As the pendulum of the General Conference swings between secularization and the Anabaptist vision, the
author discovers E. G. Kauffman, college president and pioneer missionary to China who believed that the General Conference could balance on this high wire.

Sawatsky takes H. R. Niebuhr's classic revision of Troeltsch, *Christ
and Culture* to show that there are four reasons Mennonites cannot be
understood as basically *against* culture: (a) culture is ubiquitous; (b) sin
is omnipresent as the author quotes Luther, *Simul justus et pecator*; (c)
the dynamic of missionary outreach shatters isolation which led to the
key General Conference text: "In essentials unity; in non-essentials
liberty; and in all things love"; (d) the heterogenicity of General Conference backgrounds requires diversity.

What is the answer? The denomination, with its task enormously
complicated, must nonetheless seek *norms* in order to say no, even
though it must say yes more than conservative Mennonites consider
necessary. This is a dialectical process between Divine authority available to the church without quenching the freedom of the Spirit to critique and renew every and all institutionalization of this authority.

In rejecting historic Mennonite dualism and separatism, Sawatsky's
affirmation of a prophetic, critical independent church is an audacious

course. The forces of acculturation and assimilation are formidable. The pessimists like J. H. Yoder and Theron Schlabach are unconvinced. But Sawatsky is firm in his conviction as he works in one of Canada's most impressive technical universities which has a small Mennonite college on campus as a sub-culture. For 25 years, the University of Waterloo Mennonites have been catalysts engaging in dialogue. Perhaps after 50 years the success of this noble experiment will require another hard look by Sawatsky, now President of Conrad Grebel College, a new model of Mennonite post-secondary education.

SCHIPANI, DANIEL S. (ED.)
*Freedom and Discipleship: Liberation Theology in an Anabaptist Perspective*
Maryknoll, N.Y.: Orbis Books, 1989

The classic Mennonite problem has been acculturation and assimilation. This book reveals that the Latin American Christians are confronting Anabaptist-Mennonites with a new challenge from the poor and the oppressed to start with ortho-praxis not orthodoxy. Here, the Christian obeys the Gospel in the struggle for justice. In this context, the church is involved with radical politics. In the book, ten Mennonite theologians and ethicists are joined by four non-Mennonites in examining the new challenge both from *within* the church and in the conflicts *outside* of the church.

The turf of this new encounter has many Marxists on it and many advocates of just-war theory and practice — both difficult concepts for Anabaptist Mennonites.

Liberation theology is the most difficult challenge twentieth-century Mennonites have ever faced. This is the first book setting forth key issues.

It is significant that Daniel Schipani, the editor, is an Hispanic (Argentine) Mennonite who teaches in an American Mennonite theological school. The Swiss, Dutch, North German and Russian backgrounds no longer dominate the dialogue. Schipani has also written *Conscientization and Creativity; Paulo Freire and Christian Education* (Lanham: University Press, 1988), and *Religious Education Encounters Liberation Theology* (Birmingham: Religious Education Press, 1988).

SCHROEDER, ANDREAS
*The Mennonites*
Vancouver, B.C.: Douglas and McIntyre, 1990

Designed for initial sale at the huge 1990 Mennonite World Conference in Winnipeg, this wide ranging study of the Canadian Mennonites is lavishly illustrated with scores of archival and contemporary photographs. Not since the Walter Quiring and Helen Bartel picture book, *In the Fullness of Time, 150 Years of Mennonite Sojourn in Russia* (1974), have we had such an impressive collection of photographs. Yet, there is an accompanying text which opens with a description of world Mennonite history from 1525 to the present and then continues by portraying current Mennonite life: the social and religious traditions that make the community unique, the impact of many forced emigrations, and the

Mennonite way of life in the late twentieth century. There is heavy
reliance on the major works of the late Frank H. Epp, pre-eminent historian of Canadian Mennonites.

An immigrant from Germany living in British Columbia,
Schroeder's knowledge of the Swiss Mennonites is not fully adequate.

SCRIVEN, CHARLES
*The Transformation of Culture: Christian Social Ethics After
H. Richard Niebuhr*
Scottdale, Pa. and Kitchener, Ont.: Herald Press, 1988

It is a new experience for Mennonites to discover a scholar who argues
that the Anabaptist answer to H. Richard Niebuhr's *Christ and Culture* is
superior to the Augustinian-Calvinist conception of social transformation favoured by Niebuhr. "Theorist by theorist," notes James W.
McClendon of the Graduate Theological Union, Berkeley, in the
introduction, "school by school, he examines Niebuhr's successors in
social theory, seeking those who can point the way. Protestant idealists
and existentialists, old Catholic moralists and new Catholic liberation-
ists, militant feminists and militant evangelicals are examined here
through their best representatives. And they are cross-examined along
with Scriven's ultimate favourites, the heirs of Anabaptism."

Scriven's book places Anabaptist-Mennonites at the centre of the
debate on social policy. This new centrality is also affirmed by Stanley
Hauerwas of Duke University and John Howard Yoder of Notre Dame
University but other supporters of Scriven are difficult to find. This
book will provoke stimulating controversy in the years ahead.

SHANK, AEDEN and RICHARD MOJONNIER (EDS.)
*Professionalism: Faith, Ethics and Christian Identity*
Philadelphia, Pa.: Eastern Area Mennonite Student Services, 1978

North American Mennonites moved from closed, relatively small rural
communities to large urban communities to work as academics, social
workers, lawyers, doctors, nurses, journalists, and ministers. These
new urban professionals could no longer depend on the church-world
dualism. The new vocations are inextricably bound up with the major
institutions of the city: hence, a conference for young professionals in
Philadelphia.

In the opening address, Harvard theologian Gordon Kauffman
reviewed the new situation where the old authoritarianism faced a
whole wave of complexity flowing into the simpler earlier ethos. Moreover, the new view of the Bible also contributes to the problem. Kauffman called for a more open, more personal struggle with the basic
moral dilemmas of urban professionalism. But to go beyond a conscientious individualism Kauffman suggested that small groups of urban
Mennonite fellow-seekers and fellow-professionals struggle with the
challenges of the new existence.

John W. Eby also lectured to the conference, drawing upon sociological scholarship. He also stressed the need for Christian community in
the urban professional milieu.

Unfortunately, much of the discussion could not draw upon Canadian research among urban Mennonites who have successfully walked on the tightrope between urban professionalism and an ethno-religious city sub-culture. The research of Leo Driedger would have helped.

STAEBLER, EDNA
*Whatever Happened to Maggie and Other People I've Known*
Toronto: McClelland and Stewart, 1983

The unique feature of these ten interviews by the Waterloo free lance journalist who has written dozens of articles on Mennonites and a handful of bestselling Pennsylvania Dutch Mennonite cook books, is three biographical sketches: Bevvy Martin of the Old Order Mennonites of St. Jacobs, Ontario (the sketch is called "How to Live Without Wars and Wedding Rings"); Jacob Wurz of the Old Elm Hutterite Colony in Alberta ("The Lord Will Take Care of Us"); and Leah Keupfer of the Old Order Amish Community in Milverton, Ontario ("Why the Amish Want No Part of Progress").

Staebler's sketches are full of keen insights rejecting quantification via the questionnaire used in most sociological research. All the chapters are based on extensive interviews with people featured in the writing. Staebler appended a note to her interview with the Amish family indicating that Sam Keupfer's married children, many years later, had moved up several rungs on the Mennonite ladder in order to utilize cars and tractors. This meant that they were no longer Amish. Yet their attrition rate is not greater than most voluntary associations, religious or secular, in our society. The depth interview is obviously an important research tool.

STUCKY, SOLOMON
*The Heritage of the Swiss Volhynian Mennonites*
Waterloo, Ont.: Conrad Press, 1981

This book is a creative and informative historical account of the Swiss Volhynian branch of Mennonites who migrated to Russia for a brief period before moving to the U.S. mid-west. The author, himself of this background, obtains his information from other historical work, a built-up oral history, his own family's story, and a great deal of research. The historical background is well-documented, and provides a helpful context for the story being developed.

A unique aspect of Stucky's book is his use of "personal reminiscences"; while the characters who tell the story from Their own place and time are fictional, they do provide an authentic "window" into the personal side of the historical drama.

The book is illustrated with pictures and maps, as well as a pull-out chart outlining the migrations of the Swiss Volhynian Mennonites. It is a unique and valuable contribution to the study of this particular people.

TOEWS, JOHN A.
*People of the Way: Selected Essays and Addresses*
Abe J. Dueck, Herbert Giesbrecht, Allan R. Guenther (eds.)
Winnipeg: Christian Press, 1981

This collection of articles, sermons and lectures by John A. Toews has been compiled in memorium by the Historical Committee of the Mennonite Brethren churches of Canada. The editors seek to recognize Toews' service to the church throughout this life, and as well to carry his influence to coming generations.

As well as works by John Toews, the book includes a preface by Helmut Huebert, a foreword by Abe J. Dueck, a chronology of John Toews and an *In Memoriam* by David Ewert.

URRY, JAMES
*None But Saints: The Transformation of Mennonite Life in Russia, 1789-1889*
Winnipeg: Hyperion Press, 1988

Urry was trained in anthropology at Oxford, researched Russian Mennonites in Canada, and is now teaching at Victoria University of Wellington in New Zealand.

Urry's writings always have been surprising, documented assertions and original conceptualization. A surprise in this book is the pro-Russian nationalist sentiment of the Mennonites approximately 25 years before the outbreak of the Russian revolution. The Mennonite cultural elite declared that in no other country on earth had the Mennonites achieved such prosperity and security. There were, on the other hand, connections with other Mennonites in Germany, Holland, and North America, and a knowledge of church history, especially since the Reformation. There was a rising ecumenical feeling for non-Mennonite Christians.

While rapport was growing, Urry was the first social scientist to locate clues for this sense of well-being in the changing language, rhetoric and discourse as a linguistic key to social change.

It is chastening to read this résumé of good will knowing that underneath the surface of Czarist society were the rumbles of a volcano which would erupt in 1918, venting destruction on both the old Russian establishment and the relatively new Mennonite colonies of 129 years. The Mennonite vision of a sub-culture within a culture is seriously challenged by this work. They read the face of the sky but did not discern the signs of the times.

WEAVER, J. DENNY
*Becoming Anabaptist*
Scottdale, Pa., and Kitchener, Ont.: Herald Press, 1987

Anabaptist (re-baptizers) is the name of the sixteenth-century forebears of the now complex people known as Mennonites, Hutterites and Amish. This book is based on the huge number of books, theses and articles delineating the multiple origins and diversity of these Protestant radicals who originated in Europe.

Sociologists from the sixteenth century until the present have seen dissenters as a counter-culture posing itself as a prophetic alternative to the existing, conventional social order. John H. Yoder, a Mennonite scholar at Catholic Notre Dame, South Bend, wrote *The Politics of Jesus* to support this view.

Granted the vast differences among the three groups, Weaver cautiously suggests there are four normative principles: community (not individualism), discipleship (not creedal Christianity), pacifism (not saviours with the sword), and separation (expressed in tension with service and witness). These regulative principles permit considerable variation in application without making charges of "errant departures from a normative Anabaptist tradition." The author calls for an open future in which one becomes an Anabaptist drawing on the past.

WIEBE, KATIE FUNK
*Who are the Mennonite Brethren?*
Winnipeg: Kindred Press, 1984

This pamphlet is an introduction to the Mennonite Brethren's faith and doctrines, organizations and practices. It discusses early Mennonite history, the experiences of the Mennonite Brethren in Russia, their migration to America, the expansion of the denomination and its connections with other Mennonite groups, its missionary and evangelical activities and its efforts in the area of education and publishing. The booklet is written from a primarily theological viewpoint, which it seeks to promote in simple, readable language. It is descriptive not critical.

WIEBE, KATIE FUNK (ED.)
*Women Among the Brethren: Stories of Fifteen Mennonite Brethren and Krimmer Mennonite Brethren Women*
Hillsboro, Kans.: The Board of Christian Literature of the General Conference of Mennonite Brethren Churches, 1979

This collection of fifteen stories by and about Mennonite Brethren women (nineteenth century to the present) inspires a genuine interest in a sector of that community most often left invisible within historical documents. Edited by Katie Funk Wiebe, it highlights women's struggle and courage, sorrow and defeat through the turbulent and formative years from life in Russia, the upheaval of war-time, and to the present day. One is almost overwhelmed by the drama and impact of this untold history. One recurring theme is the importance of children. Bearing, rearing, and burying children, as well as the risks of childbearing, dominated the lives of these women. The book is not only a moving document, but also a pioneering study of Mennonite women still able to tell and record their own story.

For other contributions to the story of Mennonite women, see Elaine Sommers Rich, *Mennonite Women: A Story of God's Faithfulness, 1683-1983* (Kitchener, Ont.: Herald Press, 1983) and Ruth Unrau, *Encircled: Stories of Mennonite Women* (Newton, Kans.: Faith and Life Press, 1986).

WITTLINGER, CARLTON O.
*Quest for Piety and Obedience*
Nappanee, Ind.: Evangel Press, 1978

This book documents and analyzes the history of the Brethren in Christ church, particularly in the United States, from its eighteenth-century beginnings until the 1970s. Wittlinger discerned four distinct periods in the history of the Brethren.

The group emerged out of Mennonite culture in Pennsylvania, in the eighteenth-century Holiness revivalistic movement. They emphasized evangelistic piety along with the Anabaptist understandings of obedience and brotherhood. The first one hundred years were characterized by separation from the world, but also during this period the Brethren expanded geographically. They migrated both westward and north to what was then known as Upper Canada (Ontario). The second period was one of transition where the nineteenth-century evangelistic movement and Wesleyan Holiness influenced the Brethren. As a result, missions, Sunday schools, revival meetings, and church schools emerged. The third period was one of adjusting and adapting to these changes, resulting in a swing towards legalism in the 1930s. The fourth period began in the 1950s, the church became increasingly concerned with evangelism and numerical growth.

The documentation and analysis in this book is thorough and extensive, making it an essential research tool for anyone studying the history of the Brethren in Christ, a denomination affiliated with the Mennonite Central Committee.

YODER, JOHN HOWARD and WALTER PIPKIN
*Balthasar Hubmaier: Theologian of Anabaptism*
Scottdale, Pa., and Kitchener, Ont.: Herald Press, 1988

Twenty-four years of editing and translating have been devoted to this book about one of the major figures in the sixteenth-century Anabaptist movement, martyred in Austria 462 years ago.

The publication is included in this volume because during the Reformation, Hubmaier wrote the first book pleading for complete religious toleration: *Concerning Heretics and Those Who Burn Them.* Mennonites have resisted, negotiated and dialogued with many governments while seeking freedom under the law.

# B. Graduate Theses

APPAVOO, MUTHIAH DAVID
"Religion and Family among the Markham Mennonites"
Ph.D. dissertation, York University, 1978

This is a well organized empirical study of the Swiss Mennonite community in Markham, Ontario, located due north of the Borough of Scarborough in Metropolitan Toronto. The Mennonites have been in Markham since 1803. Appavoo chose to study the religious, family, and community-cohesion aspects of their lives by measuring the effect of urbanization and secularization on Mennonite identity in the context of their ideology of nonresistance and service. The researcher used six major hypotheses. He adopted factor analytic procedures which yielded a number of scales usable with marriage, sex role attitudes and ideal expectations, and utilized a control group of non-Mennonites who lived nearby.

Despite nearly two centuries next door to the dynamic Toronto metropolis, the core values of pacifism and nonresistance have been maintained. The research further revealed that even those who broke away from the Mennonites maintained many of the core values in other churches. Deviant attitudes and tension management were maintained by founding four congregations in which different emphases were institutionalized. Strong family ties were another important resource for survival and maintenance of group values. Success and achievement were not primary goals in Markham. Finally, Appavoo's study revealed that interaction, cooperation and community cooperation were distinctly greater among Mennonites than non-Mennonites. The six hypotheses stated at the start of the study were maintained.

Despite 144 pages of statistical data, the optimistic and supportive conclusions of this dissertation are greatly at variance with other empirical studies of Mennonites. The most extensive scientific study was made in 1975 by J. Howard Kauffman and Leland Harder working with forty-two professionally trained sociologists.[1] Kauffman and Harder's 87 tables and 391 footnotes describe considerable ambiguity and erosion of original values, especially via fundamentalist orthodoxy, which undermines pacifist commitment, social concern and inter-Mennonite activities. Hence, two extensive empirical studies need to be compared. It is significant that the Harder-Kauffman research was based on the methodology of Lenski and Glock while Appavoo utilized King, Hunt and Crysdale.

BENDER, TITUS WILLIAM
## "The Development of the Mennonite Mental Health Movement: 1942-1971"
Ph.D. dissertation, Tulane University, 1976

During World War II fifteen hundred conscientious objectors from Mennonite churches in the U.S. served in 22 state mental hospitals and four training centres. Appalled by the conditions in these hospitals, the COs determined to establish a network of private hospitals with more compassionate, more therapeutic and more skilful care. By 1948, the Mennonite Mental Health Services was organized and ready to launch its first mental hospital—Brook Lane, near Hagerstown, Maryland. Today six MCC hospitals in the U.S. and Canada provide excellent alternatives to overcrowded and understaffed state institutions.

Bender's dissertation explores the relationship of the conceptions and methodologies of these mental health centres with the culture and beliefs of the Mennonite minority that sponsors them. Fairly quickly the Mennonites discovered they did not have enough clinical psychologists and psychiatrists to fully staff these hospitals. Hence, Bender also analyzed the cultural diversity of both clients and the service-providing agencies under the Mennonite Mental Health Services. He found that the hospitals had an outward and an inward impact: outward, to the whole mental health field through skilled compassionate innovative treatments; inward, to the Mennonite minority inclined to be moralis-

---

1. *Anabaptists Four Centuries Later: A Profile of Five Mennonite and Brethren in Christ Denominations* (Scottdale, Pa.: Herald Press, 1975).

tic and legalistic. Nothing ever stretched the Mennonites like this constant encounter with clients and professionals outside the church, and endless requests for funds from state mental health budgets. Bender's study reveals the impact of the Mennonite mental health experiences in World War II; compassion became more important than excessive discipline, and the need for both private and state mental institutions was demonstrated.

For another version of this experience see Vernon H. Neufeld, *If We Can Love: The Mennonite Mental Health Story* (Newton: Faith and Life Press, 1983).

BRUBACHER, PAUL H.
## "Dimensions of Social Interaction Between Old Order Mennonites and Non-Mennonites in the Mount Forest Area"
M.A. thesis, University of Guelph, 1984

Using discussions, interview questionnaires and open-ended queries, the author documented the social interaction presently taking place between non-Mennonites and a recently settled group of Old Order Mennonites in the Mount Forest area in south central Ontario.

The non-Mennonites were most concerned about the decline of the school system as a result of the growing Old Order community; and the Old Orders were most pleased with the erection of hitching rails in town to accommodate their horses and buggies. Value differences (farming as a way of life versus farming as an investment) were indicated and methods of resolving conflict delineated (personal dialogue). The intransigent stand against Workmen's (now Workers') Compensation made it difficult for non-Mennonites to participate in Old Order building projects. In short, Brubacher's study found peaceful interaction of two cultures without any abrasive conflicts.

CHESEBRO, SCOTT E.
## "The Mennonite Urban Commune: A Hermeneutic-Dialectical Understanding of its Anabaptist Ideology and Practice"
Ph.D dissertation, University of Notre Dame, 1982

The author terms this study, three self-contained but interrelated essays centring around the topic "The Mennonite Urban Commune," as actualized in the Mennonite community, Fellowship of Hope, a "research trilogy." The object of study common to all three essays is the religious tradition of Anabaptism. The first essay deals with an interpretation of the ideological influence and character of Anabaptism in the Fellowship of Hope. In the second, Chesebro evaluates the dynamic character of Anabaptism in the Fellowship; he proposes it to be as adaptable to the historical context of communal Mennonites, who are experiencing the affects of alienation from their culture and tradition, as it was to the politically and socially oppressive conditions which motivated its development in the sixteenth century. The final essay draws the arc between the interpretations given to Anabaptism in the preceding two; it proposes that the Anabaptist "praxis" of the urban commune, besides being a practical critique of dominant cultural patterns, represents a form of structural therapy.

For related studies, see Leo Driedger, J. Winfield Fretz and Donovan E. Smucker, "A Tale of Two Strategies: Mennonites in Chicago and Winnipeg," *MQR*, 52, 4 (October 1978): 294-311; Leo Deidger, "Fifty Years of Mennonite Identity in Winnipeg," *Mennonite Images*, ed. Harry Loewen, 123-36; and Dale W. Brown, "Communal Ecclesiology: The Power of the Anabaptist Vision," *Theology Today*, 36, 1 (April 1979): 22-29.

CLAASSEN, CONSTANCE
## "Utopian Aspects of the Mennonite Commonwealth in Russia"
M.A.thesis, Concordia University, Montreal, 1986

Based on mutual aid and a sense of mission to Russia and the world derived from Kingdom theology, the Russian Mennonites developed what Claassen considers a utopia. It was a self-instituted and controlled commonwealth with effective social institutions. It was not a millennial expectation but a Kingdom of God actuality in the here and now. But the demons of war and anarchy in 1917 and thereafter wounded their state within a state severely and almost mortally. After over a century of the commonwealth came suffering and then a quest for migration, principally to Canada. (If there are areas under demonic influences, the author notes that Chernobyl exploded its lethal gases near the colonies of the now defunct Mennonite commonwealth.)

The shattering of the commonwealth has given North American Russian Mennonites an awareness of tragedy as a dimension of history. A corporate utopian community only lives on in the small number of urban communes of Mennonite young people, and the many Hutterite communities in the U.S. and Canada. A privilegium support from the government of self-contained utopian rural communities, as prevailed in eighteenth- and nineteenth-century Russia, has been rejected as out of context in democratic America of the 1980s.

COONEY, DONALD FRANCIS
## "Changes in Attitude and Social Involvement Among Returned Overseas Volunteers"
Ph.D. thesis, Bryn Mawr College, 1983

Overseas voluntary agencies have determined as a major goal that, through the overseas experience, volunteers will return home with a different attitude and increased social involvement to raise consciousness and social involvement among those remaining at home. The study focuses on three questions: Do returned volunteers report changes in attitude and social involvement? Are there distinctive characteristics for volunteers who report major changes in social involvement? Do volunteers have suggestions for increasing the likelihood of attitude change and increased post-service social involvement?

An extensive survey was done among 735 returned volunteers from such agencies as the Mennonite Central Committee, and International

Voluntary Service LAOS. The study found a high percentage (88%) of volunteers reported attitude change. A high percentage (69%) reported increased post-service involvement in international social issues. A smaller percentage (44%) reported increased post-service involvement in domestic social issues. Analysis of major changes showed few distinguishing characteristics. Suggestions for increasing the impact of the experience for attitude change and increased social involvement were reported and some specific recommendations were quoted.

DALZELL, TIMOTHY WAYNE
"The Anabaptist Purity of Life Ethic"
Ph.D. dissertation, North Texas State University, Denton, 1985

While essentially an historical study, this dissertation poses once again the austerity and rigour still alive in the Old Order Mennonites, Amish and Hutterites, which surfaces among the progressives when there is an historical crisis of war and revolution as in the Soviet Union after 1917.

Dalzell underscores the manner in which a rigorous ethic and witness posed the problem of survival under persecution and the constant tendency towards disunity in the sixteenth century. The author does not see a paradigm for all to follow whereby the Cross is a strategy for living. On the contrary, he views the Anabaptists as truly heroic Christians who stood out in Christian history demonstrating in painful behaviour Luther's slogan: "Here I stand I can do no other."

For a somewhat similar study, see Kenneth Ronald Davis, *Anabaptism and Asceticism: A Study in Intellectual Origins* (Scottdale, Pa. and Kitchener, Ont.: Herald Press, 1973). For a more optimistic view beyond martyrdom, see Duane K. Friesen, *Christian Peacemaking and International Conflict: A Realist Pacifist Perspective* (Scottdale, Pa. and Kitchener, Ont.: Herald Press, 1986).

DE LISLE, DAVID DE GARIS
"The Spatial Organization and Intensity of Agriculture in the Mennonite Villages of Southern Manitoba"
Ph.D. thesis, McGill University, 1974

This study aims toward fuller understanding of the contemporary Mennonite village farming system and its development in Manitoba. It begins by describing the present land-holding system, outlines an infield/outfield pattern of cropping and organization, details crop production practices and costs on infield and outfield locations and, finally, examines the role played by economic, technological and socio-cultural forces in shaping the contemporary spatial structure of the farming system and the way in which the infield/outfield pattern developed through time.

The dissertation provides new research in several key areas that merit attention; it investigates current land-holding in sixteen villages of Rhineland and Stanley municipalities; it reveals a highly complex landholding arrangement in the villages resulting from the nucleated settlement pattern; and it unravels, for the first time, the historical development of the property pattern from initial settlement to the present day.

For related studies, see W. J. Carlyle, "Mennonite Agriculture in Manitoba," *Canadian Ethnic Studies*, 13, 2 (1981): 92-97; Richard J. Friesen, "Saskatchewan Mennonite Settlements: The Modification of an Old World Settlement Pattern," *Canadian Ethnic Studies*, 9, 2 (1977): 72-90; and Richard Friesen, "Old Colony Mennonite Settlement in Saskatchewan: A Study in Settlement Change." M.A. thesis, University of Alberta, 1975.

DICKEY, DALE FRANKLIN
## "The Tent Evangelism Movement of the Mennonite Church"
Ph.D dissertation, Bowling Green State University, 1980

Dickey investigated the tent evangelism movement which began in the Mennonite Church in 1946 at the instigation of the Brunk brothers. Dickey's analysis viewed tent evangelism as a rhetorical movement, using the methodology suggested by the dramatistic model of Kenneth Burke and developed by Leland Griffin and Robert Cathcart. That is to say, Dickey studied the conflict between the tent evangelists and the traditional leaders of the Mennonite church by critically analyzing the language used in the articles published by both parties in the Mennonite papers. The tent evangelism movement has collapsed. Its leaders still criticize the colleges and seminaries but the criticism represents a very small minority.

DYCK, HENRY
## "Jacob John Siemens and the Co-operative Movement in Southern Manitoba: 1929-1955"
M.A. thesis, University of Manitoba, 1982

This study focuses on the regional co-operative movement in Southern Manitoba from 1929 to 1955, a time period parallel with the career of Jake Siemens, a leader of the co-operative movement. The subject of the study is the origin, evolution and consolidation of co-operatives among Mennonites of Southern Manitoba. Considerable emphasis is placed on Mennonite attitudes and their relationship to co-operative ideology and institutions.

For related studies, see Frank H. Epp, *Mennonites in Canada* (Toronto: Macmillan of Canada, 1982), pp. 360-74 and J. David Flynn and Albert Koop, "A Sense of Community: Three Mennonite Towns in Manitoba, Canada," paper presented to the International Sociological Association, 1986.

ENGBRECHT, DENNIS D.
## "The Americanization of a Rural Immigrant Church: The General Conference Mennonites in Central Kansas, 1874-1939"
Ph.D dissertation, University of Nebraska, 1985

The purpose of this study is to investigate the Americanization of an immigrant church in rural Kansas. These Mennonites, who came from autonomous communities in Russia and East Europe, sought an ethno-religious distinctiveness in the United States also. Instead they were offered individual self-sufficiency. Some evidence of the group's "Americanization" is found in a language shift, public schools and higher education, the infiltration of American Protestantism, and the modification of certain church customs. By 1939, Mennonite congregations in central Kansas displayed an identity that was less ethnocentric and more religiocentric; it was less immigrant and more denominational. After six decades they were both Mennonites and Americans—"a people of two kingdoms." The yoke between the Kingdom of God and the "kingdom" of the U.S. needed a more critical analysis.

EPP TIESSEN, ESTHER RUTH
## "The Origins of the Mennonite Central Committee (Canada)"
M.A. thesis, University of Manitoba, 1980

This thesis charts the origins of the Mennonite Central Committee, Canada, as the only organization to which all sixteen different Mennonite and Amish groups belong. It unites these diverse groups in order to pursue activities in the areas of relief to victims of war, famine and natural catastrophes; mutual aid, peace and social concerns. Canadian headquarters is in Winnipeg.

The organization developed from needs and pressures emerging in the first and second World Wars, the subsequent Cold War, the developing nations and large network of voluntary service and exemption for conscientious objectors—an historic conviction of Mennonites.

Epp Tiessen outlines the organizational development which led to the founding of MCCC in 1963. She views it as an important focus of identity and a basic channel for expression of concern for the needy people of the world. Moreover, the MCCC has also served to delineate the similarity and differences between the United States and Canadian Mennonites. There are now separate Canadian and U.S. committees with a bi-national office in Akron, Pennsylvania.

Absent from this study is an adequate context to understand the nature of the service activities in direct relief, development and institutional voluntary service. Dealing with the symptoms and victims of violence, conflict and injustice is not the same as dealing with the causes of these structures of injustice. Several MCC workers who served in Vietnam have declared they would not repeat the experience under similar circumstances because of the dilemmas posed by the American occupation of Vietnam under conditions of war. A distinction should be made between social service, social action and political responsibility.

FAST, DARRELL W.
## "Where Are All the Children Going? The Faith and Identity of Children of Mennonite Parents in Toronto"
D.Min dissertation, Emmanuel College, University of Toronto, 1986

In this study, Fast addresses the question of how a religious minority—in this case the Mennonite church—passes on its heritage of faith to the next generation in an urban setting. In the context of an increasingly urban Mennonite church in Canada, the author examines the models of Christian education in the Believers' Church; he proposes a model of developmental discipleship as an alternative to the nurture and conversion approaches to children. This prepares the way for the *choice* of adult baptism.

Further in the study, Fast uses findings from conversations with Mennonite children in Toronto to determine the implications of growing up in an urban Mennonite setting. He later relates this ministry aspect with other religious research in contemporary Canadian society, and concludes that these theories do not account for the ability of the Mennonite Church to adapt to the urban challenge, and to create a context in which children are able to make a free choice regarding Christian faith.

The report concludes that the urban Mennonite church must make a distinction between a rite of passage into adolescence at age twelve and the religious rite of baptism. The former is universal, and a matter of human development. The latter is a matter of personal choice (which comes later) and a matter of faith development.

This study is particularly relevant within the context of an increasingly urban Mennonite church. Based on field research in Toronto, the study is an original contribution to Mennonite sociology completely apart from rural and small-town life.

FELSTEAD, ALLAN G.
"A Socio-Historical Analysis of the Sectarian Divisions of the Mennonite Church of Waterloo County, Ontario, 1849-1939"
M.A thesis, University of Waterloo, 1978

This thesis investigates the role of specific status, age, economic, and interpersonal factors in the development of religious conflict and schism in the Mennonite Church of Waterloo County during the years 1849 to 1939. Building on previous research that has indicated that schism is generally the end result of pressures acting upon the community from sources external to the group and from within the community itself, this analysis of historical material applies functionalist theory to five cases of religious conflict and demonstrates that sectarian division is a complex social phenomenon resulting from the combined effects of the acculturative impact of a dominant external society, interpersonal conflict and systematic differences in church rank between the opposing factions in the conflict.

In 1988, the Mennonites of Ontario — Russian and Swiss — turned their backs on schism when they merged into one conference. It is not clear whether Felstead's use of functionalist social theory to interpret the collapse of unity 1849-1939 can explain why two groups of Mennonites with totally different histories and cultures could demonstrate unity and union fifty years later. Symbolic interaction could be a better social theory than functionalism in the late 1980s.

FRANSEN, DAVID WARREN
"Canadian Mennonites and Conscientious Objection in World War II"
M.A. thesis, University of Waterloo, 1977

World War II confronted the leadership of Canada, as a nation, and the Mennonites, as a people within that nation, with two historical prob-

lems—the first was the quest for internal unity, and the second was the
quest for acknowledgement of their integrity as citizens in their respective
communities. Within this context, the confrontation of these two realities
came with the issue of military exemption and conscientious objection in a
time of war. This was also part of the larger question—for Mennonites—of
their obligation to the state, this in a time of the newly emerging concept of
Canada as an authentic entity separate from Britain. This study delves into
the dynamics of this interaction and confrontation.

Through this process, Mennonite groups identified with each other,
Mennonites identified with other pacifist groups, and most impor-
tantly, they identified with Canada. They had begun moving towards a
somewhat more ecumenical, and Canadian, collectivity.

This thesis is an important historical study, as well as being a significant examination of the Mennonite identity as it developed in the Canadian context.

FRIESEN, RICHARD
"Old Colony Mennonite Settlement in Saskatchewan: A Study
in Settlement Change"
M.A. thesis, University of Alberta, 1975

This study looks first at the origins of the Mennonite faith in the Protestant Reformation, and then traces the development and movement of
Mennonites from Europe to Russia, and finally to North America.
While in Russia, the Mennonites established a social organization and
settlement that promoted and complemented the religious isolationism
they desired and fostered Mennonite ethnic identity. When political
changes in Russia suspended these special rights, Mennonites migrated
to reserves of land in Southern Manitoba. When this agricultural village
system disintegrated—due to the inability of the settlement to adapt to
the evolving commercial grain industry in the Canadian West—two
daughter colonies were established in the Rosthern and Swift Current
area of Saskatchewan (1895 and 1906). It was found that these later settlements had a higher survival rate than their counterparts in the Manitoba Reserve. Friesen explores the related factors, and looks at development to the present day. For example, many villages are seeking legal
status as hamlets, thus lending permanence to an unusual settlement
form that finds its origins in Medieval Europe.

For a related study, see W. J. Carlyle, "Mennonite Agriculture in
Manitoba," *Canadian Ethnic Studies*, 13, 2 (1981): 92-97.

FROESE, DONNA M.
"A Comparison Between Urban and Rural Mennonite Women
in the Housewife and Wage Earner Roles on Self Actualization
and Attitudes"
M.A. thesis, University of Kansas, 1978

Froese addressed the much-debated feminist critique of the traditional
female role as resulting in a lower level of self actualization than the

contemporary female role. Using an in-depth analysis of Abraham Maslow's theory of the hierarchy of needs, Froese examines feminist literature and posits the question of whether there may be exceptions — perhaps women can develop fully within the traditional role. The study groups are rural and urban Mennonite women.

On the basis of this study, Froese concludes that self-actualization and belief in the traditional female role seem to be in contradiction; Mennonites have taught their women the traditional submissive role, while at the same time the church teaches the principles of self actualization. While Froese concludes that the housewife is not necessarily less self actualized than the wage earner, the church does need to re-examine its teachings concerning the appropriate role for women if it wants each member to make full use of her potential.

This study is presented from a counselling perspective, and as such will provide a valuable resource for those dealing with this aspect of the female role in society — particularly within the Mennonite context.

GOLDFUS, ROSS MARTIN
"The Development and Testing of a Design for Conflict Mediation in Congregations"
D. Min. dissertation, Eastern Baptist Theological Seminary, 1985

The main objective of this thesis/project — done in eastern United States Mennonite churches — was to develop conflict mediation for congregations, to identify the issue and contribute to a constructive resolution. The scriptural basis was a study of the concept of reconciliation, followed by an examination of the socio-psychological aspects of conflict. After a discussion of the qualifications of a mediator, Goldfus formulated a process for mediation in conflict. The process, used in four conflict situations in Mennonite churches, was written up into four case studies. It received strong affirmation, but it was learned that its effectiveness depends in part on the skill of the mediator and the openness of the participants to change.

GOOD, E. REGINALD
"War as a Factor in Mennonite Economic Policy: A Case Study of Insurance Institutions, Sponsored by the Ontario Conference, 1864-1954"
M.A. thesis, University of Waterloo, 1984

Good rejects the Winfield Fretz-Guy Hersberger thesis that altruism and mutual aid played a significant role in the development of Mennonite insurance institutions. He is also dissatisfied with John H. Yoder's alternative thesis that the mutual aid in most Mennonite and non-Mennonite rural communities was based on economic self-preservation. Mennonite insurance was a sophisticated version of that egocentric model. The Good veto is also wielded over Mary Young's Ph.D. dissertation at Alberta in 1974 in which she utilized anthropological theory to interpret Mennonite insurance as a part of boundary maintenance.

With the negative task completed the author sets forth a new theory that the Mennonite insurance was due to the church's peace testimony (*Waffenlosigkeit*). In time of war particularly, the Mennonites safeguarded their pacifist convictions by providing an alternative to commercial insurance and government welfare.

How to explain, then, today's decline of Mennonite insurance? It is not abandonment of the peace conviction, but rather the broadening of it through a wider ministry. Good's original thesis has not persuaded the altruism school which argues that insurance is too narrow a test of Mennonite mutual aid. The Mennonite Central Committee has dozens of altruism activities bigger and more effective than the old insurances patterns.

GRABER, ROBERT BATES
"The Sociocultural Differentiation of a Religious Sect: Schisms Among the Pennsylvania German Mennonites"
Ph.D dissertation, University of Wisconsin, Milwaukee, 1979

This study is an examination and analysis of schisms among the Pennsylvania German Mennonites. It distinguishes between "firmly bounded" and "weakly bounded" groups, and examines various factors such as wealth and age which influence the nature of these groups. Data were collected on fifteen schisms occurring in Pennsylvania between 1778 and 1969.

The results of this study suggests that the selection of schisms for intensive analysis might profitably be based on a broad schism scope, and further, definite conclusions would be facilitated if schisms could be found in which a sizeable proportion of the lay members as well as leaders could be identified.

It is hoped that this first attempt at comparative analysis of Mennonite schisms will stimulate further and more sophisticated efforts toward a general, more scientific understanding of the great complexity of Pennsylvania German Mennonite history.

For a comprehensive study of divisions between the Mennonite groups, see Frank H. Epp, "Federation and Fragmentation," in his book *Mennonites in Canada* (Toronto: Macmillan of Canada, 1982), chap. 9, pp. 395-446.

JAGER, EDWARD C.
"The Anabaptists' Resistance to Modernization: A Study in the Sociology of Religious Ideas"
Ph.D. dissertation, New School for Social Research, 1983

This dissertation affirms Max Weber's thesis that a constellation of religious ideas can help change or stabilize the very social structures which gave rise to it, using the example of the Amish and Mennonites in Lancaster County, Pennsylvania, and Hutterites elsewhere. He does this even though they deviate considerably from most of the sects Weber analyzes by eschewing "modernization" and industrialization rather than assisting in the movement toward modern capitalism. The dissertation concludes, in agreement with Weber, that investigation of the stability in social groups and communities must examine the groups' ideological structures, including structures of religious belief, along with other social structures, if they would understand persistence and resistance to change in the direction of modernization and assimilation.

JANZEN, WILLIAM
## "The Limits of Liberty in Canada: The Experience of the Mennonites, Hutterites and Doukhobors"
Ph.D. dissertation, Carleton University, 1981

As director of the Mennonite Central Committee office in Ottawa, William Janzen has both the opportunity and the obligation to observe and to influence the federal policies which have impact on the Mennonites, Hutterites and Doukhobors. In this doctoral thesis, Janzen brings systematic analysis to the *limits* and the possibilities of liberty while encountering the Canadian government. It is a formidable task in view of the differences among and within the three groups but there have been common concerns for communal living, operation of their own schools, avoidance of military service and, often, avoidance of federal and provincial welfare programs. The more progressive Mennonites would mainly focus on the exemption from military service without confrontation over communal land and autonomous welfare programs.

Janzen is not much interested in social and political theory. He is inclined to make his analysis on an issue-by-issue basis. On initial consideration, the three most separate groups are non-political even though frequently in conflict and negotiation with government. It is a kind of political/non-political paradox.

The author set forth the uncertain, ambiguous accommodation of the government because of three factors: the historical context; second, new influences after immigration; and third, pro-accommodation forces in the Canadian political system. On the whole, it is the story of radical Christian groups interacting with a flexible but rugged government. It revealed government as the art of the possible with no rigid ground rules.

KLIPPENSTEIN, LAWRENCE
## "Mennonite Pacifism and State Service in Russia: A Case Study in Church-State Relations: 1789-1936"
Ph.D. dissertation, University of Minnesota, 1984

With a sweep of 150 years, Klippenstein looks at the Russian Mennonite refusal to take up arms, a conviction he labels as "the heart of Mennonite political, religious belief and thought." This chronicle is a sad one since the 50,000 or 60,000 Mennonites remaining in the USSR have abandoned their peace convictions; and earlier, they had a terrible struggle with dilemmas posed by the German occupation and World War II in the Ukraine. Today one Mennonite scholar noted that "there remain only the individual heroic pacifists to admire but seldom to emulate."

Two centuries ago the Mennonites came to Russia with a government contract with permitted peace convictions to exist for 100 years.

In the 1870s, alternative service developed. It persisted in World War I but faced disaster in World War II. Ambiguous as is the present, individual pacifist convictions here and there are still alive. But the Soviets will never re-sign a group agreement offering special privileges to pacifist Mennonites. Even Gorbachev will not go back to the old privilegium.

Today, Russian Mennonites of Canada and the U.S. have strong peace convictions as they analyze Soviet policy very closely. Church and state in North America are greatly in contrast to the USSR. Changes may be in the offing. Leo Tolstoy, after all, was Europe's most famous pacifist. Klippenstein's book is a valuable survey of the past, and the 16 appendices contain documents of inestimable value.

MARTENS, HILDEGARD MARGO
"The Relationship to Socio-Economic Divisions Among the Mennonites of Dutch-Russian Descent in Canada"
Ph.D dissertation, University of Toronto, 1977

Building on the denominationalization theory of Richard Niebuhr, Liston Pope, S. D. Clark and Rodney Stark, Martens seeks to demonstrate that economic and material realities were central in shifting the Canadian Russian-Dutch Mennonites from a separated sect to an assimilated denomination.

Using both secondary studies and primary sources of data in newspapers, archives and interviews, the writer concludes that the increasing prosperity of the Dutch-Russian Mennonites was the crucial ingredient of the new status as a denomination.

The conclusions of this dissertation have been seriously challenged by the cross-cultural research of Leo Driedger in Manitoba and Alan Anderson in Saskatchewan. Jews, French Catholics and the Mennonites emerge as unassimilated "ethnic villages" in metropolitan areas. The changes from the simple, rural cultural context are primarily changes in style. A new urban subculture develops which is held together by a special identity, language, church membership, residential clusters, endogamy, voluntary associations and choice of friends. This is what Yinger calls an established sect.

A final critique is that Martens mistakes the plain, simple living of the rural sect for poverty. The rural sectarian farmer is land-rich and cash-poor. Until the recent agricultural crisis, this land-rich, cash-poor farmer could always sell the farm for a large sum of money or give it to his son or son-in-law. The absence of conspicuous consumption concealed substantial economic resources. These facts break the bond between sectarianism and poor people.

MIHEVE, JOE
"The Politicization of the Canadian Mennonite Peace Witness in the Twentieth Century"
Ph.D. dissertation, St. Michael's College, University of Toronto, 1988

It is an event when a Catholic theologian in a Catholic college writes a doctoral dissertation on the changing situation among Canadian Mennonites in their peace witness. President Rodney Sawatsky of Conrad Grebel College has called attention to this scholarly work as further evidence that the Mennonite Central Committee has served throughout the world of the twentieth century with inevitable changes expressed by a faith-action dialectic. Hundreds of MCC workers have experienced the political disturbances throughout the globe and in doing so, there have been changes in Mennonite thinking. The politicization of the Canadian Mennonites in Miheve'e thesis refers to the increasing acceptance of movements for justice. This, in turn, has played back into the new Shalom theology and ethics of Mennonites as seen in Perry Yoder's *Shalom: The Biblical Word for Salvation, Justice and Peace* (1987).

The major criticism of Miheve's dissertation is making the Mennonite Central Committee coterminous with grassroots local congregations. There is a sense in which MCC is a frontier agency, taking positions ahead of local consensus. On the other hand, there is no doubt about some basic changes demonstrated by the new faith/action dialectic.

ROSE, MARILYN PREHEIM
"On the Move: A Study of Migration and Ethnic Persistence Among Mennonites from East Freeman, South Dakota"
Ph.D dissertation, University of Iowa, 1982

Marilyn Preheim Rose left a Swiss Russian Mennonite community in South Dakota thirty years ago. She decided to undertake a doctoral study of 68 individuals who had also moved from this pioneer nineteenth-century settlement to other areas of the U.S. and Canada. She used questionnaires to ascertain what elements of the ethnic and religious backgrounds persisted. The data suggested that the out migration resulted in the loss of ethnic traits and the retention of "ideological" Mennonite beliefs and practices: pacifism, family, mutual aid, stewardship, discipleship and thrift.

Data of the most reliable character would have to cover more than thirty years' experience outside the home community in South Dakota, and the concept of an "ideological" re-settled ex-Mennonite needs clarification.

SMUCKER, JOHN I.
"Reflections and Implications of Urban Mennonite Mission in the South Bronx church,"
Ph.D. dissertation, The Union for Experimenting Colleges and Universities, 1985. *Dissertation Abstracts International*, 47, 3: 944

This study analyses and evaluates the mission relationships of an urban Mennonite congregation in its East Tremont neighbourhood in the South Bronx. It sheds light on the current Mennonite mission in New York City, as well as suggesting implications for the current urban strategy in the USA. Reflections on urban church leadership in this mission imply that the Mennonite denomination must develop a consistent urban church leadership training program in order to move the church toward aggressive urban Mennonite mission. The rural Men-

nonites are on new terrain — and they are surviving and perhaps suc-
ceeding.

TAYLOR, BETH-ANN COREY
"Conflict Management Styles Preferences of Mennonite and
Methodist Missionaries"
Ph.D. dissertation, Fuller Theological Seminary School of Psychology,
1984

> The conflict management styles of seventy-one missionaries attending
> annual conferences were examined using Jay Hall's conflict manage-
> ment survey (CMS). Thirty-six were experienced Mennonite mis-
> sionaries, while thirty-five were inexperienced Methodist workers who
> had not been on the field. The mission board members also completed
> Hall's conflict management survey as they imagined the "ideal" mis-
> sionary would complete it. There was a significant correlation between
> the board representatives' "ideal" and Hall's theoretical "ideal" hierar-
> chy of conflict management styles, favouring the synergistic and yield-
> lose styles. A basic conclusion to the study was that there is a need for
> increased training in the management of conflict in a cross-cultural set-
> ting.

WARNER, MIRIAM E.
"Mennonite Brethren: The Maintenance of Continuity in a
Religious Ethnic Group"
Ph.D. dissertation, University of California, Berkeley, 1985

> This study of a Mennonite Brethren congregation in California seeks
> to find the social and cultural processes by which the group has main-
> tained its ethnic identity in the urban environment. This group, with
> common religious and cultural traditions, strong kinship networks and
> interlocking ties, numbers approximately 400 members. Warner speaks
> of two "statuses" in the Mennonite Brethren church — the ascribed
> ethnic and achieved religious. Non-ethnic converts acquire only reli-
> gious membership while ethnic members acquire both. This has far-
> reaching implications for the religious and social behaviour of the
> group. Warner analyzes and describes ways in which the collective
> identity of the church is maintained, resisting the cultural assimilative
> trends of the twentieth century.
>
> For another perspective on the dynamics of the Mennonite Brethren
> church extension, see Edwin Wiebe, "Coming Off the Bench: Ontario
> Mennonite Brethren Mobilize for Church Extension," Fuller Theo-
> logical Seminary School of Theology, D.Min. dissertation, 1985 (193
> pp.).

WIEBE, BERNHARD
"Self-Disclosure and Perceived Relationships of Mennonite
Adolescents in Senior Highschool"
Ph.D. dissertation, University of North Dakota, Grand Forks, 1974

> The purpose of this study was to determine the significance of some
> patterns for Mennonite adolescents' self-disclosure *to* and perceived

relationships *with* their parents. Of specific interest for analysis were the differences in measures of total self-disclosure, the differences in measure of the perceived relationships, and the way that self-disclosure is affected by the perceived total relationships and by individual relationship conditions.

With a study group of 82 female and 77 male Mennonite senior high school students, Wiebe administered various tests to reach his conclusions. His findings dealt with which parent adolescents relate to more readily, differences in patterns of boys and girls, and various topics of self-disclosure.

WINTER, DOROTHY McCLEAR
"An Ethnographic Study of a Mennonite Christian Elementary School in Lancaster County, PA"
Ed.D. dissertation, University of Pennsylvania, Philadelphia, 1982

This study concerns the ways in which children in a particular private Mennonite elementary school are taught those matters considered essential and important to the Mennonite culture and society. Its purpose was to provide a descriptive analysis of classroom and other school activities related to the perpetuation of Mennonite beliefs and values, as well as the perceived importance of this. A specific focus was to discover teacher self-perceptions as reflected in the classroom, and to determine their relevance to producing a successful school.

Five major findings regarding perceived importance in the school were: curriculum planned to achieve a Christ-centred education; knowledge consistent with Biblical truths; teaching as an inspired and guided calling; the significance of parental involvement; and the church and school as extensions of each other.

The study shows that unity of purpose among parents and educators produces a school where clear objectives can be established and attained.

For related studies, see Bruce E. Hunsberger, "A Reconsideration of Parochial Schools: The Case of Mennonites and Roman Catholics," *MQR*, 51, 2 (April 1977): 140-51, and Donald B. Kraybill, "Religious and Ethnic Socialization in Mennonite Highschool," *MQR*, 51, 4 (October 1977): 329-51.

YOUNG, MARY M.
"Boundary Maintenance in a Religious Minority Group in Western Canada"
Ph.D. dissertation, University of Alberta, Edmonton, 1974

This study uses the concept of boundaries and boundary maintenance and applies it to an Old Mennonite community in Alberta, a sectarian group separated from the dominant society on ideological grounds, yet retaining certain close and symbiotic ties with it. It is argued that cultural content is not reliable in defining the group; its identity may be better approached in terms of the boundaries it adopts to separate itself from others. It is assumed that these boundaries are recognized by insiders and outsiders alike, and that the devices maintaining these boundaries change over space and time.

A typology of boundary-maintaining devices categorizes such devices in terms of their function in relation to the degree of self-isolation desired. The ultimate purpose of the typology is to analyze the relations between types to present a dynamic picture of persistence and change in the group under study in its socio-cultural environment.

It was found that events in the larger society have brought changes to the different types of boundary-maintaining devices of these Alberta Mennonites. This has reduced the distinctive lifestyle of the group, and there is increased contact with and participation in worldly activities.

The typology and its application provides a dynamic model for the analysis of sectarian groups by indicating how exclusiveness is maintained, the factors responsible for change and the direction of change. This approach may contribute to the clarification of study of any subcultural groups stressing separation from the culture as a whole. The symbiotic relationship with the dominant society needed more attention and definition.

For related studies, see Hugh Getty Laurence, "Change in Religion, Economics, and Boundary Conditions Among Amish Mennonites in Southwestern Ontario," Ph.D. dissertation, McGill University, 1980; J. Howard Kauffman, "Boundary Maintenance and Cultural Assimilation of Contemporary Mennonites," *MQR*, 51, 3 (July 1977): 227-40; and James A. Knight, "Pluralism, Boundary Maintenance and Cultural Persistence Among the Amish," M.A. thesis, Wichita State University, 1977.

# C. Articles

AINLAY, STEPHEN C. and JAMES DAVISON HUNTER
## "Religious Participation Among Older Mennonites"
*MQR*, 68, 1 (January 1984): 70-80

This article explores the participation of Mennonite elderly people in religious activities by using data from a survey polling five different groups of Mennonite denominations. It finds that while there is evidence of decreased organizational participation there is a dramatic increase in more subjective nonorganizational religious activity (such as prayer and Bible-reading). This raises important questions about the relationship between aging and personal religiosity, as well as church polity and the way it may encourage marginalization of the elderly. This article is an important contribution to the study of the relationship of the elderly to the church community.

ANDERSON, ALAN and LEO DRIEDGER
## "The Mennonite Family: Culture and Kin in Rural Saskatchewan"
*Canadian Families: Ethnic Variations*, ed. K. Ishwaren. Toronto: McGraw-Hill Ryerson, 1980

Using data collected by longitudinal community studies of 1955 and 1977, and a sample study of eighteen ethnic-religious bloc settlements in north-central Saskatchewan of which two were Mennonite communities, the authors posed the central question of whether the changing Mennonite culture and family represent any or all of the following four social forces: social change in the general society; the urbanization of rural people; the assimilation or acculturation of ethnic groups, or change affecting Mennonites in particular. Driedger and Anderson conclude, "It must be our contention that the data which we have presented in this paper are indicative of social change at all of these levels."

Despite the cultural changes affecting the size and roles within the family, the authors declare that "there are still strong religious and ethnic boundaries which seem to encourage endogamy and retard extensive family separation and divorce. Urbanization and industrialization are changing the Mennonite family, but it would seem that the family will remain strongly Mennonite, albeit in a changed form."

Since Saskatchewan Mennonites are primarily from the 1874 Russian migration, it would be a further test of data to study the migrations of the "Russländers" — that is, those families who came to Canada after the Revolution between 1924 and 1948. The optimism of our authors needs to consider those who have endured the traumas of revolution.

APPAVOO, DAVID
"Ideology, Family and Group Identity in a Mennonite Community in Southern Ontario"
*MQR*, 69, 1 (January 1985): 67-93

The author examines how values and ideologies affect family and kinship group maintenance and community cohesion in the face of urban industrialism and secularism. The author focuses on a small group of Pennsylvania Dutch Mennonites in Ontario. The article uses collected statistical data to test a number of different hypotheses. The author finds that there is a continued commitment to close kin and to Mennonites in the community despite urban pressures. Religious ideology reinforces ethno-cultural cohesion. The strength of this article lies in its documentation. It contains an impressive array of statistical tables on numerous different subjects.

See Appavoo's York doctoral thesis on the same subject under graduate theses dealing with Mennonites.

ARNETT, RONALD C.
"Conflict Viewed from the Peace Tradition"
*Brethren Life and Thought*, 23 (Spring 1978): 93-103

Interviewing forty-seven individuals who affirm the non-violent peacemaking position revealed the diversity which surfaces when one attempts to define terms such as conflict, non-violence and non-resistance. The interviewees' reflections on peacemaking in conflict situations are summarized by categorizing them into four different conflict areas — intraphysical conflict, interpersonal conflict, conflict within the peacemaking community and international conflict.

ARONSON, LISA
"Environmental Education – A Unique Therapy"
National Audubon Society, January 1979

Under the direction of the National Audubon Society Expedition, a special nine-month school tours the United States and in the process its students learn about the country and come to a better understanding of themselves as well. The group draws questions from the social and natural environment around it and finds answers through talks with experts such as farmers, scientists, historians, musicians and rangers. During one expedition year, the young people spent two weeks working on a Mennonite farm. This paper summarizes the experiences of one of the participants in the program with particular emphasis directed toward the psychological benefits to be gained.

ASSHETON-SMITH, MARILYN and KELLEN TOOHEY
"School-Centered Community Conflict: The Holdeman Mennonite Case in Alberta"
Alberta Journal of Educational Research, 25, 2 (June 1979): 77-88

Providing background information on a dispute between the Holdeman Mennonites and two Alberta farming communities in which the Mennonites established schools, this article seeks to explain the differences in conflict level through analysis of ideological and structural differences in the two communities. It describes an agreement for reciprocal interaction through regular school policies.

BAAR, ELLEN
"Patterns of Selective Accentuation Among Niagara Mennonites"
Canadian Ethnic Studies, 15, 2 (1983): 77-91

Employing the concept "selective accentuation" this article argues that aspects of one's heritage are accentuated or downplayed in response to the environmental conditions facing an ethnic group. Using interviews with several generations of Mennonite church members in Ontario's Niagara peninsula, the research found that the 1920s and the 1950s have now become central, while emphasis on the Anabaptist component has sharply declined. In the Process, a people whose identity was primarily ethnic now emphasize religious rather than ethnic identification. These findings support the view that changes in ethnic identification are intermittent not irreversible. The article includes a good deal of primary evidence, including examples of the questions used to measure attitudes.

BARKER, RICHARD
"The Farm Experience: Its Importance in a Child's Life"
Alexandria, Va.: ERIC Clearing House, ED265958, Montessori Teachers Association (Spring 1986), 13 p.

For the past ten summers a rural Ohio farm family, convinced of the merits of involving children in farm experiences and/or plant and animal care, has shared its farmstead with approximately 3,000 urban elementary school children. This paper discusses the impact of farm experiences on children's development, exploring rural community life among the Amish, Maria Montessori's views of the value of farm experience and British integrated day schools. American Amish society, particularly, is seen as lacking the neurotic symptoms of industrial society. Specific character traits which might develop among children involved in small-scale relevant-learning environments such as Amish society are respect and understanding of nature, the habit of observing life, foresight, responsible community participation and a certain equilibrium of conscience resulting from the knowledge that one has given one's best effort at all times.

BIRD, MICHAEL
## "Ontario Fraktur Art: A Decorative Tradition in Three Germanic Settlements"
*Ontario History*, 68, 4 (December 1978): 247-72

> See Bird, *Ontario Fraktur: A Pennsylvania-German Folk Tradition in Early Canada* (Toronto: M. F. Feheley Publishers, 1977).

BOLDT, EDWARD D. and LANCE W. ROBERTS
## "Mennonite Continuity and Change"
*Canadian Journal of Sociology/Cahiers canadiens de sociologie*, 4, 2 (Spring 1979): 151-54

> In this article, Boldt and Roberts respond to Rod Sawatsky's comparative analysis of Canadian and American Mennonite experience (*Canadian Journal of Sociology*, Spring 1978). They challenge Sawatsky's assertion that denominalization in the United States — "the institutionalization of religious pluralism" — has resulted in a fractionization, and therefore a loss of ethnic group identity. Sawatsky has further identified a contrast in Canadian Mennonites who still perceive themselves as an ethnic group. Boldt and Roberts critique Sawatsky on the basis of his argument, saying that there are too many variables in a comparison of this kind.

BROWN, DALE W.
## "Communal Ecclesiology: The Power of the Anabaptist Vision"
*Theology Today*, 36, 4 (April 1979): 22-29

> Brown begins his discussion by identifying the continuing attraction of the "New Left" to the "old left" of the sixteenth-century radicals. Calling it a recovery of the Anabaptist vision, he sees it brought about by scholars such as Harold S. Bender working with original historical sources. Brown also draws a comparison between sixteenth-century reformers and present-day Christian groups such as the Sojourners community in their attempts to break the intimate relationship of church and state. Brown states that Anabaptist ecclesiology offers a theology of community within a pluralistic society — a small vision of God's kingdom not "of this world." We need to find new ways of being political; "the option of prophetic, witnessing, suffering and supporting communities may become more necessary and viable."

Brown sees the community of believers—part of the Anabaptist focus on "peoplehood"—as a model, in a sense, of God's kingdom on earth. This bears interesting similarities to Stanley Hauerwas who, in his books *The Peaceable Kingdom* and *A Community of Character*, envisions the "story" of God's people living in community as the medium or model of His work on earth.

BROWN, PEGGY (ED.)
"Peace Studies"
Association of American Colleges, Washington, D.C., *Forum for Liberal Education*, 5, 4 (March 1983)

In this study, selected college peace studies programs are described, and perspectives on such efforts in higher education are considered in an article by Robert C. Williams, "Sounds of Silence: The Academy and the Nuclear Question." Following the essay, peace studies activities of six colleges (Goshen, Syracuse, Ohio State, Juniata, Illinois and Earlham) are described. For example, the Mennonite Goshen College's peace studies program assists other departments to include peace content in their materials.

BRUNK, CONRAD G.
"Reflections on the Anabaptist View of Law and Morality"
*Conrad Grebel Review*, 1, 2 (September 1983): 1-20

This is an excellent discussion of two different conceptions of law—the "legal positivist" and the "natural law" view—and their relation to Anabaptist conceptions of law. While the "natural law" doctrine considers law to be the expression of morality, whether this morality be ordained by God, reason or natural law, the "legal positivist" view divorces law from morality and sees law as simply the expression of the will of the sovereign, whether that be a king, a dictator or a parliament, legitimized by the sovereign's ability to enforce the law, not by its moral worth. Brunk argues that the "legal positivist" view is part of the Lutheran heritage with its dichotomy between the kingdom of God, where love and grace reign, and the kingdom of the world, where the state reigns, and that the Anabaptists have accepted this view. He considers the dichotomy between morality and law a false one and the Anabaptist identification of law with the state a confusion of terms, illustrated by the fact that when Anabaptists tried to separate themselves from the state, they were nevertheless obliged to formulate their own laws. Law must therefore be based on the moral consensus of the society.

Brunk welcomes the growing perception in conservative Christian circles that law ought to express moral norms, but he argues that this undercuts the right-wing minimalist view of the state, which is based on "legal positivism." He argues that the era of extensive legislation in issues of social justice is inevitable, but that a closer link between the societal morality and law must be re-established to prevent the emergence of tyranny. He calls on the church to regain its "prophetic role" in calling the state to be "truly lawful," i.e., "moral," but to avoid usurping the role of the state in enforcing the law, etc.

The article does not address a serious dilemma: how can one base the legal system of a pluralistic society on the morality of one particular religion? On the other hand, can the "civil religion" delineated by Robert Bellah provide an alternative through a vague deism of consensus? In any case, this is an original contribution to Anabaptist philosophy and ethics.

CARLYLE, W. J.
## "Mennonite Agriculture in Manitoba"
*Canadian Ethnic Studies*, 13, 2 (1981): 92-97

This study attempts to determine whether Mennonites in Manitoba practise a form of agriculture which differs from that of other ethnic groups. Two physically different Mennonite areas were compared to physically similar non-Mennonite areas. The article finds that a homogeneous Mennonite agriculture does not appear to exist in Manitoba. At the same time, Mennonite areas tended to have smaller farms and larger families than non-Mennonite areas and each Mennonite area was more agriculturally intensive than the non-Mennonite areas.

CHRISTENSEN, HAROLD T.
## "Attitude Toward Marital Infidelity: A Nine-Cultural Sampling of University Student Opinion"
*Journal of Comparative Family Studies*, 4, 2 (Fall 1973): 197-214

This 1986 study surveyed attitudes toward marital infidelity among 1,543 male and 1,221 female college students in Sweden, Denmark, and Taiwan, a Catholic university in Belgium, two Black colleges in the southern U.S., a state university, a male Catholic college, a small Mennonite college and a Mormon university. Data were compiled with a similar study done by the author in 1958. Extramarital coitus was rejected by more than half, but proportion varied across cultures. Rejection was disproportionately higher in Asian and religious cultures, higher for females than males, and higher with those who had not experienced premarital coitus. Generally the rejection of marital infidelity and acceptance of the double standard were associated.

It is interesting to note that Mennonites are called a "religious culture" in relation to the national terms of Sweden, Denmark and Taiwan.

COHEN, PAUL W.
## "Can the Mennonites Survive Success?"
*New York Times Magazine*, November 8, 1987

A writer on farming topics, Paul Cohen visited the plain Mennonites of Lancaster County, Pennsylvania, where he observed three centuries of a special, rigorous, quaint life style threatened by a $400-million-a-year tourist industry and commercial, industrial and population growth. Cohen believes that the plain Mennonites must live in self-contained communities if they are to survive, even granting the stubborn resistance to assimilation also evident. He cites the case of Simon Kraybill, whose family arrived in 1772. Kraybill had seven children, all of whom have moved away. Ron Kraybill, head of Mennonite Conciliation Services and Harvard Divinity School graduate, says that in his youth "it was like we were living on an island of redeemed people in the middle of heathen." Ron Kraybill and his lawyer brother see the conflict between wealth and faithfulness. Consciousness of that tension survives.

The Old Order answer still operates on the same turf as the increasingly affluent and professionalized Mennonites. Cohen also discovered a modern Mennonite Franciscan type who works with blacks and Hispanics, stressing simple living and affirming social action and integration with underclasses.

Descriptively, this is one of the best surveys of the tensions within the plain people of Lancaster County, who struggle with what one may call Protestant monasticism as it encounters the power of social and cultural conditioning.

CORBETT, BILL
## "Mennonites Break New Ground in Northern Alberta"
*Canadian Geographic*, 108, 3 (April-May 1988): 34-40

In La Crete, Alberta, 650 kilometres north of Edmonton, the provincial government has land lotteries in Canada's most northerly grain-farming area. La Crete, with land at $50 per acre and $123 per hectare, is the fasting growing farm community in Canada—and one of the youngest.

There are five Mennonite congregations in La Crete, each of different conferences or denominations: Old Colony, Sommerfelder, General Conferences, Bergthaler and Evangelical Mennonite. A sixth group, the Holdeman Mennonites, are located nearby.

La Crete is re-creating some of the old frontier homesteading conditions of an earlier time period. Yet it is a struggle requiring diversification and a deep faith in farming as other options like logging beckon them to experiment with another approach. The restless urge to find cheaper land in new, remote areas is at work in Mennonite communities of northern Alberta.

CURRIE, RAYMOND, LEO DRIEDGER and RICK LINDEN
## "Abstinence and Moderation: Mixing Mennonite Drinking Norms"
*MQR*, 53, 4 (October 1979): 263-81

Building upon a statistical study of alcohol use among various groups of Mennonites in Canada, the authors isolate and examine those factors in the development of Mennonite mores which have tended to incline some toward moderate drinking and others towards abstinence. Their study is both historical and sociological on an issue of great importance to present-day Mennonites of differing persuasions.

DILL, VICKY SCHREIBER
## "Land Relatedness in the Mennonite Novels of Rudy Wiebe"
*MQR*, 68, 1 (January 1984): 50-69

By examining the concept of land in Rudy Wiebe's novels, the author shows the connectedness between farming and Mennonite self-identity. The insight of Wiebe's novels lies in his message that the land is not a necessary ingredient of the Christian life, although it is a security which Mennonites have always craved. This is an interesting article which explores Mennonite self-identity from a literary angle.

DRIEDGER, LEO
## "Changes in Types of Boundary Maintenance in a Canadian Ethnic Minority"
Paper presented at the 1967 annual meeting of the Western Association of Sociology and Anthropology in Banff, Alberta, December 28-30

The author analyzes the community life of the Old Colony Mennonites, suggesting that they are an example of the plural subculture that is characteristic of Canada. Driedger shows how the Old Colony Mennonites have maintained distinctive boundaries through four community types — the European village, the isolated community, the suburban satellite and ethnic urbanism. He suggests that this group has maintained their ethnic boundaries by several means including separate locations, language, occupations, education, family life, and religion.

DRIEDGER, LEO
## "Fifty Years of Mennonite Identity in Winnipeg"
*Mennonite Images*, ed. Harry Loewen. Winnipeg: Hyperion Press, 1980, pp. 123-36

In exploring the evolution of Mennonite self-identity, Driedger takes a panoramic glance at Mennonite history from the Reformation to the present. He uses the image of a "sacred canopy"; Mennonites have always upheld the "stakes" of Biblical theology, believers' community, Germanic culture, and land to support their canopy amid the buffeting worldly winds. Driedger's focal point in this article is the emerging Winnipeg Mennonite community of the last fifty years, and its search for self-identity in a new urban setting. He sees this identity as being endangered because urban Mennonites no longer support their canopy with the stakes of land and physical community. Driedger's hope for the urban Mennonites' survival is in a re-commitment to Biblical theology, and in a sense of heritage to replace a lost cultural identity.

Driedger's image of a canopy is helpful, but it loses some clarity as urban, educated Mennonites contribute to and become integrated into larger society. His example of amoebic protrusion and fission seems to be a more appropriate image; urban Mennonites protrude far into their surrounding environment, while still maintaining identity and action as a body.

DRIEDGER, LEO
## "Minority Conflict: Ethnic Networks versus Industrial Power"
*Ethnic Canada: Identities and Inequalities*. Toronto: Copp Clark Pitman, 1987, pp. 293-315

Using the Bargaining and Oppositional Models of Laumann and associates, and the "Lost," "Saved" and "Liberated" Communities approach of Wellman and associates, the author examines the 1980 conflict between the Warman, Saskatchewan Mennonites and Eldorado Nuclear, which sought to build a hexafluoride refinery in a largely pacifist rural Mennonite community and had to drop the plan after federal hearings.

Driedger tested the hypotheses that (1) crucial to community support for an active proponent of community invasion will be the effective use of instrumental issues coupled with a bargaining position; (2) crucial for success in opposing a community invasion will be consummatory issues to arouse opposition, so that an adversarial strategy can be developed; (3) members of a "saved" community are most likely to have the will, commitment and ability to fight an invasion, and members of a "liberated" community will have neither the conviction nor the commitment to fight community invasion.

A careful analysis of the Federal Environment Assessment Report, No. 13, 1980, and observation of the public hearings and interviews with "liberated" and "traditional" members who had not become involved supported these hypotheses and the combination model for conflict processes Driedger had proposed. The chapter is an interesting and valuable study of conflict.

DRIEDGER, LEO, J. WINFIELD FRETZ and DONOVAN E. SMUCKER
"A Tale of Two Strategies: Mennonites in Chicago and Winnipeg"
*MQR*, 52, 4 (October 1978): 294-311

This article compares Mennonite mission strategies in Chicago and Winnipeg over the past one hundred years. The authors are interested in the role of rural communal influence in shaping the manner of Mennonite forays into larger urban centres, especially as the idea of community was used to counter the starker individualistic spirit that permeated many urban environments. The article speaks of "atomistic mission outpost and community continuity strategies," and points us now to the availability of cumulative social services insights gained from years of Mennonite Central Committee activities useful for shaping present strategies for city mission work.

DRIEDGER, LEO and J. HOWARD KAUFFMAN
"An Urbanization of Mennonites: Canadian and American Comparisons"
*MQR*, 66, 3 (July 1982): 269-90

This article examines the historical factors which moulded Mennonite populations in Canada and the United States. The paper's central theses are (1) Mennonites of Dutch North German descent have urbanized more rapidly than those of Swiss South German extraction (Russian Mennonites urbanized even more rapidly); (2) American Mennonites in the West moved toward urban centres much more rapidly than those in the East, and Canadian Mennonites are more urban than American; and (3) urbanization of Mennonites in itself does not appear to affect basic religious beliefs, but it does affect the attitudes of Mennonites on a variety of personal, moral and social issues. Driedger and Kauffman turn out to be controversial enough to be highly stimulating. They are among the first researchers to work on substantive differences between Dutch North German Russian Mennonites and those from Swiss South German regions.

ARTICLES

DRIEDGER, LEO and JACOB PETERS
"Ethnic Identity Among Mennonite and Other Students of
German Heritage"
*Religion in Canadian Society*, ed. Stewart Crysdale and Les Wheatcroft.
Toronto: Macmillan of Canada, 1976, pp. 449-61

The authors attempt to show that ethnic identity among Mennonite students in Manitoba is significantly greater than among other German students there, as measured by the six factors of religious participation, endogamy, use of ingroup language, participation in ethnic organizations, amount of parochial education and choice of friends. Both attitude and behaviour with respect to these factors is measured. Mennonites rank significantly higher in all six factors, both with regard to behaviour and to attitude, than other Germans of various religious denominations combined.

The authors reject theories that community size, socio-economic status or generation in Canada have any significant association with ethnic identity. On the other hand, institutional Completeness is positively associated with stronger ethnic identity, and this proposition seems to apply particularly to the Mennonites. The authors suspect that institutional completeness is the product of ideological and social psychological factors nourished within the in-group which these institutions support. What these factors are, the authors do not examine in detail. This would have been interesting, especially since the authors reject the above-mentioned points as factors determining the degree of ethnic identity, and seem to regard institutional completeness as a product of ethnic identity.

The authors conclude by pointing out that when Germans in Manitoba are studied, the Mennonites must be "controlled," so as not to distort findings on ethnic identity among Germans.

DRIEDGER, LEO, ROY VOGT and MAVIS REIMER
"Mennonite Intermarriage: National, Regional and
Intergenerational Trends"
*MQR*, 67, 2 (April 1983): 132-44

"What percentage of Mennonites marry non-Mennonites, and what is the rate of increase of such intermarriages?" With these and similar questions, the authors examine data on Mennonite intermarriage in Canada. By studying trends in Mennonites in Manitoba, and particularly in Winnipeg, this article discovers that rural, more segregated Mennonites tended to marry inside the Mennonite church, while more urban Mennonites had a higher incidence of intermarriage. This article tends to favour endogamy, but the authors restrict themselves largely to a research report on trends as against writing a highly interpretive, polemical essay. Sociologists provide data for policy but they do not formulate policy.

DRIEDGER, LEO, MICHAEL YODER and PETER SAWATZKY
"Divorce Among Mennonites: Evidence of Family
Breakdown"
*MQR*, 59, 4 (October 1985): 367-82

With previous studies of divorce among Mennonites "rare and
sketchy," this study has nine statistical tables and a good grasp of the
larger societal context in which the Mennonite trends must be placed.
Early Anabaptists tolerated little divorce in their fellowships and only
when adultery was involved. They may not have agreed on many
things, but they did agree that marriage should be a lifelong commitment. Modern Mennonites find themselves in countries like the
United States and Canada where divorce rates are very high and climb-
ing, thus creating enormous pressures on the family. Compared to
other religious groups, Mennonites still have a low divorce rate, but it
is increasing significantly.

While most Mennonites in North America agree that marriage
should be a lifelong commitment, they are less certain about what to do
when divorce occurs in their churches. About 80 percent of all Mennonite churches now have to deal with divorce, and some have large
numbers of divorced people in their midst. The Mennonite divorce
rate is four times as high in the United States as in Canada; also, within
the two countries the rates vary considerably by region. While urbanization and industrialization seem to accelerate marriage breakdown,
urban regions do not necessarily have the highest rates.

Among active church members separation and divorce rates are
much lower than among inactive members. Ethnicity is also an important factor, with Asian and white European Mennonites, who tend to
come from quite stable family backgrounds, showing lower rates of
breakdown and Mennonites from black and Indian backgrounds much
more involved in breakdown.

When all Mennonite youth are compared with those from broken
homes, the latter are found to be not as strong in their religious beliefs,
to attend church less often, to have more trouble getting along with
others and to more often exhibit deviant behaviour. Unstable homes
seem to affect youth negatively.

While Mennonite divorce rates are still among the lowest in North
America, considerable evidence suggests that marriage breakdown is
increasing. In most churches broken marriages create considerable
agony, and on occasion, conflict and disruption. There seems to be
little hope that the problem will abate in the future. The nuclear family,
designed for greater freedom and mobility, seems also to break down
more under pressure.

One of the central conflicts among progressive Mennonites is the
clash between the rigorous and perhaps perfectionist nature of Mennonite ethics, including the ethics of marriage, and the deep involvement of Mennonites with the non-judgemental mental hygiene movement confirmed by the presence of eleven Mennonite mental health
centres in the U.S. and Canada, with headquarters as follows: Mennonite Health Services, 21 S. 12th Street, Akron, Pa. 17501.

DUECK, AL
## "Prolegomena to Mennonite Approaches in Mental Health Services"
*MQR*, 66, 1 (January 1982): 64-81

Dueck tackles the problem of relating religious conviction and mental health programs. He outlines five basic steps. First, there must be a critique of existing mental health approaches. Second, analogies between God working in history and certain processes of therapy should be recognized. Third, efforts must be made to translate religious constructs and mental health vocabularies. Fourth, there must be reciprocal dialogue between faith and profession. Fifth, the implications of religious commitments for mental health practices must be explored. This excellent article is comprehensive and well-documented and it addresses the issue of how Mennonites can make a unique contribution to mental health as a result of their faith.

DYCK, E. F.
## "The True Colours of Plain Speech"
*Books in Canada*, October 1988

Stimulated by the role of Winnipeg as the Mennonite literary capital of Canada, Dyck has written an original essay in Mennonite literary criticism.

The major characteristic of Mennonites, Dyck argues, is a unique peasant ideology. A peasant is one who lives in the country and works on the land. There is a strong commitment to Anabaptist Christianity. But the clearest example of Mennonite ideology is found in their language. And the Mennonite — *Russian* Mennonite — language is *plattdeutsch*, the Low German patois which provides a plain speech pattern. Thus, to be a Mennonite writer is to exploit the peasant ideology encoded in this Low German dialect.

Dyck illustrates his argument with citations of Fritz Senn, Arnold Dyck, Rudy Wiebe, Patrick Friesen, Armin Wiebe, Sandra Birdsell, Lois Braun, Victor Jerrett Enns, Di Brandt, Audrey Poetcker and Maurice Mierau.

This provocative essay is poorly timed because Winnipeg Mennonites are the most urban and culturally sophisticated in North America. The use of plattdeutsch is fading. The peasant ideology is not the key to the urban Winnipeg Mennonites. Perhaps there is a way in which writers reach back into the collective memory of their forefathers and mothers. Those memories deserve artistic expression but this is not the real world of the forty-five Mennonite Ph.D.s who teach in the city's two major universities.

EDIGER, ELMER M.
## "Influences on the Origin and Development of Mennonite Mental Health Centres"
*MQR*, 66, 1 (January 1982): 32-46

This article traces the history of and motivation for starting Mennonite Mental Health Services (MMHS) centres, and describes how these centres are run. The tension between psychiatry and the church is held in a delicate balance; this has produced an excellent selection of programs. These programs are enhanced by the chaplaincy program. Government funding has helped shape but has not fully controlled the direction of these centres. While informative about the structure of MMHS centres, this article does not describe the programs themselves, nor does it explain how Mennonite hospitals differ from state-run institutions.

EDIGER, MARLOW
*Mennonites in American Society.*
1985 Research Report, Mennonite College of Nursing, Bloomington, Ill

Designed for elementary and secondary school social-studies educators, this examination of the beliefs, values, customs, and philosophies of diverse groups of American Mennonites focuses specifically on major differences between and among the Holdeman Mennonites, the Hutterites, the General Conference, the Mennonite Brethren and the Old Order Amish. Specific comparisons are made in regard to dress and physical appearance, attitudes toward formal schooling, acceptance of modern appliances and machines, acceptable occupations and living arrangements, attitudes toward military and community service and differences in the teachings of the church.

EPP, FRANK H.
"Problems of Mennonite Identity: A Historical Study"
*The Canadian Ethnic Mosaic*, ed. Leo Driedger. Toronto: McClelland and Stewart, 1978), pp. 281-94

In this article, Epp traces what he calls the "Mennonite quest for identity" throughout this people's 450-year history. He cites the theme of identity as integral to understanding the Mennonites of Canada. Epp begins with a basic historical survey of Mennonite migrations since the nineteenth century, and then delves more deeply into its implications and the resulting internal dynamics. He deals in a clear and informative way with such classic Mennonite dilemmas as separation versus accommodation, progressive and conservative elements and internal fragmentation.

Epp concludes that Mennonites in Canada are still undergoing the active and dynamic process of developing a self-identity; he cites the growth of institutions such as the Mennonite Central Committee as helpful in this process.

While Epp's focus is on the historical Mennonite "people," it would have been helpful to mention the increasingly international nature of the Mennonite Church as significant in terms of Mennonite self-identity. This has introduced national, ethnic, cultural and racial pluralism into the church.

FRANCIS, E.K.
"Group Formation as a Result of Migration — The Mennonites in Manitoba"
*Interethnic Relations*. New York: Elsevier Scientific Publications, 1976

The author traces the development of the Mennonites from a religious to an ethnic group. The policies of cultural and economic segregation of the Mennonites monitored by the Russian imperial government led to a distinctive ethnic group. Changes in Russian government policy induced many Mennonites to migrate to North America in the latter part of the nineteenth century.

In Manitoba, organizational forms developed by the Mennonites in Russia were initially maintained, due to the absence of a provincial bureaucracy which might have interfered with it. However, the later introduction of Canadian government supervision moved toward a policy of cultural assimilation in the period preceding World War I. In addition, Mennonites were integrated into the capitalist economy. Both represented a challenge to ethnic distinctiveness. These developments were partly reversed during the Depression when Mennonites reverted to traditional forms of farming and organization in order to survive.

The author concludes by observing that ethnic groups emerge from various strong motives, but that the boundaries which separate them from their host society may change. Such symbolic differences include distinctive religion, language, economic system, kinship relations, etc. Where several such characteristics are combined, they tend to reinforce each other and perpetuate the separate ethnic character.

This case study's value lies in its inclusiveness; it touches on ideological, social, economic, cultural, linguistic and kinship elements and provides concrete examples of how they contribute to the formation of an ethnic group.

E.K. Francis' first study of the Russian Mennonites of Western Canada appeared in 1955.

FRANZ, DELTON
"How We Do Our Work. The Mennonite Voice to Government: Then and Now"
*Washington Memo*, Mennonite Central Committee, 21, 1 (January-February 1989)

An eye-opening account describing how the non-political progressive Mennonites started to abandon the church-world dualism of three centuries, beginning in 1940 and climaxing in the 1960s, but continued through the present. On twenty-three occasions Mennonites have testified at Congressional hearings. One hundred twenty-five delegations have visited Washington to discuss pending legislation.

The new test of faithfulness, according to the writer of this statement, is not doctrinal orthodoxy but *orthopraxis*. Christians should be judged by what they *do* and not merely by what they say. The goal both in North America and the Third World is to establish justice in economic and political systems. This is a language which can be communicated to Congress.

The writer of this statement is Delton W. Franz, director of the Washington office of the U.S. Mennonite Central Committee, who is in effect a Mennonite lobbyist in the nation's capitol. The Canadian counterpart to Delton Franz is William Janzen, director of the Ottawa office of the Mennonite Central Committee.

FRETZ, J. WINFIELD
## "Newly Emerging Communes in Mennonite Communities"
*Communes Historical & Contemporary*, ed. Ruth Shonle and Man Singh Das.
Delhi: Vikas Publishing House, 1979, pp. 112-24

This article is a report on an ongoing study by the author of the recent phenomenon of a number of intentional communities arising out of Mennonite congregations. These new communities are not "daughter" congregations planted by the mother church, nor are they splinter groups which have broken away from a parent body. For the most part, their members retain memberships in their former churches and frequently continue to participate in conventional church activities.

Nevertheless, these communities imply a judgement of the traditional churches as not offering enough opportunity for personal growth and interpersonal caring relationships. The communities do not, however, represent a hostile rebellion against the established church, but a "gentle prod to change." Economically, the communes afford their members a greater sense of security by freely sharing possessions, and help them break out of the competitive mass-consumption oriented capitalist system. Interpersonal relations take place on a communal level, with the result that psychological resources are greater than in the small nuclear family. Religious activity is informal and allows all members to participate and address their deepest needs. The communes attempt to re-capture the Anabaptist vision.

A majority of the leaders and many members of these communes are well-educated, and the author suggests that the intentional communities are a by-product of Mennonite Church college influences, as they are usually close to Mennonite college campuses. The article represents only preliminary findings, and the author refrains from making long-term conjectures, but the phenomenon he describes is very encouraging, and it will be interesting to follow the further development of these communes. One might even suggest that increased proliferation of such communes might have some effect on the values of non-Mennonite capitalist society.

FRIESEN, J. W.
## "Mennonites and Hutterites in Twentieth Century Alberta Literature With Special Reference to Educational Implications"
*Alberta Journal of Educational Research*, 22, 2 (June 1976): 72-90

This study reports on an analysis of a variety of sources of literature dealing with the attitudes of Albertans toward two minority groups. These are the Mennonites — an evangelical Protestant sect, and the Hutterites — another religious sect with an atypical lifestyle. The time span of the study is from the turn of the century to the present.

FRIESEN, J. W.
## "Mennonites in Canada"
*When Cultures Clash: Case Studies in Multiculturalism*. Calgary: Detselig
Enterprises, 1985, pp.143-58

This is one of five case studies of ethnic and cultural groups in Canada by Friesen. He briefly traces the history of the Mennonites, from the life of Menno Simons and the rise of Anabaptism at the time of the Reformation to the persecution-induced migration of Mennonite groups: of the Swiss Mennonites to America from the eighteenth century on, and of Dutch and North German Mennonites to Russia and thence later to North America. He provides a compendium of Canadian Mennonite groups, briefly describing each and illustrating the diversity of Mennonite groups. He argues that it is grossly inaccurate to refer to the Mennonites as a single cultural group with a common set of peculiar social practices. Nevertheless, there are some common distinctive characteristics: (1) the common background of language and stock; (2) certain common Anabaptist beliefs and practices; (3) a Mennonite orientation stressing the conscience of the individual believer (which often leads to schisms); (4) great concern about distinctive baptismal practices; (5) a quest for simplicity. Friesen then discusses the Mennonite view (or views) of education, describing the history of Mennonite education, and its role in preserving Mennonite identity. As with everything, Mennonite groups differ in their educational philosophy, from very conservative views favouring a minimal education and Biblical awareness, to more liberal views favouring higher education and study of a wide range of subjects. This article is a good introduction to the Mennonites in all their diversity.

FRIESEN, RICHARD J.
"Saskatchewan Mennonite Settlements: The Modification of an Old World Settlement Pattern"
*Canadian Ethnic Studies*, 9, 2 (1977): 72-90

In this detailed and descriptive article, Friesen traces the development of the Mennonite settlements in Saskatchewan from their European origins, and more directly, from the patterns of the Manitoba Mennonite villages. He describes the East and West Reserves of Manitoba, held together by voluntary cooperation, and further the partial abandonment of this system after which many Mennonites moved to settle in Saskatchewan. The basic motivation was a desire to "establish and to maintain a certain social and religious organization." With the use of map drawings and detailed descriptions, Friesen gives a clear picture of the major types of Saskatchewan village settlements: the organized village, the unorganized village and the four-corner hamlet. As in the Manitoba villages, the church played the key role in leadership.

Friesen's work is very helpful as an historical document, as well as being an interesting sociological study.

GAEDE, STAN
"Religious Participation, Socioeconomic Status, and Belief-Orthodoxy"
*Journal for the Scientific Study of Religion*, 16, 3 (1977): 245-53

This study seeks to determine the correlation, if any, between religious participation (church attendance, other involvement) and belief-orthodoxy and, as well, socioeconomic status. Gaede relies on a secondary study done by J. H. Kauffman and Leland Harder of approximately 1,800 male workers. Previous studies have found increased status correlative with religious participation; education was found to be a significant factor of status. Belief-orthodoxy also seemed to add to increased participation. Gaede's research basically supports these findings, with some notable derivatives. He found education to play a significant role. Religious participation increased as both education and belief increased, but belief decreased as education increased. Through further analysis, Gaede concludes that "education rather than economic status may be the more determinative factor in the socioeconomic status/religious participation relationship."

While difficult to follow at times, this study appears to reflect accurately the present situation in light of higher education among church members and increasing socioeconomic standards. Yet, belief orthodoxy is not incompatible with the climate of many church-related colleges and theological schools.

GLICK, ORELL and JAY M. JACKSON
## "A Longitudinal Study of Behaviour Norms and Some of Their Ramifications in a Small Liberal Arts College"
Kansas City, Mo.: Institute for Community Studies, 1969

This study sought to discover changes occurring in attitudes, values and life orientations of American college students. With a target population of 183 students of a small Midwestern Mennonite liberal arts college, Glick used Jackson's (1960) model to determine norms and changes in behaviour over a four-year period. Some conclusions were: the ideal or preferred behaviour was stable, intensity of feeling decreased through the study (the highest being in the first three months of the freshman year) and students who remained through the junior year were less divergent from the mean responses of the total group at the beginning of the freshman year than those students who left before completing their junior year.

GOERING, JACOB D.
## "Sigmund Freud, Carl Jung and Religion"
MQR, 66, 1 (January 1982): 47-56

This article provides a brief summary of Freud's and Jung's attitudes toward religion written by a Mennonite clinical psychologist. The contrast between these two men's attitudes leads Goering to discuss the importance of religion in psychotherapy. He sides with Jung, suggesting that the psychotherapist's religion and belief system plays an important role in the healing process, not so much in what is said, but rather in how religion is lived out by the therapist. This area needs further study, and it has ramifications for the Mennonite Mental Health Services.

GREEN, STUART
## "Victim-Offender Reconciliation Program: A Review of the Concept"
Social Action and the Law, 10, 2 (1984): 43-52

This study describes the philosophical basis and structure of the victim-offender reconciliation programs (VORPs) administered by the Mennonite Central Committee. An alternative to incarceration, victim-offender provides third-party-assisted meetings between offender and victim to explore the facts of the crime, express feelings and to reach a resolution. While emphasizing conflict resolution instead of punishment, VORP deals with the victim's psychological injuries, allowing them to confront the offender. This also alters the offender's "dehumanized" perception of their victim, and hopefully prevents further offences.

Green and Stuart make good use of this study in giving a constructive analysis of this reconciliation ministry and its benefits to society as a whole.

HEINRICHS, DANIEL J.
"Parental Contributions to the Mental Health of Their Children"
*MQR*, 66, 1 (January 1982): 92-98

Parents play an important role in laying the foundation of their children's personality and character. The quality of relationships in the home lead to a sense of identity and self-worth. The home is a God-given structure which helps to form the basic character of the children and affects their ability to relate to and trust in God. The latter part of the article, dealing with the structure of the home, leans heavily on scripture. The use of biblical quotations is too simplistic and sidesteps the very real problems of biblical interpretation, particularly in light of oppressive patriarchal family structures which are frequently justified by reference to scripture.

HILTY, DALE M., RICK MORGAN and JOAN E. BURNS
"King and Hunt Revisited: Dimensions of Religious Involvement"
*Journal for the Scientific Study of Religion*, 23, 3 (September 1984): 252-66

This study tested the hypothesis that religious involvement is a multidimensional phenomenon by having 758 sixteen to ninety-year-old members of the Mennonite Church complete a questionnaire used in previous studies by M. B. King and R. A. Hunt. Factor analysis resulted in the extraction of seven factors: personal faith, intolerance of ambiguity, revised orthodoxy, social conscience, knowledge of religious history, life purpose and church involvement. Minimal support was found for the dimensions reported by King and Hunt. Findings support the proposed multidimensional hypothesis and suggest the suitability of these seven factors for measuring the nature of religious involvement.

HOSTETLER, BEULAH STAUFFER
"Midcentury Change in the Mennonite Church"
*MQR*, 60, 1 (January 1986): 58-82

In this paper, Beulah Stauffer Hostetler looks at changes taking place in the Mennonite Church — particularly the Franconia conference — from

1950 to 1960. There was dramatic change in religious forms and patterns of life during this period of time, and yet the Mennonites
remained a stable and integrated community.

Hostetler examines these changes, dealing with areas such as the
growing peace emphasis, the challenging of defensive structuring, as
well as authoritarian control, the withdrawal of conservatives and "new
wine in new wineskins."

In her conclusion the author states that, even when stresses were the
most acute, new forms were being shaped that continued to express key
values (p. 81). The 1950s were undeniably the beginning of an awakening in the Mennonite church – an adjustment of religious understandings to the cultural milieu. Hostetler examines key forces and influences in this transformation.

A larger view of this issue is presented in Beulah Stauffer Hostetler's
University of Pennsylvania doctoral dissertation, "Franconia Mennonite Conference and American Protestant Movements, 1840-1940," and
the revised thesis in her book, *American Mennonites and Protestant Movements* (Scottdale, Pa.: Herald Press, 1986).

HUFFINS, MARION LOIS
"Pennsylvania German: Maintenance and Shift"
*International Journal of the Sociology of Language*, 25 (1980): 43-57

The author examines the use of Pennsylvania German, based on interviews with 119 individuals of Pennsylvania German background, of
whom twelve were Old Order Amish or Mennonites. Although, as
Huffins points out, the sample cannot be considered representative of
Pennsylvania Germans generally, not being based on random selection,
it shows a pronounced decline of the use of Pennsylvania German
among those not of Amish or Mennonite background, while the Amish
and Mennonites (plain people) tend to use and transmit Pennsylvania
German more often.

This difference is due to the fact that Pennsylvania German has a
specific "domain" among plain people, being used to maintain religious
identity. Among non-plain Pennsylvania Germans, the language does
not serve this function, since these people do not have a strong sense of
distinctiveness from the culture of American society and do not have a
strong ethnic consciousness. Since Pennsylvania German, for them,
serves no unique function that could not be equally well served by
English, it is disposable.

Furthermore, the author contends that social value attached to languages helps to determine their use or neglect. For non-plain Pennsylvania Germans, Pennsylvania "Dutch" has no social value, being
regarded as the dialect of uneducated rural folk. A language's accept-
ability rests on four attributes: standardization, autonomy, historicity
and vitality. Pennsylvania German is perceived to have none of these
attributes (and not without reason, as Huffins shows). Hence most
non-plain Pennsylvania Germans are indifferent about transmitting the
language to their children.

Huffins' study shows that while Pennsylvania German will probably
survive in Amish and Mennonite communities, it is dying out in non-

plain groups, and illustrates the factors contributing to the use or disuse of a language, as well as the transitional, unstable character of bilingualism without diglossia, as opposed to a situation where each language plays a specific role.

HUNSBERGER, BRUCE
"Background Religious Denomination, Parental Emphasis, and the Religious Orientation of University Students"
*Journal for the Scientific Study of Religion*, 15, 3 (September 1976): 251-55

Hunsberger administered a forty-four-item questionnaire regarding religious background, beliefs and practices to 312 university students. These were from Catholic (156), United Church (240) and Mennonite (61) backgrounds. The results showed Mennonite students were in significantly greater agreement with parental religious teachings than were United, with Catholic students being intermediate. Reported emphasis placed on religion in the childhood home was only partially related to these differences in agreement. The findings of this study also are discussed in light of earlier seemingly contradictory studies.

HUNSBERGER, BRUCE E.
"A Reconsideration of Parochial Schools: The Case of Mennonites and Roman Catholics"
*MQR*, 51, 2 (April 1977): 140-51

Hunsberger follows earlier sociological investigations on the degree of religiosity and religious commitment among students, both Mennonites and Roman Catholics, who attend parochial post-secondary schools and students of the same denominations who attend public schools. He investigates and compares those students on the degree of agreement with their parents' religious views, on their private religious practices (church attendance, private prayer, private reading of scripture), on basic Christian beliefs and on choice of friends from their own or other denominations. He learns that differences between parochial and public school attenders are minimal, reaching significance only in religious practice. But he also suggests that his particular choice of parochial schools may have affected his findings.

JAWORKSI, M. A., A. SEVERINI, et al.
"Genetic Conditions Among Canadian Mennonites: Evidence for a Founder Effect Among the Old Colony (Chortitza) Mennonites"
*Clinical and Investigative Medicine*, 12, 2 (1989): 127-41

Distinctive disease patterns exist among the Canadian Old Colony (Chortitza) Mennonites, who are characterized by medical researchers as religious and genetic isolates. The world's largest reported familial aggregations of insulin-dependent diabetes mellitus, of auto-immune diseases and of Tourette syndrome were initially ascertained in a small Alberta public-health district. Clusterings of malformations, inborn errors of metabolism and other conditions were also found in the sub-district and in group descendants living in other provinces. A founder effect, or genetic drift, accounts for the familial aggregations of autosomal recessive and dominant conditions, some diseases of multifactorial determination and other inherited conditions in Canadian kinships descending from this ancestral group.

A genetic isolate like the Old Colony people offer special opportunities for studying genetic epidemiology and molecular biology of inherited diseases.

This dark picture of Old Colony health must be added to the many social problems which have developed in their communities in Canada. The Mennonite Central Committee is now providing staff service to the Old Colony in Canada where there are continuous arrivals from Mexico.

In the same issue of *Clinical and Investigative Medicine*, see the brief introduction to the foregoing article by Charles R. Scriver of McGill Medical School, "New Experiences: Old Genes—Lessons from the Mennonites."

JILEK-HALL, LOUISE, WOLFGANG JILEK and FRANK FLYNN
## "Sex Role, Culture and Psychopathology: A Comparative Study of Three Ethnic Groups in Western Canada"
*Journal of Psychological Anthropology*, 1, 4 (Fall 1978): 473-88

The authors obtained the clinical records of psychiatric patients over age sixteen who represented three ethnic groups: the Coast Salish Indians (SI), the Doukhobors (D), and the Mennonite (M). Chi-square techniques were used to identify eighteen symptom items on which one culture group scored significantly higher than the other. Diagnostic categories significantly differentiating among the groups were (a) schizophrenic psychosis for the D, (b) reactive-neurotic depression for the SI, and (c) affective psychosis for the M. Overall results indicate that while sexes could to some extent be differentiated on the basis of clinical symptoms, cultural factors were the more important differentiating criteria of symptom formation.

JUHNKE, JAMES C
## "Mennonite Church Theological and Social Boundaries, 1920-1930—Loyalists, Liberals and Laxitarians"
*ML*, 38, 2 (June 1983): 18-24

As Juhnke states, "Theological questions and social issues were intertwined in the troubled quest for group identity in the MC (Old Mennonite church) in the 1920s and 1930s." In an interesting and detailed account, he describes the debates, arguments and even battles which took place as part of the fight against modernism. For leaders such as John Horsch (a Mennonite scholar and teacher), theology and daily living were closely linked, and both needed to reflect a godly life. The title of "his most significant publication" illustrates this well: "Modern Religious Liberalism: The Destructiveness and Irrationality of the New Theology" (1920). Focusing on the hotbed of the Mennonite colleges and on the interaction of Mennonite scholars and teachers, Juhnke provides a helpful perspective on the development of Mennonite theology, living and thinking.

This study had a three-fold purpose: (1) to report on the development and use of a "Religious Life Scale" as a composite measure of religiosity or, more particularly, "spiritual maturity"; (2) to examine the relationship between spiritual maturity and a number of independent and dependent variables potentially related to it; and (3) to note whether such relationships discovered within a Mennonite population differ in significant ways from reported findings in other populations.

Although the study is based on data previously collected by Kauffman and Harder (1975) on five co-operating denominations, the Mennonite Church, the General Conference Mennonite Church, the Mennonite Brethren Church, the Brethren in Christ Church and the Evangelical Mennonite church, it introduced a new composite scale and presented the results on the Mennonite population, for purposes of comparison, with the findings of investigators of other groups. The new composite scale provides a fresh methodology for the integration of the massive data of Harder and Kauffman.

KAUFFMAN, DUANE and AVERY ZOOK
## "Reply to Mellor and Andre's 'Religious Group Value Patterns and Motive Orientations': Data and Comment"
*Journal of Psychology and Theology*, 10, 3 (Fall 1982): 256-58

In a response to S. Mellor and J. Andre (see *Psychological Abstracts*, 66: 1138), who used the Rokeach value survey (RVS) to measure the value patterns of a variety of religious traditions, these authors present data from a study that used the Rokeach to survey fifty-eight Mennonite college students. A number of procedural and analytic comments and comparisons of the two studies are provided.

KAUFFMAN, J. HOWARD
## "Boundary Maintenance and Cultural Assimilation of Contemporary Mennonites"
*MQR*, 51, 3 (July 1977): 227-40

Kauffman draws from his larger study (Kauffman and Leland Harder, *Anabaptists Four Centuries Later* [Scottdale, Pa. and Kitchener, Ont.: Herald Press, 1975]) some new conclusions about cultural assimilation of Mennonites. He decides that those Mennonite groups which display less favourable attitudes toward the maintenance of social boundaries against the "world" turn out to be less supportive of Mennonite views in several particulars: general Christian orthodoxy, uniquely Anabaptist theological positions, and current Mennonite ethical emphases. On September 1, 1976, at a special session of the American Sociological Association, Kauffman read an earlier version of this essay, "The Plain People: Their Place in Sociological Study."

KAUFFMAN, J. HOWARD
## "Social Correlates of Spiritual Maturity Among North American Mennonites"
*Sociological Analysis*, 40, 1 (1979): 27-42

A fourteen-item "Religious Life Scale" was developed and tested in an attempt to define and objectify the measurement of religiosity among North American Mennonites. Religiosity is used by sociologists to refer to the religious beliefs, attitudes and behaviours which permeate the life of the individual based on the assumption that some persons are more religious than others. Kauffman is aware that the term religiosity has a variety of parallel terms from which he selected David O. Moberg's concept of "spiritual well-being" and then revised it with the new synonym of "spiritual maturity."

The fourteen-item "Religious Life Scale" was then used to explore the degree of statistical association (using Kendall's Tau B or C) or correlation (Pearsonian r) between spiritual maturity and a number of other social and religious variables. Data for the study originated in a 1972 survey of the members of five Mennonite denominations in the United States and Canada. The two-stage systematic random sampling procedure yielded 3,591 respondents, each of whom completed a lengthy questionnaire which utilized fixed-alternative responses. As measured by scores on the Religious Life Scale, spiritual maturity was found to be: (1) positively and strongly related to age, (2) weakly (but significantly) related to socio-economic status, rural residence, and sex (females higher), and (3) not significantly related to educational achievement. Correlations with additional religious variables were examined and discussed.

In the conclusions, Kauffman uses a correlational model to predict that the most religious Mennonite would be an elderly female with a professional occupation, residing in a rural non-farm area and having a low to moderate income. It would not matter how much education she has.

The marked difference between the U.S. and Canada, whereby the Canadian Mennonites are now dominantly urban from Halifax to Vancouver, strongly suggests that Kauffman's Canadian data may well be outdated after fifteen years. But Kauffman's methodology is in the mainstream of contemporary sociology of religion.

KEENEY, WILLIAM
"Experiences in Mental Hospitals in World War II"
MQR, 56, 1 (January 1982): 7-15

This article is a factual treatment of how Mennonites became involved in mental hospitals through their status as conscientious objectors and through the Civilian Public Service. There are three ways to respond to a social problem: on an individual, on an institutional and on a systems level. Mennonites with their tendency towards separation from the world, did not attempt to change the system but rather developed parallel institutions. This article introduces this subject but does not develop it fully since subsequent articles in this issue of the *Mennonite Quarterly Review* were written for this purpose. This article suffices as a brief introduction to a much larger topic.

KING, OMER E.
"From Pennsylvania Dutch to English in the Brethren in

Christ Church"
*Brethren in Christ History and Life*, VIII, 1 (April 1985): 37-46

This article outlines the language transition from German to English which took place among the Brethren in Christ in the late nineteenth century. The Brethren in Christ split off from the Mennonites in 1770. King suggests that while the use of English opened up new options to the Brethren for missions, revivalism and the Sunday School, there were also costs which have yet to be assessed. The Brethren lost contact with their historical roots and their theology of separation from the world.

KLINGELSMITH, SHARON
"Women in the Mennonite Church, 1900-1930"
*MQR*, 54, 3 (July 1980): 163-207

"How can the role of women in the Mennonite Church be expanded?" In the first few decades of this century, perceptive women came to grips with this question. Klingelsmith focuses her attention on the correspondence of those leaders who personally guided the fledgling Mennonite Women's Missionary Society on through to the bitter disappointment of seeing it absorbed by the Mission Board. It was within this organization that they could find the fullest employment of their own talents and give vent most candidly to their deepest feelings about their roles in the Mennonite Church. This is an important article which addresses the neglected topic of women's involvement in the church. Klingelsmith provides the reader with a wealth of illustrative material, itself primary source material for other scholars.

KRAHN, CORNELIUS, J. WINFIELD FRETZ and ROBERT KREIDER
"Altruism in Mennonite Life"
*Forms and Techniques of Altruism and Spiritual Growth*, ed. Pitirim Sorokin. Boston: Beacon Press, 1954

This chapter was added to Sorokin's symposium on altruism by asking how a small coalition of Mennonites can contribute millions of dollars to financing programs for the alleviation of human suffering in every continent and staffing these programs by hundreds of volunteers serving without pay.

The first answer in the essay comes from a survey of the history of suffering among Mennonites starting with the sixteenth-century Reformation where separation of church and state and pacifism elicited persecution. This new group sought to de-emphasize creeds, sacraments and state churches with a new emphasis on *applied* Christian love. "Let us do good to all men, especially unto them who are of the household of faith" (Gal. 6:10). The Sermon on the Mount became the key part of the New Testament.

Against this background, there is an expression of altruism by responding with assistance for victims of natural catastrophes, famine, war, epidemics and refugees from oppressive societies.

At this point in the essay the authors created conceptual confusion by insisting that Mennonites prefer the term "mutual aid" in place of altruism. This was an unfortunate decision since altruism is unselfish

concern for welfare of others. There are no tests of faith or church
membership before giving help. It is disinterested benevolence in contrast to the mild egoism of mutual aid: "You help me; I will help you."

On the other hand, the altruistic Mennonites did develop, and continue to develop, a vast network of mutual aid institutions with a mild
form of egoism. They have a large number of insurance societies providing protection from fire, storms, death, burial costs and, later, automobile accidents. In these insurance programs one is only helped if one
contributes premiums specified in the contract and if one is an
"insider." The Mennonites also innovated through institutions primarily focused on their own members such as retirement homes, hospitals
and summer camps. More precisely, both the insurance and the welfare institutions are forms of mutual aid.

The supreme test of Mennonite altruism on an emergency basis was
the desperate need in Russia after the Bolshevik revolution of 1917-18
where 100,000 Mennonites were in trouble as Christians, affluent
farmers, pacifists and German-speaking people. The Mennonite Central Committee was organized in 1920 to deliver food and, later, immigration assistance in the movement of Mennonites from Russia to Canada and the United States. Twenty thousand came to Canada in 1924.
From this dramatic start, the Mennonite Central Committee has developed into an impressive global peace, social concerns, social service and
development agency.

Meanwhile Mennonites, with 698,000 members in fifty-two countries, are regularly encountering the complex issues of justice and freedom in every part of the world. This encounter now requires Mennonite ethicists to develop a more sophisticated typology which not only
distinguishes between altruism and mutual aid but also between types
of social change and patterns of social service and the ratio between aiding "outsiders" and "insiders."

KRAYBILL, DONALD B.
"A Content and Structural Analysis of Mennonite High School
Songs"
*MQR*, 51, 1 (January 1977): 52-66

Kraybill has drawn an article on religious ideas of students in a Mennonite high school from his dissertation at Temple University, "Ethnic
Socialization in a Mennonite High School." Using class songs com-
posed by students between the years 1944 and 1973, he isolated and
analyzed certain religious attitudes portrayed in those songs in order to
identify this subculture's belief system. He provides an interesting
analysis of changes in their ideals over the years. By viewing the class
song as a type of myth or social document which attempts to "make
sense" out of the symbolic universe, Kraybill has produced a fascinating
and revealing article.

KRAYBILL, DONALD B.
"Religious and Ethnic Socialization in Mennonite High
School"
*MQR*, 51, 4 (October 1977): 329-51

ARTICLES

This article summarizes the findings from a one year longitudinal study of a Mennonite high school in Lancaster, Pennsylvania. Surprisingly, Kraybill finds that Mennonite students in public schools are very similar to their ethnic peers in private Mennonite schools. Family background has a definite, positive impact on student attitudes in the areas of religious orthodoxy, ethnic ritual and the avoidance of normative American social practices. The article's four appendices are the questionnaires used to measure religious orthodoxy, ethnicity, ethnic ritual and avoidance. The conclusions of this article are tentative, as the author himself admits, as larger longitudinal studies over many years are needed. At the time this article was written there was a lack of detail on ethnic schooling—Kraybill's thorough study is an important contribution to the area.

KREIDER, ROBERT S.
" 'Let a Hundred Flowers Bloom' and 'One Lord, One Faith, One Baptism' "
*MQR*, 57, 3 (July 1983): 181-93

In this primarily autobiographical article, Kreider relates his own experiences in pluralism. He claims that contemporary living means coming into contact with people of different religious backgrounds. A tension must be maintained between one's own belief and the belief of others, between toleration and faithfulness, between love and purity of doctrine. Kreider's experience leads him to embrace and learn from the pluralism around him. This article encourages acceptance of diversity, yet its tone is overly optimistic. Realistically, diversity is often more than simply annoying or unsettling; profound differences lead to conflict. A question which Kreider could have addressed is how can one handle constructively the conflict which pluralism sometimes generates.

KROEKER, WALLY, DAN RATZLAFF, WILFRED MARTENS and KATIE FUNK WIEBE
"Worldwide Mennonites Celebrate Their Peoplehood"
*Christian Leader*, 42, 16 (August 15, 1978): 2-14

This series of five articles and one poem in the *Christian Leader* deal with diverse aspects of the Mennonite World Conference held in Wichita, Kansas in July of 1978. The writers explore prominent themes such as "unity in diversity," celebration of peoplehood, the kingdom of God in a changing world, and "What is a Mennonite?" The last question is a challenging one, as there were Mennonites attending from forty-four different nations! These articles also spoke of the many smaller events which added colour to the conference.

While the coverage in the *Leader* was quite comprehensive, it would have been helpful, and interesting, to see a report from the "outside" perspective of a non-Mennonite observer.

LAUNAY, GILLES
"Bringing Victims and Offenders Together: A Comparison of

Two Models"
*Howard Journal of Criminal Justice*, 24, 3 (August 1985): 200-12

This study briefly reviews previous research which suggests that crime victims and criminal offenders can benefit from meeting. Two models of such encounters are described and compared: (1) the victim-offender program of the Mennonite Central Committee, which involves the victim meeting his/her offender to discuss terms of repara-tion, and (2) the Rochester model, where victims and unassociated offenders meet as a group. The study concludes that the Rochester model is more effective.

For more information on the victim offender model, see Stuart Green, "Victim-Offender Reconciliation Program: A Review of the Concept," *Social Action and the Law*, 10, 2 (1984): 43-52.

LEDERACH, JAMES
"A Case for Mandatory Public Service for Conscientious Objectors"
*Conrad Grebel Review*, II, 2 (Spring 1984): 139-48

Lederach argues that conscientious objectors can better practise Chris-tian obedience if they co-operate with the United States government by registering with Selective Service than if they protest as a nonregistrant. Although advocates of nonregistration claim that to register with Selec-tive Service is to co-operate with the military they forget that anything less than subversion similarly serves the state. Nonregistrants are not better able to proclaim opposition to militarism because they forfeit personal freedoms and hence their ability to proclaim. Finally, the non-registrant's ability to serve is strictly delimited, whereas traditional alternative service is exclusively concerned with servanthood.

As a solution, Lederach submitted that a draft law which would impose a term of Alternative Service for all those who elected conscientious objector status would allow all conscientious objectors to serve, not just those called up by the Draft Board. Such a program would provide the opportunity to demonstrate a strong commitment against militarism.

LEHMAN, HAROLD D.
"Teachers Abroad Program: A Model of Rural Primary Education in Bolivia"
Paper presented at Meeting of the Comparative and International Education Society, New York, N.Y., March 18-21, 1982

The Teachers Abroad Program (TAP) was developed as a project of the Mennonite Central Committee to meet the education needs of devel-oping nations. Its activities in Bolivia involve North American volun-teer teachers, a committee to start a school in a rural community, com-munity development and nonformal adult education.

LEVY, JOANNE
"In Search of Isolation: The Holdeman Mennonites of Linden, Alberta and Their School"
*Canadian Ethnic Studies*, 11, 1 (1979)

Just as Canadian history and political events are sometimes viewed as dull and ordinary, so too are the courts criticized as less than innovative. But in February 1977, the Assistant Chief Provincial Court Judge of Alberta made a decision that offered a settlement on a disputed point in the history of Mennonites in Canada, gave new recognition to the civil rights of a minority group, and made Canadian legal history. For the first time a provincial Bill of Rights was used to override part of another provincial statute. In this case, freedom of religion triumphed over compulsory attendance regulations contained in the School Act. As a result the Holdeman Mennonites of Linden, Alberta were allowed to retain a school that was unauthorized by provincial legislation. It was a key development in the history of a unique group in Alberta's ethnic fabric.

The educational freedom of Canadian Holdeman, Old Order Mennonites and Amish is now established: an independent, private system usually with uncertified teachers but with a thin line of accountability to the ministry of education. The U.S. Supreme Court in 1986 also decided the Amish but not the fundamentalist private schools may have uncertified teachers.

Unlike the other alternative private school systems such as the Catholic, Christian Reformed, Lutheran, U.S. segregated Protestants in the south, Jews, Muslim, or Progressive Mennonite, the Holdeman and Old Order types terminate education at the legal drop-out age, usually fourteen, hence they are dependent on the better educated outside professionals for medicine, dentistry and engineering. It is, then, a form of protest which the State tolerates rather than a comprehensive educational strategy.

This toleration is both a sincere affirmation of civil and religious rights and an awareness of the non-political nature of the Holdeman community which has political impact.

LINDEN, RICK, RAYMOND F. CURRIE and LEO DRIEDGER
"Interpersonal Ties and Alcohol Use Among Mennonites"
*Canadian Review of Sociology and Anthropology*, 22, 4 (1985): 559-73

The widely different patterns of alcohol use among groups in different countries indicate that cultural factors are important determinants of alcohol use. Research suggests that the social groups to which an individual belongs provide the mechanism through which the cultural norms regarding alcohol use influence the individual's behaviour. This study, based on questionnaire data, looks at the effect of interpersonal ties on the drinking behaviour of a national sample of 1,208 Canadian Mennonites using a theoretical model combining social control and differential association theories. Drinking was found to be related to the behaviourial preferences of others. These effects varied with the closeness of the relationship with that particular associate and with the person's visibility to each associate.

LOCKERY, A. R.
"The Value of Place Names in Teaching the History of Manitoba"
*History and Social Science Teacher*, 19, 4 (May 1984): 199-204

Place names alone can provide an illuminating picture of Manitoba's (Canada) history. This article discusses settlements of native cultures — the Hudson's Bay Company and various ethnic groups including the French, English, Mennonites, Icelanders and Ukrainians.

It is interesting to note that Mennonites are listed as an "ethnic" group, along with four nation-related groups. This is a misnomer which distorts basic sociological terminology.

LOEWEN, HARRY
"The Anabaptist View of the World: The Beginning of a Mennonite Continuum?"
*Mennonite Images*, ed. Harry Loewen. Winnipeg: Hyperion Press, 1980, pp. 85-95

Loewen places Anabaptism in broad perspective by citing the Hellenistic-Christian dialectic of faith — the physical versus the spiritual, or "this-worldly" vs. "other-worldly." Anabaptists have always lived in tension between these two, and Loewen discusses this as an important aspect of Mennonite history. Traditionally Anabaptists practised withdrawal from the world, but those who were part of the "Golden Age of the Dutch Republic," as well as those who accepted Catherine II's invitation to settle in the Ukraine became wealthy, nationalistic and integrated into all aspects of society. Loewen concludes that Mennonites maintain an "uneasy truce" with the world, but he sees hope in institutions such as MCC which live out the life of Christ while not making peace with the world.

A further, more specific comment on this issue is made by Roy Vogt ("The Impact of Economic and Social Class on Mennonite Theology," in *Mennonite Images*, pp. 137-48). Vogt discusses the "withdrawal" of urban Mennonites through the relative autonomy of professionalism. He proposes that Mennonite professionals are able to maintain a "purer" form of Anabaptism because they are removed from the class struggles of the managerial and blue collar sectors of society. Vogt's exemption of professionals from class stratification goes too far.

LOEWEN, HARRY and AL REIMER
"Origins and Literacy Development of Canadian-Mennonite Low German"
*MQR*, 69, 3 (July 1985): 279-88

This article briefly surveys Low German literature and the culture linked with that language. The writers observe that ironically the literary consciousness of Plattdeutsch developed inversely to the use of the language. The article's predication that Canadian Mennonite ethnic identity will not in the long run survive the disappearance of Plattdeutsch reveals the Manitoba Russian-Mennonite bias of the writers in that they ignore the fact that many Canadian Mennonites never spoke Low German. Their claim assumes that values, religion and kinship ties are inextricably related to language. This claim is not supported by sociologists such as Appavoo and Driedger.

LOEWEN, HOWARD J.
"One Lord, One Church, One Hope: Mennonite Confessions
of Faith in America — An Introduction"
*MQR*, 67, 3 (July 1983): 265-81

The main points of this article are first, that Mennonites have produced
numerous confessions which must be recognized as valuable tools to
chart theological self-identity, and second, that Mennonite confessions
contain a common core which transcends the factional divisions
separating Mennonites from one another. Loewen provides a brief historical survey of the confessions, compares their form, structure, and
content and raises the possibility of the confessions having not only an
inter-Mennonite function, but an ecumenical function as well. This is
an important article which deals with a seldom discussed topic. The
historical section tracing the different families of confessions is somewhat confusing. The author has sacrificed some clarity in favour of
keeping the article brief.

MARTIN, MAURICE
"The Pure Church: The Burden of Anabaptism"
*Conrad Grebel Review*, 1, 2 (Spring 1983): 29-41

Martin defines the "burden of Anabaptism" as a conflict between the
Anabaptist belief in a pure church and belief in God's unconditional
love. Contemporary Mennonites find themselves vacillating between
the desire to maintain a pure church of disciplined believers and acceptance of human finitude and suffering. Martin attempts to resolve this
burden which Mennonites have inherited from Anabaptism by clarify-
ing the theological constructs of sin and grace. He suggests that the
Mennonite idea that forgiveness is once-for-all leaves an inadequate
understanding of the ongoing need for grace and forgiveness. Contrary
to traditional Mennonite practice, then, forgiveness should be an ongoing process. Hence, reconciliation is the key to experiencing the love of
God and achieving a more adequate view of the pure church.

MAYKOVICH, MINAKO KUROKAWA
"The Difficulties of a Minority Researcher in Minority
Communities"
*Journal of Social Issues*, 33, 4 (February 1977): 108-19

This paper examines some of the problems encountered by a Japanese
researcher in Japanese communities and Mennonite communities in
California and Ontario.

MILLER, ELMER S.
"Marking Mennonite Identity: A Structuralist Approach to
Separation"
*Conrad Grebel Review*, 3, 3 (1985): 251-63

In this excellent article Miller argues that conceptions of Mennonite
identity, especially of the concept of separation, have undergone profound changes under different historical circumstances, and that the
meaning of separation for the various sixteenth-century Anabaptist

groups was significantly different from that of their twentieth-century descendants. He argues that greater weight must be attached to the economic, social and political factors operating in the sixteenth century in any attempt to understand the rise of the Anabaptists, their self-understanding, and what separation meant for them. The possibility of economic separation through the guild structures, the rise of capitalist classes dissatisfied with the Catholic Church's support of the landed aristocracy, the rise of nationalism and the desire of feudal lords for greater political independence from Rome, the Peasants' Revolt, the rise of humanism and the political activities of Catholic, Lutheran and Calvinist churches, against all of which the Anabaptists established their separate identity, often at the cost of martyrdom, must be seen in relation to one another. These factors no longer apply in the twentieth century, so that twentieth-century interpretations of separation necessarily reflect the interpreter's ideological position in the context of contemporary socio-economic, political and religious factors. Miller argues that today the concept of separation has lost its theoretical and existential meaning, as Mennonite theology has drawn closer to mainstream evangelical Christianity, as the Mennonites have become economically integrated as they have been relatively free from persecution, as language barriers and the dress code have gradually dissolved, as even the concept of non-resistance has ceased to be uniquely Mennonite. The perpetuation of a separated Mennonite identity will depend on the emergence of new "myths" or interpretations of Mennonite separation needs of the future. Considering that much Mennonite scholarship operates with a primarily theological perspective, Miller's article is a useful reminder that there are other factors to consider. It is a creative and original thesis.

MILLER, JOSEPH S.
"Mennonite Experience Between the Wars"
Fifth Mennonite Experience in America Conference, June 9-11, 1985.
*MQR*, 60, 1 (January 1986): 5-103

The articles in this issue of the *Mennonite Quarterly Review* were first presented at the Fifth Mennonite Experience in America Conference, sponsored by the Mennonite Historians of Eastern Pennsylvania. The title of the conference was "The Long Weekend: Mennonite Experience Between the Wars." The papers dealt with what the Mennonite churches from a wide variety of Mennonite denominational groups had experienced from the 1920s until the 1950s. Two of the papers pointed out that the interwar period saw a complex array of Mennonite peace and service beliefs and practices. James C. Juhnke looked at the beginnings of the Mennonite Central Committee. According to Juhnke, MCC as an inter-Mennonite organization demonstrated that after World War I Mennonites were often at odds on what peace and service actually meant. Paul Toews outlined Mennonite peace activism between the war. Toews' analysis showed the differences between those Mennonites who tended to be more politically active and those who were opposed in any degree to being involved, at least publicly, in the political process of the interwar period.

E. Morris Sider pointed up the dichotomy in the Brethren in Christ identity crisis between the wars. Their authors stressed both pietism from Brethren and United Brethren sources and Anabaptist ideals from their Mennonite roots, leaning more toward pietism before World War II and tilting slightly the other way immediately after. Only since the 1970s have the Brethren in Christ begun to synthesize the two elements.

Beulah Stauffer Hostetler selected the 1950s for an examination of changes in the Mennonite Church, especially but not exclusively in the Franconia Conference. These Mennonites fell back on defensive structuring in an effort to balance and synthesize their divergent streams of neo-traditionalism and fundamentalism, with a dash of Anabaptist vision included increasingly as the decade unfolded. One of the liveliest topics of the period was nonconformity, especially in its changing patterns.

Leonard Gross presented an analysis of that period in the Mennonite Church when Daniel Kauffman was a powerful spokesperson for doctrinal thought and practice. Unlike Mennonites and their Anabaptist forebears, Kauffman wanted to shape doctrine more exactly and to use doctrine as a measuring device for behaviour within the churches. It was Mennonite scholasticism, a rational orthodoxy. Gross's use of selected quotations from several diarists and letter-writers of the period is especially rewarding.

MILLER, PAUL
## "Pastoral Care for Posttherapy Individuals"
*MQR*, 66, 1 (January 1982): 99-110

This article is a result of the author's experience in counselling thirty-two post-therapy individuals. He found that these individuals were experiencing difficulty in re-integrating into congregational life, especially in terms of finding confidentiality and genuine acceptance. A particular problem was the social stigma which therapy generates. A good deal of the article is devoted to practical suggestions for pastors in dealing with post-therapy individuals. This is a sensitively written and helpfully pragmatic article which highlights the importance of pastoral care.

NAFZIGER, DONALD D.
## "Mennonites on Trial"
*Christian Century*, 99, 34 (November 1982): 1093-94

In 1982 Mark Schmucker, a Mennonite youth, was tried for his refusal to register for Selective Service in the American army. His resistance to the draft, based on his religious convictions, is a strong testimony of one young person's commitment to the Mennonite belief in nonresistance, expressed through civil disobedience.

NAFZIGER, E. WAYNE
## *Entrepreneurship: Equity and Economic Development.*
Vol. 53 in *Contemporary Studies in Economic and Financial Analysis*
Greenwich, Conn.: JAI Press, 1986

An experienced field researcher in the problems of economic development of Third World countries, Nafziger has written a collection of essays based on his work in India, Nigeria and Zambia and then surprisingly ends the book with a final chapter, "The Mennonite Ethic and Weber's Thesis." The Third World material is particularly interesting in its probe into the social and caste background of the entrepreneur, noting that in India, for example, there are no investors from the lower castes while the vast majority have origins in the higher castes.

Nafziger's unexpected inquiry into a cross-cultural analysis of Mennonites and the Third World, and the application of Weber's famous thesis, are marred by limiting his data to the conservative Swiss-American Mennonites, and by another distortion based on data collected from 1921-42, when only 14 percent of the Swiss Mennonites belonged to urban churches. The past four to six decades have rendered this rural bias obsolete.

In any case, Nafziger, a Kansas State University economist, concluded that ". . . though the Weberian framework can explain the relative success of Mennonites in the occupations they have entered, it cannot adequately explain their failure to enter powerful and strategic positions in the economy."

NEUFELD, VERNON
"The Mennonite Mental Health Story"
*MQR*, 66, 1 (January 1982): 18-31

This article is a history of Mennonite involvement in the mental health movement. Mennonites had a history of establishing hospitals for the mentally ill, but this effort was spearheaded in 1947 by MCC which initiated a number of mental health programs. The actions of MCC were prompted largely by the experience of Mennonites who served in mental hospitals during World War II. The article explores the development and organization of Mennonite Mental Health Services (MMHS) and concludes that the MMHS plays a positive role as a collaborative service agency that expands the ministry of the church into new areas of service. This article does not question the presupposition that the church should form parallel programs to state initiated facilities. A contrast between the effectiveness of the Mennonite response to the problem of mental illness and, for example, the Quaker response to that problem would have been helpful. These subjects, however, are treated in subsequent articles in the same issue of the *Mennonite Quarterly Review*.

PAETKAU, PETER and PETER KLIPPENSTEIN
"The Conference of Mennonites in Canada: Background and Origin"
*ML*, 34, 3 (December 1979): 4-10

This article is a concise narrative of the events that led up to the collaboration of the Rosenorter and Bergthaler churches to form the "Conference of Mennonites in Central Canada" (later known as Conference of Mennonites in Canada) in 1903. It also describes the role played by the significant leadership. Unfortunately, the article is solely descriptive, lacking any analysis or attempt to set these events in the larger Mennonite historical context. Those interested in the larger historical context should refer to Frank H. Epp, *Mennonites in Canada*, Vol. 1.

PALMER, HOWARD
"Ethnic Relations in Wartime: Nationalism and European
Minorities in Alberta during the Second World War"
*Canadian Ethnic Studies*, 14, 3 (1982): 1-23

Focusing on ethnic relations in Alberta from 1939 to 1945, this article
assesses the impact of the war on inter-group relations and notes significant shifts in attitudes toward a number of groups. In analyzing these
shifts, which were both negative and positive, the article explores the
relationship between a group's demographic profile, degree of acculturation and attitudes toward it. The effects of the social and economic
conditions of wartime on attitudes are also explored. The sense of
camaraderie that the effort fostered generally worked to undermine
class and ethnic barriers. However, there was a negative side to this
*esprit de corps* which heightened hostility toward several minorities for
varying periods of time. Groups such as Germans and Italians which
were perceived to be associated with enemy powers, and pacifist groups
such as Hutterites and Mennonites, encountered increasingly negative
attitudes — attitudes which were occasionally translated into public policy in the nationalistic fervour of wartime.

PATTERSON, NANCY-LOU
" 'See The Vernal Landscape Glowing': The Symbolic
Landscape of the Swiss-German Mennonite Settlers in
Waterloo County"
*ML*, 38, 4 (December 1983): 8-16

An analysis of Waterloo County Swiss Mennonite farm landscapes,
along with a variety of Swiss Mennonite works of art and literature
which also depict landscape themes, prompted Patterson to conclude
that certain attitudes toward the landscape are expressed. Symbolically,
this farm landscaping places the Mennonite farm family in a favoured
position within the landscape, with the world and all its dangers on the
outside. These ordered farmsteads can be considered metaphoric structures which the Waterloo County Mennonites equate with "the state of
blessedness obtained through Christian redemption."

PEACHEY, PAUL
"Free Cities, Free Churches, and Urbanized Societies"
*Brethren Life and Thought*, 27 (Autumn 1982): 199-205

In this article, Peachey offered "a few observations" on the issue of
"peace churches" and "urban ministry." This think piece takes the
reader back to the Reformation, recalling that although the Anabaptist
roots were urban, the ancestors of today's Mennonites and Brethren
fled the cities. Peachey questioned whether these people can effectively
re-enter the cities after four hundred years of rural ministry.

While Peachey raised a valid question, his argument lacks clarity when
applied today. Furthermore, he attempted no solutions for contemporary
Anabaptist descendents who are concerned with urban ministry.

88                                                                    MENNONITES

PEACHEY, PAUL
"The Lost Science of Man"
*MQR*, 66, 1 (January 1982): 82-91
This article discusses the problems of relating science and religion. It
briefly mentions the history of sociology and its establishment as a discipline. Sociology originally was envisioned as a unifying human science, and has gradually slipped into the realm of science, dealing primarily with empirical data. The task for sociologists today is to confront
the identity and meaning questions which people are asking, while continuing to engage in empirical investigation. This is a thought-
provoking article which attempts to broaden the rigidly defined hori-
zons of professional disciplines.

PETERS, JOHN F.
"Socialization Among the Old Order Mennonites"
*International Journal of Comparative Sociology*, 28, 3-4: 211-23
Using occupation and demographic data, as well as observation and
interview, this study seeks to explore the social role of the 3,600 "plain"
Mennonites in Canada. It finds the family as the primary agent of
socialization in economic and religious values, reinforcing the agrarian
lifestyle and conservatism. The plain Mennonites stand in great contrast to surrounding society, and segregate themselves on the grounds
of social and moral incompatibility. Only the Swiss-German dialect is
spoken until age six, when children attend their own parochial school.
The Canadian government's policy of multiculturalism endorses this
type of ethnic identity.

PITTS, V. PETER
"Drawing the Invisible: Children's Conceptualization of God"
*Character Potential*, 8, 1 (November 1976): 12-24
The researchers asked 180 first to third graders to draw a picture of
God. Subsamples were Lutheran, Mennonite, Methodist, Mormon,
Roman Catholic and Unitarian. The groups differed on scores of
anthropomorphism and on scores representing proportions of religious
to non-religious imagery. When asked to draw a person as well, the
children preferred to do this first. Younger children had more difficulty
in creating a drawing than older ones. The study also discusses the
implications of this for religious education.

REDEKOP, CALVIN
"Anabaptism and the Ethnic Ghost"
*MQR*, 68 Supl. (August 1984): 133-46
The concept of being the "people of God" is central to the Anabaptist
understanding of the Christian calling. Redekop gives an historical
overview of how Mennonites have attained peoplehood. His focus on
the Mennonite community in Paraguay leads him to question whether
ethnic separation of this nature is a valid way to be the "people of
God." Redekop concludes that separation to become the "people of
God" inevitably results in an ethnic identity (an ethnic ghost). There

are dangers for the "people of God" such as ethnocentrism, yet there are also creative aspects in the combining of ethnic and religious identity. Redekop spends most of the article highlighting the dangers of the "ethnic ghost" making his final optimism about its positive aspects an unexpected generalization.

REDEKOP, CALVIN
## "The Embarrassment of a Religious Tradition"
*ML*, 36, 3 (September 1981): 17-21

Redekop suggests that in the past "religious embarrassment" has caused some Mennonite groups to leave the Mennonite fold. Nor is that trend confined to history. At the time that this article was written, the Evangelical Mennonite Brethren, or EMBers as Redekop calls them, were struggling with whether or not to retain the name Mennonite, fearing that an ethnic label would hinder evangelism. Redekop cautioned the EMBers that on the contrary, they should beware that "without tradition there is no faith." Redekop reasoned that the heritage or "community of common experience" is important even for a newly developing evangelical fundamentalist church.

While some readers might find Redekop's challenge to the EMBers harsh at points, this article is valuable in aiding our understanding of one of the human motives which has influenced church history.

REDEKOP, CALVIN
## "Mennonite Displacement of Indigenous Peoples: An Historical and Sociological Analysis"
*Canadian Ethnic Studies*, 14, 2 (1982)

Under the relentless pressure of persecution and the loss of human rights, Mennonites have a 400-year history of migrations. This important study examines four crucial settlements in the USA, Canada, Mexico and Paraguay, with the common problem of an encounter with indigenous people who occupied the land to which Mennonites had come. Sometimes the state commanded expulsion on behalf of the new immigrants. The preferred answer was co-existence and a symbiotic relationship.

In the nineteenth century, the Oklahoma and Manitoba Mennonite migrations were similar since the land was legally opened to white settlements by government decree, leading to the removal of the native population. Yet, the original settlers occupied the land in varying degrees when the Mennonites arrived.

The situation in Mexico in the twentieth century is a story of continuous conflict with the natives or *agraristas* resenting efforts at eviction, a resentment leading to reprisals. The area to which the Mennonites came was a 230,000-acre parcel of land that was sold by one Mexican family. On the whole, the anarchy and hostility of this environment caused many Manitoba Old Colony Mennonites to return to Canada.

The most interesting case of the four is the twentieth-century migration to the Chaco in Paraguay. This is the classic study in co-existence between Caucasian Europeans with strong backing from North America interacting with Indians threatened by a precarious life in a dysfunctional social system. The Mennonites responded by purchasing 220,000 acres of land for the Indians, supplemented by schools and literacy programs, seven hospitals and a growing network of jobs in small industry and agriculture meant to end centuries of nomadic life. In 1935, the Mennonites started to preach the Christian faith to the Indians. Unlike the traditional missionary who comes from the outside in a temporary assignment, this religious ministry came from a large permanent community relating to the indigenous people. And this ministry was part of an economic, social and cultural encounter.

A veteran of many visits to the Chaco, Redekop is a Mennonite sociologist trained at Chicago who is fully aware of the attacks on the Chaco Mennonite colonies by anthropologists from both the U.S. and Paraguay. For example, Miguel Chase in *La Situacion actual de los Indigenas en el Paraguay,* published by the Asuncion Centre for Anthropological Study (1972), views the Mennonites as agents of colonialism who disparage and destroy indigenous cultures, including social structures and institutions. Chase makes a final charge of race prejudice and discrimination.

Redekop rejects the charges of exploitation and unfair treatment and then argues that the bush and forest people of Paraguay were being destroyed by a fragile, inadequate and hostile natural environment. The new network of jobs in a settled environment, schools, excellent health facilities and churches provided an alternative social system leading to genuine growth in numbers, literacy, improved health, a higher standard of living and a social equilibrium. Above all, they have retained their identity as indigenous Indian people, surviving through social change brought about by the peaceful co-existence and interaction of two groups of permanent settlers.

REDEKOP, CALVIN
## "The Promise of Work"
Benjamin Eby Lecture. Waterloo, Ont.: Conrad Grebel College, 1983

First presented as the 1983 Benjamin Eby Lecture, this essay examines work, not as an economic issue, but as a moral problem. Redekop addresses the paradox in Western society in which we look to new technology for an end to the necessity of human labour, while at the same time we are desperately concerned about employment.

Answering this paradox, Redekop draws on Durkheim and Toennies for a *Gemeinschaft,* a communal definition of the good society in which the collapse of meaningful work is less likely to take place. In this *Gemeinschaft* work is good, loving, creaturely, fulfilling and a means of glorifying God. These developments permit work to become personalized and de-bureaucratized.

The issue in this brilliant essay is whether these are disembodied concepts without functional and institutional roots. It is a convincing platform to restore meaning to work, but does the platform have supports on the ground of reality? Which is to say, are the computers overwhelming crafts, arts, work and service?

REDEKOP, CALVIN and JOHN A. HOSTETLER
## "The Plain People: An Interpretation"
*MQR*, 51, 4 (October 1977): 266-77

In this article the authors attempt to bring more clarity to the classification "Plain People" and to the sociological reality and nature of these people. Sociologists have defined the plain people in many different ways—as a social movement, an ethnic group and a sect group. While Redekop and Hostetler agree that in some respects the plain people fit these definitions, they hold that they are substantially different because their social collective is formed by a value system or social reality that is radically different from the prevailing core society. Not convinced that religion can create the integration of the entire society, the plain people believe that religion can integrate small communities. This article serves as an introduction and conceptual framework to Volume 51, No. 4 (October 1977) of *Mennonite Quarterly Review* which has as its theme "The Plain People". It is a concise and straightforward evaluative introduction to sociological concepts and categories used at various times to understand the plain people.

REDEKOP, PAUL
## "The Mennonite Family in Tradition and Transition"
*Journal of Mennonite Studies*, 4 (1986): 77-93

The family has always been of central importance to the Mennonite way of life. Yet until recently, little has been written about this important institution. The purpose of Redekop's article was to bring together recent sociological research on the Mennonites which has included at least some analysis of the Mennonite family. His overview included such topics as the nature of courtship and mate-selection practices among the Mennonites, marital relationships, parenthood and child rearing and Mennonite kinship.

In the literature he surveyed Redekop found two major themes to be significant to Mennonite family life. The transition from being a rural people towards urbanization and Mennonite faith both have had important influences on Mennonite family life. Redekop also identified areas where further study of Mennonite family life is necessary—kinship networks and relationships, the influence of social class within the Mennonite community, and the influence of feminism among modern Mennonite women. With regards to the latter topic, his own hypothesis that "Mennonite women appear to be in the forefront of the feminist revolution" cannot be substantiated and illustrates the need for more research.

REGEHR, T. D.
## "Mennonites and the New Jerusalem in Western Canada"
*Visions of the New Jerusalem: Religious Settlement on the Prairies*, ed. Benjamin G. Smillie. Edmonton: NeWest Press, 1983, pp. 109-20

This article discusses the experience of the Mennonites in the context of other religio-ethnic groups who also contributed to Western Canadian history. Some of these people who settled the west had the vision of establishing the new Jerusalem there, but each group's perception of what the kingdom of God should be like was narrowly defined by their own religious and ethnic experience and beliefs. The Mennonites were no exception. Like the other groups who settled Canada's prairies, they participated in relegating the Indians and Metis to the periphery of society. The Mennonites were less concerned with the people they had displaced than with their vision of building an isolated community similar to the one that they had left in Russia.

The isolation that the Mennonites had hoped to maintain on the reserves of land in Manitoba and Saskatchewan was never complete. As separation became increasingly impossible, Mennonites began to spiritualize their view of the kingdom of God and began to work at improving Canadian society through such in-house organizations as the Mennonite Central Committee and some even entered Canadian politics.

Regehr's article sets the Mennonite experience in the larger context of Canadian religious history and as such, makes an important contribution to both Canadian and Mennonite history.

REGEHR, WILLIAM
"Research Notes: Evangelical Mennonite Brethren"
*ML*, 27, 1 (March 1982): 29-30

This response by the Administrative Secretary of the Evangelical Mennonite Brethren Conference, to Calvin Redekop's "Embarrassment of a Tradition" (*ML*, 36, 3 [September 1981]: 17-21), appears to justify Redekop's challenge. Regehr missed Redekop's concern entirely, stating outright that he failed to understand Redekop's integral argument, that "without tradition there is no faith."

RINGENBERG, WILLIAM C.
"Development and Division in the Mennonite Community in Allen County, Indiana"
*MQR*, 50 (April 1976): 114-31

This study traces the history of the third largest Indiana Amish settlement from the group's emigration in 1840 from Alsace Lorraine through the development of five distinct branches of the original group in northeastern Allen County. These divisions included the Amish-Mennonites, the Egli Amish (now Evangelical Mennonites), the Apostolic Christians, the Missionary Church Association and the group which retained the Old Order Amish identification. Such splintering was characteristic of the Amish (and other Mennonite groups) during the late nineteenth century; thus one may view the pattern in Allen County as a study in microcosm of the problems of disunity in the larger American Amish society.

RUTSCHMAN, LA VERNE
"Anabaptism and Liberation Theology"
*MQR*, 55, 3 (July 1981): 255-70

The first part of this article is a summary of the basic tenets of Latin American liberation theology. The second part outlines the possible interaction between liberation theology and Anabaptism. Rutschman acknowledges significant theological differences between the two movements yet he critiques the Mennonite church in Latin America for its lack of commitment to the cause of justice. He suggests but does not develop the concept that economic class differences between Mennonites and the poorer classes play a role in Mennonite reluctance to commit themselves to the struggle for justice.

SAWATSKY, RODNEY J.
"Defining 'Mennonite' Diversity and Unity"
*MQR*, 67, 3 (July 1982): 282-92

Mennonite pluralism is theologically rooted because Anabaptists emphasized subjectivity and historicity. This has meant that the church must define obedience from within its own cultural situation. As Mennonites spread and confront different situations pluralism is inevitable. The diversity of Mennonites is easy for historians and sociologists to chart, Sawatsky observes, yet the unity of Mennonites must be articulated by theologians.

SAWATSKY, RODNEY J.
"Domesticated Sectarianism: Mennonites in the U.S. and Canada in Comparative Perspective"
*Canadian Journal of Sociology/Cahiers canadiens de sociologie*, 3, 2 (Spring 1978): 233-44

The acculturative forces influencing Mennonites have been recognized within specific national environments. Little, however, has been published contrasting the acculturative forces between different national contexts. This essay argues that, although as sectarians Mennonites ought ideally to be uninfluenced differentially by varying national environments, the contrasts between Canadian and American Mennonites belie the theory. Comparisons based upon demographic characteristics and degree of adoption of the American denominational pattern suggest that Canadian Mennonites have a stronger sense of ethnic identity than their American counterparts, but find themselves simultaneously more indigenous to their national milieu. Furthermore, it is proposed that as progressive assimilation renders the Mennonite sectarian ideology dysfunctional, any functional construct will seek to accommodate diversity based on national contexts.

An alternative view to Sawatsky's thesis is that Mennonites are an international people who migrate back and forth among three continents with interchangeable common faith, common language, common history and literature, and a common ethos and common schools. These pilgrim people adapt to national and cultural contexts without succumbing to them. Where acculturation has taken place, as in Germany, Russia and the United States, the mainstream international scholars and prophets offer sharp criticism and censure.

For related studies, see Leo Driedger, "Ethnic Identity in the Canadian Mosaic" (pp. 9-22), and Frank H. Epp, "Problems of Mennonite Identity: A Historical Study" (pp. 281-94) in Leo Driedger (ed.), *The Canadian Ethnic Mosaic — A Quest for Identity* (Toronto: McClelland and Stewart, 1978).

SAWATSKY, RODNEY J.
"Ten Things You Should Know About Canadian Mennonites"
*Festival Quarterly*, 16, 1 (Winter-Spring 1989)

President of Conrad Grebel College, University of Waterloo, Rodney Sawatsky is representative of young Canadian Mennonite intellectuals who are growingly aware of the differences between the Canadian and American Mennonite communities. This is particularly interesting in the case of Sawatsky because his B.A., M.A. and Ph.D. were earned in the United States. Indeed, he says that one of the things he likes best about his southern neighbour is "the almost unequalled creativity of privately-funded American colleges and universities."

Sawatsky takes the borders seriously since even theology and ethics must incarnate the particularities of one's national culture and society. He makes much out of the different origins of the two countries, with the U.S. emerging out of an Enlightenment and Revolution, whereas Canada became a nation in a counter-revolution with monarchy, established churches and respect for tradition. It will come as news to the socialist party in Canada that Sawatsky considers it conservative.

Many other differences are recorded with the most important being the larger participation of Mennonites in Canadian political and cultural life. Another key factor was the greater urbanization of Mennonites in Canada. The overall picture is a Canadian scene in which the Mennonites are moderate, responsible, creative, urban, professional, affluent and artistic. These traits have led in recent decades to more Mennonite institutions in Canada. Behind the institutions is a new identity.

Sawatsky has struggled in this paper with a permanent problem of all Christians: how to be indigenous in a particular culture and also how to be ecumenical, international and pluralistic. Canada has wrestled with the French and native peoples questions with only modest success. It now faces a flood of Asiatic immigrants posing yet another challenge from the old philosophical question: The one and the many. The U.S. faces the one and the many, too. In encountering it, the Americans are dominated by an ambiguous conservatism that seems far from the French, American, Russian or Third World revolutions.

With this paper Sawatsky has laid to rest any further caricatures of Canadian Mennonites as crypto-Americans.

SAWATSKY, RODNEY, HAROLD MILLER, RICHARD MACBRIDE and WALTER SAWATZKY
"Mennonite Central Committee: A Faith/Action Dialectic"
*Conrad Grebel Review*, 6, 3 (Fall 1988)

Four essays and an introduction reveal the fresh winds of social and ethical policy blowing over the Mennonite Central Committee, the large international service and peace agency serving in fifty countries with 1,000 workers.

After twenty-two years of Mennonite service in the midst of turbulent Africa, Harold Miller rejects the development model, generally considered superior to the direct aid and relief models. Miller replaces it with a listening and learning paradigm with reciprocity between host and donor societies, while affirming the primal strengths of Africa, transcending its weaknesses.

Richard Macbride, a veteran of MCC service in Lesotho, cites the bold prophetic Kairos document of 1985 which challenges the legitimacy of South Africa's government and questions the faithfulness of its churches. With the government turning a deaf ear to these cries of judgement, Macbride commits the Mennonite heresy of wondering if violence could be supported in the face of frustration and desperation.

Mark Neufeld of Carleton University is a Mennonite graduate student who has been overseas. He rejects the liberal-reformist emphasis on conflict resolution as the major Mennonite assumption in favour of social transformation by *struggle*. Neufeld's piece has the ring of liberation theology.

Walter Sawatsky, a Mennonite scholar trained in Russian studies, writes with qualified appreciation of *glasnost* and *perestroika*, thus reflecting an enormous shift in Mennonite thinking since the terror of the Russian revolution in 1918 and after.

These essays are the boldest and best expression of the new action-faith dialectic of contemporary Mennonites via its global peace and service organization. These essayists are ahead of the church as a whole.

SCHLABACH, THERON F.
"The Humble Become 'Aggressive Workers': Mennonites Organize for Mission, 1880-1910"
*MQR*, 52, 2 (April 1978): 113-26

During the period 1880-1910, the Mennonite and Amish Mennonite churches in North America rapidly accepted change and innovation. The ideal that Mennonites held up for Christian personality was changed, and new institutional structures were set up to serve that ideal. A psychology of aggressivism, more in line with American Protestantism, replaced the old psychology of humility. The author charts this change by examining the language of Mennonites in primary sources such as letters and newspaper articles. Two main difficulties resulted from this change. Theologically this new aggressiveness conflicted with traditional Mennonite beliefs such as obedience, non-conformity and non-resistance. Organizationally, this aggressiveness led to the building of a new infrastructure and a centralizing of power. The tension between the Sunday School movement of the younger more aggressive Mennonites and their conservative leaders is highlighted. This article raises some excellent questions about the effect Protestant theology has had on the Mennonite church. Schlabach's perceptive examination of the Mennonite Church during this critical time in its history provides valuable insights in examining the Mennonite Church and its relationship to Prostestantism today.

SHELLY, MAYNARD
"Mennonites: Affirming the Model of Martyrdom"
*Christian Century*, 95, 27 (August 1978): 781-82

This brief report on the tenth Mennonite World Conference, which was held in Wichita, Kansas in July 1978, concentrates on the Mennonites who are still persecuted in Russia, Africa, Asia and Latin America. The article points out that the Anabaptist concern for obedience is still an essential part of Mennonite practice, even at the risk of martyrdom.

SMUCKER, DONOVAN E.
## "Report from Vancouver: Faith Overcomes Ambivalence"
*Conrad Grebel Review*, 2, 2 (Spring 1984): 107-22

In his report of the Sixth Assembly of the World Council of Churches, Smucker made several observations. Overall, ecumenical Christianity must come to terms with a certain tension, because within biblical faith there are two opposite responses to organized religion. The high priestly prayer for unity in John 17 points to ecumenicity and unity in the church. On the other hand, Jesus attacked the hypocrisy of the religious establishment of his day. The ecumenical Christian must keep these apparently opposing ideas in creative tension, by affirming a common faith with fellow Christians but fearlessly criticizing empty ritual, moral decay and religious hypocrisy. He made two further observations about the present state of ecumenical dialogue: the collapse of the old Constantinian settlement of church and state (state churches) has opened the gates for a more Anabaptist view affirming separation of church and state, and the neo-evangelicals like Ron Sider and Jim Wallis are emerging as a critical new voice. Finally, Smucker affirmed that the World Council is an advisory body of consensus among many groups of Christians rather than a superchurch. German and Dutch Mennonites attended Vancouver as delegates. Nearly thirty Mennonites were present as fraternal delegates — observers without voting privileges.

SMUCKER, JOSEPH
## "Religious Community and Individualism: Conceptual Adaptation by One Group of Mennonites"
*Journal for Scientific Study of Religion*, 25, 3 (September 1986): 273-91

The experiences of Mennonites are not unlike those of other people moving from rural to urban areas. What is unique, however, are the conceptual adaptations made by this sample of Mennonites. In this paper, Smucker, a Montreal sociologist, reviews the major influences which have loosened individual commitments to Mennonite rural communities. He then examines the conceptual adaptations made by a sample of Mennonites living in one metropolitan area, as they attempt to maintain their identities. Key processes in their adaptation are the revised definitions of "community" and "service." Associated processes are the high degree of involvement in philanthropic projects and the use of psychological terminology which appears to bridge the gap between a heightened importance assumed by the self in an urban setting, and images of what it means to be a Mennonite.

Besides Mennonites, Smucker has introduced a category that he calls non-Mennonites. These are the individuals in his sample who are recent converts to the Mennonite church. Smucker failed to include their responses in his analysis, designating them as outsiders. Perhaps this group should be called non-ethnic Mennonites or new Mennonites, thus acknowledging them as *bona fide* Mennonites.

STAHL, JOHN DANIEL
"Conflict, Conscience, and Community in Selected Mennonite Children's Stories"
MQR, 55, 1 (January 1981): 62-74

Stahl explores the values exhibited in three Mennonite children's books written after World War II. He finds that selfless love and nonresistance are emphasized. He cautions that the suppression of anger and aggressive emotions, as exhibited in the stories, can encourage unhealthy tendencies towards passivity and avoidance of conflict, especially since some of the stories don't distinguish between self-renunciation for its own sake and self-renunciation for high moral principles. Stahl concludes by stating that it is important to examine literature to discover what personality patterns, self-concepts and standards of behaviour it encourages. Stahl assumes that the stories he examines in this article are of higher literary quality and are thus more likely to have a greater impact on readers; this claim is unsubstantiated by the article.

STEINER, SUE C.
"Mennonites in Politics"
Christian Century, 102, 16 (May 1985): 463-64

This is a brief report on the second in a series of "Conversations on Faith," entitled "The Church's Relationship to the Political Order." Here two hundred Mennonite leaders had the opportunity to air theological and ethical differences in the church.

SUZUKI, MICHAEL G.
"Differences Between Self-Concepts of Mennonite Adolescents and Public School Adolescents"
Alexandria, Va.: ERIC Clearing House, EDO90073. Resources in Education, 1974, 17 pp

The purpose of this study was to find out if there are any significant differences in the self-concepts of Mennonite high school adolescents and public school adolescents. The comparative results tend to show very little difference. There was some variation in relation to religion, conformity and relation to community.

TIECHROW, ALLAN
"Military Surveillance of Mennonites in World War I"
MQR, 52 (April 1979): 95-127

As sectarian pacifists who were German-speaking, American Mennonites, Amish and Hutterites were subjected to various kinds of government surveillance in World War I. The extent and character of this is described in a lengthy memorandum by Captain R. J. Malone of the military intelligence division of the U.S. war department. Published in toto, this report, which held a security classification until 1973, shows the tactics used, the men targeted, and the quality of the army's information. It is a chronicle of over-reaction and dubious or illegal practices. In addition to numerous explanatory footnotes, the editor has prefaced the report with an explanation of the military intelligence division's effect on the Mennonite faith. The introduction cites primary source materials not treated in the report itself.

TOEWS, J. B.
## "Mennonite Brethren in the Larger Mennonite World"
*MQR*, 67, 3 (July 1983): 257-64

The thesis of this article is that the underlying issues of the Mennonite Brethren and *Kirchliche* split in Russia, and the Mennonite Brethren self-understanding that emerged from that split have continued to be issues in the relationship of the Mennonite Brethren to other Mennonite groups. The author briefly surveys the history of the relationship between the Mennonite Brethren and other Mennonites, and concludes by calling for more open dialogue with the larger Mennonite fellowship. The merit of this article lies in the author's honest and open appraisal of his own tradition, and the call to acknowledge the benefits of Mennonite pluralism.

TOEWS, JOHN B., ABRAM G. KONRAD and ALVIN DUECK
## "Mennonite Brethren Church Membership Profile, 1972-82"
*Directions*, 14, 2 (Fall 1985)

In 1975 Howard Kauffman of Goshen and Leland Harder of Associated Mennonite Biblical Seminary, Elkhart, made a monumental sociological study of North American Mennonites. They had a budget of $40,000 and the help of forty skilled researchers. For accurate, descriptive data about Mennonite attitudes and behaviour, this is an authoritative study utilizing the most sophisticated research methods known to modern social science.

Ten years later the Mennonite Brethren scholars replicated the Harder-Kauffman study. Mennonite Mutual Aid, Goshen, Indiana, joined four major Mennonite Brethren Boards in financing the follow-up research. The study shortened the list of items studied but selected the same churches from a decade ago. Questionnaires were the basic instrument for the new research.

The data shows that the Mennonite Brethren are more urban, older, male, married, better educated, professional but less mobile than a decade ago. On general orthodoxy and fundamentalism the scores are very high; indeed, almost unanimous on everything except a six-day creation.

Regarding peace and reconciliation, fewer than half agree that the peace position should be actively promoted and that they would select alternative service if drafted. Personal moral practices such as alcohol, drugs and promiscuity are strongly rejected but there is a change toward tolerance on inter-faith marriages, movies, moderate drinking and dancing.

Also in the report are sprightly essays by leading Mennonite Brethren scholars. Delbert Wiens of Fresno labels the older patterns as "tribalism" from which the church is moving with sophistication, risking the byproduct of individualism. Wiens' famous essay "New Wineskins for Old Wine," published in 1968, was one of the first attempts to bring a critical but appreciative analysis into the inner circles of the church.

John E. Toews of the Mennonite Brethren Seminary, Fresno, boldly declares that the "Mennonite Brethren commitment to Anabaptist faith and ethics is weakening." Not only was the peace position declining but the scores on separation of church and state disclosed "danger signals for historic Anabaptist-Mennonite Brethren understandings."

John H. Redekop of Wilfrid Laurier University, Waterloo, believes that advanced education has strengthened the church. He pointed out an error of omission in the study: it researched the attitudes of those who have remained Mennonite Brethren but "the data do not indicate to what extent the pursuit of higher education has produced casualties and loss of membership."

In any case, between the Harder-Kauffman research of 1975 and this study ten years later one can gain much insight into a vigorous community of Christians who walked out of the *Kirchliche* Mennonite establishment in Russia 130 years ago. The major limitation of this study is that all of the scholars come from *within* the Mennonite Brethren Church.

URRY, JAMES
"Who are the Mennonites?"
*Archives Europeenes de Sociologie*, 24, 2 (1983): 241-62

Urry worked at the question of the identity of one group of Mennonites known as the "Russländer." The "Russländer" were Russian Mennonites who migrated to Canada in the 1920s in the wake of the Bolshevik Revolution. Urry explained how and why the "Russländers" have sought different identities in several periods of their history, in recent years adopting the historic concept of identity developed by the "Kanadier" who migrated from Russia in the 1870s, and the faith definition of Mennonitism as understood by the Swiss Mennonite theology of Anabaptism.

Urry's work gives valuable insights into the self-identity of the "Russländers," his non-Mennonite background allowing him an objectivity foreign to most Mennonite academics who have written on Mennonite themes.

VOGT, ROY
"The Impact of Economic and Social Class on Mennonite Theology"
*Mennonite Images*, ed. Harry Loewen. Winnipeg: Hyperion Press, 1980, pp. 137-48

Through analysis of social structure, Vogt examines the "withdrawal strategy" of modern urban Mennonites. His hypothesis is that the increasing professionalism among urban Mennonites is in reality a means of following the Anabaptist tradition of nonconformity and withdrawal from society; the relative autonomy of professionalism allows the freedom to maintain a "purer" faith based on Anabaptist ideology. The professional is removed from the "dehumanizing class struggle of the urban world." Vogt relies on a study done by J. Howard Kauffman and Leland Harder in his comparison of professional, business, farming and blue-collar workers concerning their adherence to Anabaptist theology. One observation is that the professional tends to have an idealistic, analytical approach to issues as opposed to the realistic, "visceral" involvement of the non-professional.

An historical perspective on the question of Mennonites in society is found in Harry Loewen's article, "The Anabaptist View of the World: The Beginning of a Mennonite Continuum?" (also in *Mennonite Images*, pp. 85-95). He traces the "withdrawal strategy" back to early Anabaptist beginnings.

WEAVER, J. DENNY
"Where Mennonites are Headed in the 1980s"
*Christianity Today*, 27, 9 (1983): 74

Weaver identifies several issues critical to the direction of the Mennonite denominations in the 1980s. He suggests that Mennonites need to define several questions of denominational identity which include such theological emphases as Christocentrism, peace and the communal nature of the church. Also necessary is a recognition of a variety of cultural and ethnic forms in a valid theology of community.

WEAVER, LAURA H.
"Forbidden Fancies: A Child's Vision of Mennonite Plainness"
*Journal of Ethnic Studies*, 11, 3 (1983): 51-59

The author describes her childhood experiences as a Mennonite and considers the problems and the benefits associated with growing up "different" and "plain" in American society.

WIEBE, BERNIE and THOMAS B. SCOTT
"Self-disclosure Patterns of Mennonite Adolescents to Parents and Their Perceived Relationships"
*Psychological Reports*, 39, 2 (October 1976): 355-58

This study addressed the concern which parents consistently express to ministers and counsellors – the lack of close relationships with their adolescent children. However, according to scores on the self-disclosure inventory for adolescents, 159 Mennonite youth (tenth-twelfth graders in three schools) self-disclosed like other observed adolescents, as selected topics were discussed by them with parents and friends. Perceived relationships with parents were positive, even though disclosure was less to parents than to best friends. Also, perceived relationships and self-disclosure were qualitatively different to mothers and to fathers.

WIEBE, BERNIE and CALVIN W. VRAA
"Religious Values of Students in Religious and Public High Schools"
*Psychological Reports*, 38, 3, Pt. 1 (June 1976): 709-10

This study seeks to analyze the effectiveness of Mennonite religious high schools in transmitting religious values. The Allport-Vernon-Lindzey study of values was administered to 124 Canadian high school seniors – forty from religious Mennonite schools, fifty-six Mennonites in public schools, and twenty-eight non-Mennonite students at a large public high school. Attending Mennonite private schools made no significant difference in the religious values held by Mennonite students.

While this study shows some interesting results, the somewhat unbalanced ratio of Mennonite to non-Mennonite students may lead to some question.

WIEBE, DON
## "Philosophical Reflections on Twentieth-Century Mennonite Thought"
*Mennonite Images*, ed. Harry Loewen. Winnipeg: Hyperion Press, 1980, pp. 149-64

In this article Wiebe seeks to defend his thesis concerning the "impoverished state of [the Mennonite] mind." While restricting his discussion to the Mennonite Brethren community, he explores what he identifies as "anti-intellectualism." Although giving some merit to H. S. Bender's emphasis on discipleship being the reason for a lack of Mennonite Brethren theological output, Wiebe argues that "radical rejection of free and critical thought" is the primary cause. As well, intrinsic to the "Anabaptist vision," Mennonites have nurtured a fear of assimilation; in keeping with church doctrine, they have given the state to the realm of "the world." The problem, states Wiebe, is that the *mind* has also been given to this realm, creating an Anabaptist "intellectual ghetto."

Wiebe specifies his study as relating to one sub-group of Mennonites, the Mennonite Brethren, and so his observations are necessarily somewhat particular. As Wiebe's title, "Reflections on Twentieth-Century Mennonite Thought" indicates, it may be helpful to see some comparison with other Mennonite "sub-groups" to give a more balanced and complete picture.

WIEBE, KATIE FUNK
## "Mennonite Brethren Women: Images and Realities of the Early Years"
*ML*, 36, 3 (September 1981): 22-28

Most history includes few references to women, and church history is no exception. It has been assumed that women have been excluded from most of our recorded history because they were passive and unassertive, but this essay argues otherwise. Writing from the perspective of Mennonite Brethren history, Wiebe demonstrates that while women rarely held positions of power and authority in the church, they contributed to the life of their church in a multitude of ways. Besides serving as missionaries and members of the women's societies, history shows that they influenced their husbands' decisions, suffered much and endured during times of crisis when their men were imprisoned, conscripted and exiled.

In *Women Among the Brethren* (1979), Wiebe gathered fifteen such stories of Mennonite Brethren women who made significant contributions to their church's history. Wiebe's discussion of Mennonite Brethren women illustrates how history can be rewritten to include women.

WRIGHT, RICHARD A.
"A Comparative Analysis of Economic Roles Within the
Family: Amish and Contemporary American Women"
*International Journal of Sociology of the Family*, 7, 7 (1977): 55-60

This article uses an economic methodology to assess the origin of modern feminism. Using Amish women as an example of women in traditional agrarian families, Wright compares their role with the position of American women in modern industrial households. He argues that Women's Liberation arose as a result of the loss of productive economic functions by modern women. In our post-industrial society, which equates monetary gain with human value, housewives are dependent on their husbands economically and often feel alienated and frustrated. In contrast, although Amish women are not considered to be equal to their husbands, their well-defined economic roles within their families gives their lives meaning.

While this article is more about women's liberation than about Amish women, it gives useful insights into the role of women within Amish society.

YODER, JOHN C.
"True Watchers: A Study of Social Order Among the Mennonites in Eighteenth-Century Pennsylvania"
*MQR*, 67, 4 (October 1983): 339-53

Although Mennonites separated themselves from the official state government, the Mennonites in Pennsylvania in the eighteenth century in no way rejected the need for leadership. The church leaders were responsible not only for the spiritual well-being of the community but also for the care of the poor, for legal questions and other community affairs. Thus authority was maintained in a very structured and hierarchical way. This article compares the structure of the schoolroom (as exemplified by the school of Christopher Dock) and the structure of the Mennonite community. The article provides valuable insights by viewing the schoolroom as a microcosm of the larger community.

YODER, MICHAEL L.
"Findings from the 1982 Mennonite Census"
*MQR*, 69, 4 (October 1985): 307-49

The census that this article is based on was collected from a scientifically selected sample of 271 congregations from all twenty-two district conferences of the Mennonite church in the United States and Canada. The census yielded data on such basic characteristics as age, sex, membership status, race and ethnicity, church background, residence, education and occupation. Additional data were gathered on education in church schools and colleges, church service experience, marital status and, for women only, number of children ever born or adopted. The article provides and interprets the basic results of the census on these items, giving special attention to differences among Mennonites according to race and ethnicity. In addition, the article compares Mennonites to the larger American population and examines social change among Mennonites by using data from previous roughly comparable studies.

YOUNGREN, T. ALAN
"Mennonite Won't Play the Game"
*Christianity Today*, 26, 11 (June 1982): 44

This brief article pats Mennonites on the back for their role in relief and development, suggesting that Mennonite volunteer work through the Mennonite Central Committee, Mennonite Relief Sales and the Mennonite stores are all examples of "grassroots motivation" among the Mennonites.

# D. Unpublished Sources

DUECK, KATHRYN
"Learning Resources Information of Orientations by Students in a Subculture"
Paper presented to the 59th Annual Meeting of American Education Research Association, Chicago, 1974

The purpose of this study is to assess the relative impact on Mennonite high school students of various orientations toward the issues of war and peace. With factors involved such as family, religion, media, age and sex differences, the 438 students surveyed answered closed and open-ended questions. While the research was somewhat limited, some conclusions were: religion is the most important source of orientation, next are teachers, peers, ministers, mass media, and finally family. Also, questions about war elicited frustration, while conventional views of war and the passive nature of peace emerged.

One must argue with Dueck's conclusion that the family plays no significant role with respect to peace; perhaps in a more subtle way family has a profound effect on a child's view of conflict and of him/herself within it.

FRIESEN, JOHN W.
"Concepts of Mennonites in School Curricula"
Unpublished paper, University of Calgary, Faculty of Education, 1984

This study—conducted as part of the mandate of the Mennonite Bicentennial Commission of Waterloo—is an attempt to discern the presence and use of material related to Mennonites in school curricula. Friesen sent questionnaires to private and public schools in the five westerly provinces, all of which have a discernable Mennonite population. The questions, for which he provides tables and representative responses, range from a detailed examination of Mennonite information/content to analysis of the value of cultural awareness and multiculturalism. Friesen's questionnaire also allowed for unsolicited comments, some of which he includes in his report.

As Friesen states, content analysis of written materials is a research technique mounting in popularity. This report, timely in the year of the Ontario Mennonite Bicentennial, as well as in a time of increased interest in multiculturalism, provides a unique picture of the Mennonite presence in Canada. While some of the tables are unclear, they do serve to summarize Friesen's findings.

HAMM, PETER
## "Continuity and Change Among Canadian Mennonite Brethren"
Conference on "Dynamics of Faith and Culture in Mennonite Brethren History," Winnipeg, November 14-15, 1986

This is a shortened, revised version of Hamm's doctoral dissertation at McMaster University, now published as a book and annotated in the *Mennonite Books* section in this volume.

The original data of Hamm came from the Church Member Profile of Harder and Kauffman in 1972 which was re-checked as "Mennonite Brethren Church Membership Profile 1972-1982" published in *Direction* 1986.

The foregoing paragraphs make it clear that there is now a constant interaction among Mennonite scholars of the three major groups in North America.

Hamm's central typological term is Ernst Troeltsch's *"sect"* which he uses in a non-perjorative sense to indicate conflict and tension with the religious and cultural mainline establishment. Along with the sectarian conception, Hamm follows his McMaster mentor in using the integration/differentiation dialectic. This conception seeks to identify the integrating forces which sacralize a religious movement and therefore hold it together. It also identifies the disintegrative, erosive forces which destroy a religious movement.

Hamm is basically optimistic that the Mennonite Brethren of Canada have a viable sectarianism which "may well be the pattern for other evangelical denominations."

The author has written an important major sociological analysis of the Mennonite Brethren. His optimism that his church is a paradigm for other evangelical groups would be vigorously debated by other sociologists from within (*Directions*, 1980) and without his own denomination.

See the annotation of his book for further analysis.

JUHNKE, JAMES C.
## "Mennonite History and Self Understanding: North American Mennonitism as a Bipolar Mosaic"
Conrad Grebel College Conference on Mennonite Identity, May 28-31, 1986

Juhnke argues that Mennonite self-understanding in North America has been conditioned by a two-fold European heritage: (1) the Swiss-South German stream, transplanted to Pennsylvania in the seventeenth and eighteenth centuries and spread out from here, is mainly divided into Mennonites and Amish; (2) the Dutch-North German stream, which made its way via Prussia and South Russia to North America, where its members migrated in the 1870s, 1920s and 1940s, is mainly divided into *Kirchliche* and *Brudergemeinde*. These two streams differ in terms of historical memories, cultural characteristics, theological preferences, dialect, etc. Juhnke describes both differences and mutual influences between these streams in their European origins and in their North American development. He includes a brief analysis of Dutch-Russian and Swiss-American literature and argues that humility has been a more prominent part of the Swiss stream's virtues, while Dutch-Russian Mennonites have been more enterprising.

The author examines some preceding attempts to find a unified historical conception for the study of the great diversity of Mennonite groups. He finds the concept of the liberal-conservative continuum partially useful, but as a socio-political abstraction it fails to take into account cultural and ethnic characteristics of the diverse groups, characteristics which do not necessarily correspond to the divisions according to liberal, moderate or conservative groups. He finds the "Normative Mennonitism" approach unable to do justice to the plurality of Mennonite denominations. He criticizes Frank Epp's emphasis on the difference of historical experience between Canadian and American Mennonites; Epp's point, however, seems justifiable insofar as the experiences of the Mennonites in two national contexts has differed and shaped them to some degree.

Juhnke proposes a "double-bi-polarity," taking into account both the Swiss-Dutch difference and the dimension consisting of traditionalists and progressives. This model seems very valuable in understanding Mennonite denominational diversity both in its cultural and its socio-political aspects.

The historical perspective might not be easily portrayed in such a model, but Juhnke acknowledges that "we need multiple images."

KRAYBILL, DONALD B.
"Modernity and Identity: The Transformation of Mennonite Ethnicity"
Conrad Grebel College Conference on Mennonite Identity, May 28-31, 1986

Proceeding from the basis of the sociology of knowledge, Kraybill argues that Anabaptist identity was originally "socially constructed," externalized and then given its objective status by elaborate social control mechanisms upheld by a plausibility structure based on a rural context. By means of intensive socialization, this objective identity was internalized and formed the "personal values" of subsequent generations. (One might however question the implication that Anabaptists had originally intended to create a separate identity.)

Mennonite ethnicity, the product of a dialectical interaction between social context and individual or group thought, is not static; changes in the historical conditions on which the "plausibility structure" is based naturally affect ethnic identity. The author proposes an eclectic conceptual model for understanding the transformation of Mennonite ethnicity, based on the "three-generation hypothesis" and on modernization theory. The effects of modernization in the domains of culture, behaviour, structure and authority are well shown. Culturally, a shift from concrete to abstract conception of symbols, from a perspective concerned with the immediate situation to emphasis on common history, from homogeneous to heterogeneous beliefs, from a communal to an individual identity, takes place.

Behaviourial expression of identity becomes situational rather than continuous, participation becomes organizational more than cultural, and a sense of uniqueness is based less on practice than on ideation. Structurally, Mennonite ethnicity is no longer simple, strongly integrated, stationary and complete, but complex, less integrated or complete and portable. Authority is vested less in office than in organization; expertise has greater influence than charisma, and authority is legitimized more by rational argument than by appeals to tradition.

The three-generation hypothesis fits less well. Kraybill argues that the "Forgetter" stage was omitted, except in the case of individuals or splinter groups. The article is an interesting analysis of Mennonite identity, although more applicable to modern "mainstream" Mennonites, rather than the more traditional branches. Kraybill argues that, far from dooming Mennonite identity, its ability to modernize itself shows its vitality.

LOEWEN, JACOB
## "The German Language, Culture and Faith"
Conference on "Dynamics of Faith and Culture in Mennonite Brethren History," Winnipeg, November 14-15, 1986

A Mennonite anthropologist who knows that language and culture are intimately related, Loewen surveys many years of controversy among Mennonites concerning German as an identity mechanism, a separation device, and the special conduit for a revived branch of Mennonites who broke away from the established Mennonite church in Russia 128 years ago.

Loewen links the emergence of English among North American Mennonite Brethren with urban professionalism, affluence and American nationalism.

This is the most impressive survey now available of the Russian Mennonite movement from the use of Dutch in Holland, to Low German after migrating to East Prussia and Russia and the later use of high German and English in North America.

Now that an in-group language barrier no longer exists, this anthropologist is telling his peers that separation and identity must work in some other way than the use of German.

Missing from the paper is the impact of many different languages among the World Conference of Mennonites which has participants from fifty-two countries, speaking 100 languages. The sessions of the World Conference of Mennonites held every six years reflect the impact of migration and missionary activities, thus creating a multicultural community of Mennonite Christians who no longer possess a common language.

PETERS, JOHN F.
## "Economics of the Canadian Old Order Mennonites"
Paper presented for Conrad Grebel College Conference, "Anabaptist
Faith and Economics," May 24-27, 1990

The field research of John F. Peters among the 4,000 Old Order Mennonites of Waterloo County is now available at the very time when J. Winfield Fretz has moved to the States.

Peters is an empirical researcher with a clear sense of social theory. This paper represents both a qualitative and quantitative analysis of the Waterloo "horse and buggy" community. The research strongly endorses Max Weber's thesis that ideas and beliefs affect social and economic behaviour. At the same time this work takes strong issue with the Weberian notion of the relationship between Protestantism and capitalism.

In contrast to modern industrial workers, the Old Order Mennonites are not alienated from their work; the means of production is not the crux of their existence and their ideology controls and dominates economic activity. Finally, they do not resonate with movements of revolt against capitalism even as they have discovered how to restrain, bridle and qualify capitalism. They do not pander to the tourist trade or own a store selling Mennonite artifacts.

From Donald Kraybill Peters borrows the phrase of the "upsidedown" kingdom. The Old Order Mennonites have reversed the values of a business civilization giving economics a holistic, human face and creating an alternative economic system. Coming from a scientifically trained sociologist this is an impressive tribute to success if one is willing to pay the price of cultural conservatism.

PETERS, JOHN F. and MARLIN WENZEL
## "Ontario Old Order Mennonites: A Demographic Analysis"
Unpublished paper presented to faculty and fellows of Conrad Grebel
College, December 4, 1987

Two sociologists, John Peters from Wilfrid Laurier University and Marlin Wenzel from the University of Western Ontario, have engaged in research over a four-year span dealing with the population data of marriage, fertility, age, death and community size of Old Order Mennonites in Waterloo County and a new settlement near Mount Forest, Ontario, forty miles north of Waterloo.

The whole project was suggested by a detailed directory of the Old Order Mennonites edited by Annie Martin, a member of the church in the Waterloo area. When Peters and Wenzel expanded the directory's data, they suggested that the Wilfrid Laurier University computer could create a new and better directory of families and their births, deaths, age and defections. Annie Martin and other church members agreed. It has been published under the title, *Families of the Old Order Mennonite Church*, Wilfrid Laurier University, 1987.

The Peters-Wenzel study makes comparisons longitudinally and with the Canadian population as a whole.

Among results of the research is a disproportionate ratio of male births, the completed Old Order family twice the size of the average Canadian family, the total absence of divorce, single women outnumbering single men by 2 1/2 times, and the predominant outmigration to the Markham Mennonites who are plain and conservative but have made the concession in favour of cars and tractors.

More research is needed on the Old Order pattern of socialization, particularly with the decline of farming occupations, the possibility of deviance in the group, the increasing number of single women and the possibility of unreported behavioural patterns which research by outsiders may not discover.

REDEKOP, CALVIN
## "The Sociology of Mennonite Identity: A Second Opinion"
Conrad Grebel College Conference on Mennonite Identity, May 28-31, 1986

Redekop presents an alternative interpretation of Mennonite identity to Donald Kraybill's ethnic interpretation, which Redekop finds insufficient. He argues that the concept of ethnicity ignores the perpetual dialogue between Mennonites and society as the continuing defining criterion of the group's identity, as the premises of the sociology of knowledge would imply.

Redekop sees Mennonite identity as originating in a utopian attempt to reform society, thus not separatistic. Only through persecution of the Mennonites and the impossibility of transforming society did the emphasis on turning inward, on self-preservation, emerge. Yet despite their stance of opposition, Mennonites have not remained unaffected by the larger cultural and social contexts in which they have lived, resulting in the development of increased self-awareness as an entity, increasingly autonomous but less utopian. Redekop argues that the Mennonite phenomenon is a utopian movement "at war with the Mores,"[2] never coming to terms with the tendency to become an ethnic group; this conflict explains the continuing identity crisis.

Although both Kraybill and Redekop base their arguments on the sociology of knowledge, Redekop rejects the interpretation of Mennonite identity as ethnicity and advocates an interpretation of that identity as based on a utopian reformist ideology in interaction with changing historical circumstances. Due to this process, it has to some degree become codified or institutionalized. The net effect of external and internal changes is examined and shown to result in increasing need to emphasize the story of rejections, in a shift from enmity to the outside world to psychological and social isolation and in the conscious maintenance of a "peoplehood tradition." One wonders whether Redekop, in his criticism of Kraybill's "ethnicity," does not over-emphasize the theoretical, "ideological" component of Mennonite identity. Nevertheless the article supplies an interesting and valuable alternative perspective on Mennonite identity.

---

2. The phrase is from W.G. Sumner.

REDEKOP, CALVIN and HENRY REGEHR
"Pro-social Behaviour: Volunteering and the Good Society"
Canadian Learned Societies, McMaster University, 1987

The authors contend that, in contrast to anti-social and social (con-formist) behaviour, pro-social behaviour has been studied insuffi-ciently. Pro-social behaviour is conceived of as voluntary altruistic activity; the authors focus on such activity on a large scale or long-term basis. They illustrate such behaviour by studying Mennonite service organizations (MCC, Mennonite Disaster Service, etc.) and give some data regarding the participation of individuals in such organizations.

The authors distinguish three factors conducive to pro-social behaviour: situational characteristics — the presence of need requiring voluntary help, structural inducements, that is, the presence of organi-zations inviting participation and the influence of family, friends, etc., and the ideological charter, the philosophical and ideological motiva-tions of a person's behaviour. The authors argue that previous attempts to examine pro-social behaviour in terms of either situational factors or personal disposition can be reduced to the ideological factor.

The contention that pro-social behaviour results from self interest is rejected by the authors and it is stressed that ideological factors must not be ignored in analyzing pro-social behaviour. They adduce both the historic role of the Church and personal comments by Mennonites, which indicate that the majority regard voluntary service as an expres-sion of their Christian ideology. The thesis calls for further study, as the authors acknowledge. It seems like a formidable task to develop an unbiased method of studying ideological influence on personal behaviour, but the results of such a study would be very interesting.

SAWTASKY, RODNEY J.
"Beyond the Social History of the Mennonites"
Conrad Grebel College Conference on Mennonite Identity, May 28-31, 1986

The author writes in response to James Juhnke's paper, "Mennonite History and Self-Understanding: North American Mennonitism as a Bipolar Mosaic." He criticizes Juhnke in two ways: first, Juhnke's the-sis may "explain too much" in that it implies that mutual influences or co-operation between the two streams, Swiss-American and Dutch-Russian, is merely "ironical." Second, Juhnke explains "not enough"; Mennonite plurality cannot readily be captured in a simple duality. Possibly both these criticisms are based on a somewhat overstated ver-sion of Juhnke's thesis, which proposes a "double bi-polarity" taking cultural, as well as theological differences, between Mennonite groups into account. Sawatsky does, however, assume the general utility of Juhnke's model.

Sawatsky proceeds to identify the social history approach of Juhnke as characteristically Dutch-Russian, while the Swiss-American approach to historiography has been the normative, rather than the plu-ralistic, model and has emphasized the church history method, which interprets history from a theological standpoint. The author briefly describes both approaches and cites examples. He then argues that Juhnke's "global vision for a world of Mennonitism" implies a normativity be constructed. Sawatsky argues in favour of returning to the theological, normative church history approach, which has been largely displaced by the social science approach, in order to construct a common norm for the worldwide Mennonite experience.

SOMERS, WILLIS
## "A Theology of Investments, Mennonite Mutual Aid and Biblical Faith — A Case Study"
Paper presented for the Conrad Grebel College Conference, "Anabaptist-Mennonite Faith and Economics," May 24-27, 1990

This case study reveals the way in which the Mennonite Mutual Aid of Goshen, Indiana faced the real world, symbolized by $20,000,000 in its reserves and surplus backing up health, automobile and property insurance. Very quickly the directors of the board discovered the problem posed by American corporations with South African investments. By 1986 it was obvious that investment guidelines for multimillion-dollar reserved funds needed reviewing.

Although love had always been the key virtue for Mennonites, the Mutual Board soon found that justice needed to interact with love. They discovered that they must be aware of the South African problem; they also needed to understand the tangled web of institutions in that nation. Then the board had to communicate a very complex issue to the church constituency behind them and, finally, formulate a specific policy. Meanwhile, continuous monitoring of the policy must take place.

This long encounter caused the Mennonite managers of the $20,000,000 treasury to lose the innocence of the rural or small-town world of corner grocery stores and small businesses. Somers concluded that the quest for a new policy was "long, difficult and frustrating." The Mennonites met the real world and were not shattered by it.

TOEWS, PAUL
## "Faith in Culture and Culture in Faith: Mennonite Brethren Entertaining Expansive Separatist and Assimilative Views about the Relationship"
Conference on "Dynamics of Faith and Culture in Mennonite Brethren History," Winnipeg, November 14-15, 1986

Professor Toews of Fresno Pacific College analyzes three modes of reflection on faith and culture: the expansive era in the early 1900s when Christian education, science, social reform, missions, American culture and esthetic life were glowing with excitement. Then came a separate thrust in the 1950s. Here fundamentalist theology was a barrier against drifting into the mainstream. Along with this theology was the quest for an authoritative hierarchy. This new separation was contradictory and ambivalent.

The third and final mode, according to Toews, was the assimilationist trend. The old German ethnicity began to erode with the declaration that faith can exist without cultural forms.

Toews consults his hopes rather than his fears that contradictory signals can lead to a wiser, sounder, more tenable linkage of faith and culture. The author offers little or no evidence that this ambiguity and ambivalence will lead to a wiser and sounder view.

URRY, JAMES
## "A Religious or a Social Elite? The Mennonite Brethren in Imperial Russia"
Conference on "Dynamics of Faith and Culture in Mennonite Brethren History." Winnipeg, November 14-15, 1986

This paper examines the emergence of the Mennonite Brethren as both a social and a religious group within the larger Mennonite community which had been established in Russia by 1860. By re-examining the forms of community and society which had developed in both Prussia and in Russia before 1860, Urry was able to establish the social background from which the early leaders and membership of the Brethren arose. Suggesting that this social context was an important precondition of the Brethren's beginnings, he argued that the emergence of the Brethren was not such a radical break with the religious and social world which existed before 1860 as has often been argued. Rather, the Brethren manifested a trend apparent in the larger community as Mennonites came to terms with the rapidly changing social, economic and political atmosphere of late nineteenth-century Russia. Indeed, religious life in 1860 appears to have been rich and varied in Russia and the Brethren movement was but one section of a complex picture.

WIEBE, KATIE FUNK
## "The New Mennonite Brethren: In But Still Out"
Conference on "Dynamics of Faith and Culture in Mennonite Brethren History," Winnipeg, November 14-15, 1986

An English professor in Tabor College, USA, has written an original study which can be the envy of the sociologists. She decided to make a statistical study of non-traditional (non-ethnic Mennonite) names as reported in the leading church paper from 1962 to 1985, and non-traditional names among conference delegates, local church workers and membership on committees and boards.

She discovered a large increase between 1962 and 1984 in names of families who have joined the Mennonite Brethren more recently. Yet only a tiny percentage were on key church boards. Similarly, only another tiny percentage of Mennonite Brethren women were represented on these boards and committees.

Other startling discoveries were that seventy-three Mennonite Brethren churches in 1984 had dropped the term Mennonite to identify themselves; and a continuing trend to transfer out of the church.

A comparative study is needed of other conferences and denominations to see the rate at which non-traditional members are accepted in leadership committees. This is a candid self-criticism of a Mennonite "denomination."

WIEBE, RUDY
## "The Moralities of the Mennonite Brethren"
Conference on "Dynamics of Faith and Culture in Mennonite Brethren History," Winnipeg, November 14-15, 1986

The leading Mennonite novelist of Canada teaches at the University of Alberta. His candour and realism have evoked much criticism and much praise.

In this essay, he argues that the Mennonite ethos is a barrier to doing ethics. His preliminary examples of ethos are the changing views of dancing, radio, television, movies, smoking, drinking and finally, sexual taboos. Wiebe declares that "taboos do not develop arbitrarily; no one talks freely about those places where one is most vulnerable and where identity is most tender." In brief, Wiebe views sex as "an individual's affair," not an area of community or church law.

In a section entitled "From ethos to ethois," he sees the Reformation as "inherently secularizing and pluralizing" because faith must be removed from ethos. Wiebe has a brilliant section here on the nature of contemporary rebellion when the religious and secular ethois are tottering. One senses deep despair in this analysis because there isn't much to rebel against. Wiebe overlooks the possibility of a vacuum in which new forces rush in to replace the old.

Wiebe is very pessimistic about recreating the Mennonite Brethren tradition. He seeks a new way for his churches to be people of God without succumbing to the *Geists* which dominate our world. The new people of God will not live under the protection of culture or social enclaves.

# III. Hutterites

# A. Books and Pamphlets

HOFER, JOHN, DAVID WIEBE and GERHARD ENS
*The History of the Hutterites*
Winnipeg: W. K. Printers' Aid, 1982

This interesting booklet traces the history of the Hutterite church, beginning with the early apostolic church and including the history of the church up to the Reformation. It describes the formation of the Anabaptist movement and the foundation of the Hutterite church by Jakob Hutter, who was tortured and executed in 1536. After a period of persecution, there followed a period of relative growth and peace from 1554-92, during which the *Bruderhof* became a Hutterite institution. The Turkish War and especially the Thirty Years War resulted in renewed severe persecution and the expulsion of the Hutterites from Moravia in 1622. The Hutterites found temporary refuge in Hungary but were forced to go to Wallachia in 1767, and to Russia three years later, where they founded colonies in Vishenka and Radichev. There followed a period of deterioration during which the community of goods was abandoned, until in the 1840s when the establishment of Huttertal under Mennonite influence brought a renewal of the community of goods in 1859. In the 1860s and 1870s, the policy of Russification induced the Hutterites to migrate to the USA. During the First World War, many Hutterites moved to Canada, where during the Great Depression they were valued for their self-sufficiency and economic strength. Although they obtained conscientious objector status in the Second World War, there followed a period of increased government interference with land purchases, education, etc. Still, by adapting slowly to modernization while carefully maintaining their religious and cultural identity, the Hutterites continued to expand and prosper. The oldest communal society in the western world has proven its outstanding gifts of adaptation in many social and political contexts. Karl Peter calls it selective acculturation.

HOSTETLER, JOHN A.
*Hutterite Life*
Scottdale, Pa., and Kitchener, Ont.: Herald Press, 1983

*Hutterite Life* completes a set of three booklets by John A. Hostetler, the other two entitled *Mennonite Life* and *Amish Life*. While brief and concise, the book deals in an interesting and informative way with virtually every aspect of Hutterite communal living. Topics include religious beliefs and practices; aspects of communal living; women in colony life; marriage and family; art and humour; stability; and survival. As in Hostetler's view of Amish life, the Hutterites also face the challenge of surviving in their communal setting within the larger North American society. Hutterites have endured particularly severe harassment by religious and civil authorities in the past, and drastic means have been used to convert the Hutterites back to the state church. As Hostetler cites,

Catholic services were enforced on every *Bruderhof*, and when this did not bring results, an executioner was assigned to collaborate with the state theologian.

Despite their difficult past, however, the group has grown to the present 30,000 (p. 14). Beautiful photographs complement this volume, making it a colourful and attractive educational tool.

See also Hostetler, *Mennonite Life* and *Amish Life* and, for his major work, see *Hutterite Society* (Baltimore: Johns Hopkins University Press, 1974), annotated in Vol. 1, pp. 140-41.

HUTTERIAN SOCIETY OF BROTHERS and JOHN HOWARD YODER (EDS.)
*God's Revolution: The Witness of Eberhard Arnold*
New York: Paulist Press, 1984

The Hutterian Society of Brothers, who edited this book (with the assistance of John H. Yoder), bring together a collection of short sayings by their community's founder, Eberhard Arnold. As the introduction states, they are "a selection of those dominant strands of Arnold's instruction." The book is introduced by Yoder, who provides the historical context for the life and work of Eberhard Arnold. Included in the book are four basic divisions of Arnold's sayings: This Crumbling World and God's Coming Order; The New Order Fleshed Out; The Individual and the Community; and Peace and the Rule of God. As is clear from these headings, this man had a great vision for the community of believers and its work in advancing God's Kingdom.

The book is an important work in terms of primary sources and is an inspiration and direction for those seeking the way of Christ as understood by The Society of Brothers.

For related books, see Eberhard and Emmy Arnold, *Seeking For the Kingdom of God* (Rifton, N.Y.: Plough Publishing House, 1974); Eberhard Arnold, *A Testimony of Church Community from his Life & Writings* (Rifton, N.Y.: Plough Publishing House, 1973); and Emmy Arnold, *Torches Together* (Rifton, N.Y.: Plough Publishing House, 1971).

PETER, KARL A.
*The Dynamics of Hutterite Society: An Analytical Approach*
Edmonton: University of Alberta Press, 1987

Karl A. Peter of the Simon Fraser University sociology department collaborated with his colleague, Ian Whitaker, and two Manitoba sociologists, Ed Boldt and Lance Robert, to bring together a collection of outstanding essays on the Hutterites on the assumption that the Hutterites are not a static society but a group constantly adjusting to new environmental, political and cultural forces. Yet, this selective acculturation does not destroy their historic role in sustaining the oldest communal societies in the western world. A remarkable fact is the two losses of the communal organization of property in past history and its recovery after lapses of eighty and fifty years.

The authors are impressed by the ability of the Hutterites to support their large families and yet have surpluses for the expansion of old and new farms, using only capital generated by their own agricultural work. Hutterites are also praised for their flexibility in altering their pattern of farming from mixed to specializing in one or two crops.

Essays on the changing role of women and the rise of marital tensions break new ground.

The analysis of defection from Hutterite colonies suggests that the generally favourable view of the Hutterites in this book does not exclude the danger signal of a constant trickle of departures. The author's view is that this is due to the subversion of the collectivist ideal by the individualist view of salvation held by fundamentalist sects in the immediate environment. Moreover, the Hutterite worship service is barren of images, pictures, music and spirited preaching (all sermons are read). The authors suggest upgrading their static worship pattern.

For a review of basic trends in Hutterite research, this is a state-of-the-art book. More time might well have been spent in contrasting its different approaches from John Hostetler's *Hutterite Society* (1974) and John Bennett's *Hutterian Brethren* (1967).

# B. Graduate Theses

BAUM, RUTH E.
"The Ethnohistory of Law: The Hutterite Case"
Ph.D dissertation, State University of New York, 1977

This study deals with the Hutterite law from an ethnohistorical perspective. The Hutterites are a communal religious isolate, based on large-scale agriculture on the North American plains, whose internal legal system has been an important factor in maintaining their boundaries and their sectarian character since their origin in 1528. They are unusual in being a status society whose non-administrative substantive law is solely criminal. The reasons lie in their religion and their historical period of origin. Because their legal bases differ from the larger society, the latter's courts sometimes have problems dealing with them.

For related studies, see John W. Bennett, "Social Theory and the Social Order of the Hutterian Community," *MQR*, 51, 4 (October 1977): 292-307, and Edward D. Boldt, "Leadership Succession Among the Hutterites: Ascription or Achievement," *La revue canadienne de sociologie et d'anthropologie/The Canadian Review of Sociology and Anthropology*, 15, 3 (1978): 394-96.

HEIKEN, DIANE E. B.
"The Hutterites: A Comparative Analysis of Viability"
Ph.D dissertation, University of California, Santa Barbara, 1978

The author seeks to fill a void in the present literature concerning Hutterites by dealing systematically with the process of colony breakdown. While colony failure is still relatively rare, variations in colony cohesiveness are extensive. This study focuses on the factors which account for varying degrees of colony disorganization (including total breakdown) and the likelihood of the Hutterites' continued prosperity. The author has gained her information from time spent visiting and working on forty-six Hutterite colonies in western Canada, from economic data and demographic information derived from kinship charts.

For related studies, see Karl A. Peter, "The Decline of Hutterite Population Growth," *Canadian Ethnic Studies*, 12, 3 (1980): 97-110; Karl Peter, Edward D. Boldt, Ian Whitaker and Lance W. Roberts, "The Dynamics of Religious Defection Among Hutterites," *Journal for the Scientific Study of Religion*, 21, 4 (1982): 327-37; and Edward D. Boldt, "Acquiescence and Conventionality in a Communal Society," *Journal of Cross-cultural Psychology*, 7, 1 (March 1976): 21-36.

MELLAND, JOHN and IAN FRANCIS
"Changes in Hutterite House Types: The Material Expression of the Contradiction Between Being-on-the-colony and 'Being-in-the-world.'"
Ph.D. dissertation, Louisiana State University, 1985

Hutterite society emphasizes simple living and avoidance of the world which is reflected in ascetic colony housing. However, as more areas of life change, it is difficult to maintain avoidance as an ideal. Leaders are now confronted with demands for participation and collective consumption, particularly for modern and more private housing. This study examines how Hutterite housing has changed and why recent changes have been so dramatic. The desire for more autonomy indicates that colony members are attempting to satisfy their own expectations of themselves, not just social expectations. Secondly, although housing has been defined by the colony, the unforeseen consequences of the changes made possible by more private housing have affected the original definition and reshaped it.

OBENG-QUAIDOO, ISAAC
"Hutterite Land Expansion and the Canadian Press"
Ph.D. dissertation, University of Minnesota, 1977

Obeng-Quaidoo studied the treatment of Hutterite developments in the dailies and weeklies of Saskatchewan and Alberta, provinces with large numbers of Hutterite colonies. The period was from 1940 to 1972. Against the background of prejudice and resentment, this thesis is a study in the sociology of knowledge in a majority-minority situation.

It is a story of decreasing prejudice in the Saskatchewan dailies and silence in the small-town weeklies of the province. Alberta newspapers reflected more prejudice against the Hutterites, even though starting in 1969 the daily papers became more tolerant.

The focus of the inadequate press coverage was essentially the conflict between socialism and capitalism. The Hutterites are not Communists from Moscow or Beijing but they clearly are not capitalists as understood by a free-market businessman or farmer. The author of the dissertation was surprised that the critics of the Hutterites did not acknowledge their contribution to agriculture in an era when machines were destroying jobs in the agricultural sector.

Every variable in the context of majority-minority relationships of Hutterites and non-Hutterites was analyzed by the author in his study.

The rise of television has made this study outdated in the sense that today one would want to know if the Hutterites are caricatured, omitted or distorted by both print media and television programs. The National Film Board of Canada has presented several sympathetic portraits of the Hutterites.

STEPHENSON, PETER HAYFORD
"The Dying of the Old Man and a Putting on of the New: The Cybernetic of Ritual *Metanoia* in the Life of Hutterian Commune"
Ph.D. dissertation, University of Toronto, 1978

Stephenson wrote this dissertation to test his basic hypothesis that the persistence of communes is predicated on their use of ritual. He applied this assumption specifically to the five centuries of experience with ritual in the Hutterian societies. The key ritual he cites is adult baptism as a public expression to commitment in a communal society. This is more than the adult baptism of the Baptists but the threshold into collective rebirth, as developed by Jacob Waltner. In the collective context, adult baptism declares that childhood socialization is complete and now full status in the commune begins.

In the second half of the thesis, Stephenson examines colony-fission, a form of expansion and exploration confirmed by ritual. In the Epilogue he shows that Hutterian culture is an example of a self-simplifying system.

One senses great originality in this dissertation but Stephenson tries to prove too much by his hypothesis of ritual, particularly with the concentration on the adult baptism. Moreover, a plain, austere communal Protestantism like Hutterite Christianity limits liturgies, celebrations, memorials, dramas and litanies.

# C. Articles

ANDERSSON, BENGT E.
"Misunderstandings Between Generations: A General Phenomenon?"
*Scandinavian Journal of Educational Research*, 17 (1983): 1-10

In this study, fifty thirteen-year-olds and their parents rated their attitudes toward each other's generation. Each group was also asked to predict the other group's ratings. No evidence of a generation gap between the generations was found. However, both generations had faulty perceptions of the attitudes of the opposite generation. These faulty perceptions may be the basis for opposition or conflict. Comparisons are made with R. O. Hess and I. Goldblatt's 1957 study of American teenagers and their parents and S. Schluderman and E. Schluderman's study of Hutterite adolescents (*Journal of Psychology*, XXIX, 29-309).

BENNETT, JOHN W.
## "Frames of Reference for the Study of Hutterian Society"
*Communes Historical and Contemporary*, ed. Ruth Shonle Cavan and Man
Sing Das. Delhi: Vikas Publishing House, 1979, pp. 25-43

The author points out that while descriptive studies of the Hutterites
exist abundantly, theoretical work is sparse. In this excellent article, he
proposes as points of departure for such work, six organizational concepts: (1) The Hutterite colony may be studied as a Central European-
derived nucleated village, linking it to non-communal *gemeinschaftliche*
traditions, although the village system is maintained on the basis of
communalism. Such a study would shed light on the scope of Hutterite
communalism. (2) Hutterite instrumental organization can be seen as
a conflict-avoidance and resolution system in which destructive
interpersonal relations are allayed by communal discipline. Hutterite
communalism would be the principal means to conflict-avoidance,
based on the repression of self-seeking urges. (3) This self-negating
emphasis invites the study of Hutterite personality with respect to the
relationship between repression and aggression; among Hutterites,
extra-punitive reactions are discouraged and occur rarely, in contrast to
society at large. Intra-punitive reactions are more frequent. (4) The
Hutterite inter-colonial socio-economic system represents a form of
co-operative exchange, made more efficient because it is based on communal, not private, co-operation. This highlights a level of integration
in Hutterite society much larger than individual colonies. (5) Hutterite
agriculture can be seen as a model of conservationist practice resulting
from an economy of scale plus the temporal continuity of Hutterite
society. (6) Hutterite history and social processes, due to extreme controls placed on processes of change, are a particularly good example of a
homeostatic system, as illustrated by the cycle of economic build-up
and colonial fission.

Social theorists will remain indebted to Bennett for this brilliant
summary of concepts for the interpretation of data.

BENNETT, JOHN W.
## "The Hutterites: A Communal Sect"
*Religion in Canadian Society*, ed. Stewart Crysdale and Les Wheatcroft.
Toronto: Macmillan of Canada, 1976

This is a good description of Hutterite communal organization, focusing on the Jasper, Alberta colonies. Hutterite organization, an expression of their religious values, was developed in the sixteenth century
and has remained fundamentally unchanged. It represents a mixture of
democracy and patriarchy, dramatizing the difficulty of balancing communal cohesion and individual liberty. The colony has two principal
levels of leadership, the Elders or Executives being superior to the
Managers. Leaders are invested with considerable authority, the First
Minister being the moral, spiritual and organizational head of the community, but they are subject to elections. All baptized males are able to
vote. Women are excluded from the assembly. They have their own
hierarchy, only the head of which, the Head Cook, is elected.

Although Hutterite organization has not significantly changed, the Hutterites have adapted to modern society to survive: highly modern farm equipment is used, and even the competitive principle is creeping in under the surface, although carefully controlled. Intensive socialization in Anabaptist communal values is relied on, rather than capitalist-style incentives.

The author touches on relations between non-Hutterites and Hutterites, which have sometimes been strained, due to the latter's social isolation and economic clout. Attempts are made to improve neighbourly relations. Bennett speculates that as the Hutterite population increases and less land becomes available, colonies may become permanent settlements and some Hutterites may be forced to live in the "outside" society, thus modifying their organizational methods somewhat.

BENNETT, JOHN W.
"Social Theory and the Social Order of the Hutterian Community"
MQR, 51, 4 (October 1977): 292-307

The topic of this article is the techniques used by Hutterites to maintain internal discipline in the face of powerful external and internal inducements to deviate from the chartered rules and tradition. Bennett's general hypothesis about Hutterian social control is this: the Hutterites are committed to precedent as a means of continuously reviewing the social order so that it emerges as an adaptive mechanism. Hutterian society works not because it is static but because the pace of change is deliberate and subject to human control.

BOLDT, EDWARD D.
"Acquiescence and Conventionality in a Communal Society"
Journal of Cross-Cultural Psychology, 7, 1 (March 1976): 21-36

This study tested the hypothesis that the conventional behaviour of individuals reared in "folk" societies is attributable to their tendency to acquiesce willingly to expectations of the group. One hundred ten- to fifteen-year-old children reared in the conventional and structurally "tight" Hutterite communities were compared to a group of 100 urban and fifty rural children from the Canadian host society. Findings indicate that the Hutterites were only marginally more acquiescent than "worldly" students, whereas Mennonites scored significantly higher. An alternative explanation of Hutterite conventionality is suggested which reduces lack of deviance to lack of individual autonomy and the opportunity to be different.

BOLDT, EDWARD D.
"The Death of Hutterite Culture: An Alternative Interpretation"
Phylon, 41 (1980): 390-95

In this article, Boldt argues that the principal threat to Hutterite culture no longer lies in harassment from the outside (such as government interference with land purchases, independent school systems, etc.) but in a process of relaxation of the social structure from within.

Boldt argues that the Hutterites developed their "tight" social structure under the pressure of persecution in their early history. The relative peace and freedom enjoyed by the Hutterites in Russia from 1770 to 1874 resulted in a relaxation of the social structure, allowing for more individual role interpretation. The pressures that induced the Hutterites to emigrate to North America reinforced the tightly organized structure of the group, but the absence of serious persecution from the host society today is resulting once again in a more "loose" social structure.

The greater autonomy of colonies, formerly under stricter control from the annual general assembly of preachers, as well as the reluctance of the heads of colonies to enforce traditional values within their community has already resulted in increased "deviance." Boldt sees this movement toward greater interpretability of normative standards as a significant shift in Hutterite attitudes to change and predicts its continuance. Although it need not do so, this process of liberalization will, in Boldt's opinion, likely erode Hutterite cultural identity, because such assimilationistic tendencies are difficult to control.

Boldt's article is an alternative, but equally pessimistic, response to Frieder's prediction of Hutterite cultural erosion in 1972. Since Boldt's article (1980), enough time has passed to necessitate another examination of his thesis.

BOLDT, EDWARD D.
## "Leadership Succession Among the Hutterites: Ascription or Achievement?"
*The Canadian Review of Sociology and Anthropology*, 15, 3 (1978): 394-96

This article is a critique of Peter Clark's hypothesis that in slow-fissioning colonies, where the male membership greatly exceeds the number of available leadership positions, nepotism is involved in the selection of members to the Hutterite leadership. Boldt argues that an alternative interpretation is possible. He suggests that egalitarianism is taken seriously among Hutterites, given the *raison d'être* of their communities, but that diversified modern agricultural economy necessitates a degree of hierarchical differentiation and competent leadership, for the selection of which an impartial process exists. Ability, which Boldt sees as the prime criterion in leadership selection, is defined in terms of demonstrated aptitude for a task and since sons naturally take an interest in, and develop an aptitude for, the occupational activities of their fathers, it is not surprising that the son of a Hutterite leader often emerges as the most logical choice to take over the position, especially in slow-fissioning colonies where a choice of candidates is possible. Boldt condemns Clark's nepotism thesis as a "gross oversimplification at best." It is legitimate to suggest an alternative interpretation, but perhaps Boldt is somewhat idealistic in excluding the possibility of nepotism altogether. However, since both Boldt and Clark state that their hypotheses are "impressionistic," there may not be much of a point to their quarrel until further research is done on the subject.

BOLDT, EDWARD D.
## "On Aligning Actions in Simple Societies"
*The Canadian Review of Sociology and Anthropology*, 16, 3 (1979): 249-59

An important recent statement on the theoretical status of "aligning actions" by Stokes and Hewitt (1976) demurs on the applicability of the concept to small-scale, relatively undifferentiated societies. While critical of the normative approach to the relationship between culture and conduct in complex societies, these authors are nevertheless content to defer to such an interpretation of simple societies. It is here proposed that this represents an oversimplification and misinterpretation of the basis of social order in such societies. Patterns of joint action, while appearing stable and trouble-free, are still highly susceptible to problematic events and misalignment. Efforts to restore alignment, however, assume a different form due to the imposed nature of role expectations and the use of a restricted linguistic code. Public affirmation (both verbal and nonverbal) of collective interests replaces the large verbal elaboration of individual interests as a predominant mode of facilitating joint action. The Hutterites are cited as an illustrative case.

Boldt's summary includes the following: (1) Simple societies are not immune to the problematic events of social living. The normative account of the basis of joint action in such societies represents as much an oversimplification as when applied to complex societies. (2) This is true even of those simple societies that might be characterized as tightly structured. The over-stability and orderliness of such societies still rests on processes of negotiation and alignment, though of a different form than in looser societies. (3) The "imposed and received" nature of role expectations in tightly structured societies, with attendant conditions of high observability, betrays a fragile rigidity in social relations that require for their maintenance active and ongoing public efforts to ameliorate the impact of readily perceived misalignments between these expectations and actual conduct. (4) Speech in tightly structured societies is guided by a restricted linguistic code, and verbal communication therefore emphasizes the expression of shared attributes and concerns rather than the personal and the individual. This gives rise to a form of verbal aligning action (doctrinal conformity) which publicly affirms the legitimacy of these collective expectations as opposed to the verbal elaborations of the discreet intent of individuals. The alignment of culture and conduct becomes a primary concern which in turn facilitates the mutual alignment of conduct between actors. (5) The conditions of a restricted code are such that nonverbal channels of symbolic communication become the object of special perceptual activity, hence the extensive practice of wordless rituals in tightly structured societies, rituals that facilitate alignment just as verbal activity does.

Boldt believes that the nature of Hutterite society refutes the attempt of Stokes and Hewitt to bridge the functionalist and symbolic interactionist approach to simple societies. Boldt affirms that doctrinal conformity and nonverbal ritual assure effective joint actions. His essay, then, is an important contribution to social theory as it relates to the Hutterites.

BOLDT, EDWARD D.
## "Structural Tightness, Autonomy, and Observability: An Analysis of Hutterite Conformity and Orderliness"
*Canadian Journal of Sociology/Cahiers canadiens de sociologie* 3, 3 (Summer 1978): 349-63

Current explanations of Hutterite conventionality emphasize their socialization practices which are said to result in deeply internalized norms and values as well as a highly developed desire for the approval of others. This paper challenges such an oversocialized conception of Hutterites, and proposes an alternative approach focusing on the structural tightness of Hutterite society and the resultant restriction of individual autonomy. Structural tightness is conceptualized as one dimension of role relatedness, namely the degree to which role expectations are "imposed and received" rather than "proposed and interpreted." Reduced autonomy in turn, coupled with conditions of heightened observability, gives rise to a particular mode of conformity termed doctrinal conformity.

BOLDT, EDWARD D. and LANCE W. ROBERTS
## "The Decline of Hutterite Population Growth: Causes and Consequences—A Comment,"
*Canadian Ethnic Studies*, 12, 3 (1980): 111-17

This article is a comment on an article by Karl Peter in *Canadian Ethnic Studies*, 12, 3 (1980), pp. 97-110. The authors suggest that the declining birth rate is not a result of delayed marriage but rather is a result of birth control. Peter does not stress birth control, and these authors critique him for this. There is an official Hutterite policy against birth control and the extent to which it is being practised must represent individual choice behaviour that is sharply at odds with basic religious tenets. Thus Boldt and Roberts hypothesize that the declining population rate has implications in that it reflects a decrease in the structural tightness of the group. While this article is logical, it is based on speculation as the authors had no data on whether birth control is actually being used.

CAVAN, RUTH SHONLE
## "Public and Private Areas and the Survival of Communal Subsocieties"
*Journal of Voluntary Action Research*, 13, 2 (1984): 46-58

The author examines the roles of public and private spaces in a community's boundary maintenance or construction. She compares two such subsocieties—the Amish and the Amana communities—and their relationships with tourism. The former reject tourism and confine it to "public areas" which are often artificially created by the tourist industry, because private ownership of Amish farms has prevented the development of communal areas vulnerable to tourist intrusion. Amish private, residential areas, where their culture is maintained, are protected by strong boundaries.

By contrast, the Amana group was communitarian until 1932, when the change to private ownership was made, and so communal areas open to tourist intrusion had developed. After the change to private ownership, tourism was encouraged as a source of revenue. The private, residential areas of Amana were soon populated by people of non-Amana background, and Amana culture was mixed with and partially eroded by that of the American host society. Recently, efforts have been made to reconstruct boundaries to preserve Amana cultural identity while not rejecting tourism.

Cavan shows that, from the point of view of the subsociety wishing to guard its identity, the establishment of boundaries is easier where a clear separation of public and private spaces exists. For the dominant host society wishing to absorb non-conforming subsocieties, it is necessary to destroy barriers protecting the private lives of the subsociety. The author concludes that studies of the relationship between non-compatible groups with respect to public and private spaces may suggest ways in which to avoid or ease difficulties of adjustment between distinctive groups. This study might also be valuable with respect to francophone Canadians or the problem of Canadian identity.

DRIEDGER, LEO
## "Nomos-building on the Prairies: Construction of Indian, Hutterite, and Jewish Sacred Canopies"
*Canadian Journal of Sociology/Cahiers canadiens de sociologie*, 5, 4 (Fall 1980): 341-56

This paper attempts to bridge Berger's macro-sociological concepts of nomos-building, and social construction of reality, with some of the empirical micro-sociological studies of the native Indians, the Hutterites and the Jews of the Canadian prairies. Berger's concept of "a sacred canopy" claims that ideology, community, culture and territory are important stakes upholding a canopy under which the construction of reality takes place, and where nomos-building is sheltered. The native food gatherers are faced with the reconstruction of their canopy; the Hutterites transferred their European canopy intact; the Jews transformed their canopy from the shtetl into Jewish urbanism. Religious commitment, alert opening and closing, and social distance are discussed as important processes affecting nomos-building.

The communal nature of the Indians and Hutterites is quite different from the *gemeinschaft* community of the Jewish community with its urbanization and sophisticated professionalization.

Meanwhile further testing of Peter Berger's social canopy-nomos concept must take place.

FRIESEN, JOHN W.
## "The Hutterites"
*When Cultures Clash: Case Studies in Multi-culturalism*. Calgary: Detselig, 1985, pp. 123-42

Friesen's book contains five cases of cultural and ethnic minorities, of which this study of the Hutterites is one. The author briefly describes the history of the Hutterites, from the rise of Anabaptism and the life

of Jakob Hutter in the sixteenth century, through their migration
through Moravia, Hungary, Russland and finally North America, fleeing almost incessant persecution. He then describes the Hutterite values and religious beliefs. The attempt to live according to Christian
teaching as revealed in the Bible as they understand it entails strict faith,
submission to the Hutterite church, common ownership of property,
pacifism, obedience to the government in all matters not contrary to
the commands of God, separation from the sinful world and adult baptism. Friesen portrays these values sympathetically, and such practices
as communalism and pacifism are quite attractive. The author also
shows how the Hutterites put their beliefs into practice, describing the
organization of Hutterite colonies and the function of the council, the
householder, the head preacher, etc. Also, he describes how discipline
is enforced and what roles are assigned to the sexes — women are held
to be inferior to men. The author describes the upbringing of the Hutterite children, which stresses discipline and unquestioning obedience;
the Hutterite German school education may be largely responsible for
the maintenance and perpetuation of the Hutterite community. Finally,
Friesen responds to several accusations commonly made against the
Hutterites (that they take up too much land, that they pay no taxes, that
they do not participate in the community, etc.) and shows them to be
unfounded. A comparative analysis of the five minorities needed more
attention, but the separate cases were excellent.

HOSTETLER, JOHN A.
"History and Relevance of the Hutterite Population for
Genetic Studies"
*American Journal of Medical Genetics*, 22, 3 (November 1985)

The special and cultural origins of the Hutterian brethren are described
along with the characteristics that make the group useful for genetic
studies as the most inbred population in North America. The Hutterites are a closed population with high levels of fertility and consanguin-
ity. They keep extensive genealogical records and maintain a stable residence pattern. Throughout their colonies in Canada and the United
States, they maintain a uniform pattern of communal living as the oldest group of Christian communalists in the world. Within the Hutterite
population are endogamous subgroups.

The Hutterites have a long tradition of orderly fission by which new
colonies are started without rancour or the result of controversy. The
inbred population is useful for detecting new recessively inherited
diseases and for advancing knowledge of the effects of inbreeding and
chromosomal variations.

Hostetler underscores the durability of the Hutterites who came
from the Ukraine in 1874-79, expanding from three to 300 colonies
with 30,000 members. When they arrived in the nineteenth century,
North America had eight communal societies: Harmony, Oneida,
Amana, Bethel, Zoar, St. Nazianz, Ephrata and the Shakers. All have
vanished while the Hutterites expand. The Hutterites have also out-
lasted the hundreds of hippie communes founded during the youth

culture of the 1960s and early 1970s. Today the Hutterites are a thriving community, and the largest number of communes under their discipline are located in Alberta.

The survival of the Hutterites beyond the nineteenth-century utopias and the hippie communes underscores the role and impact of a highly authoritarian culture in which the individual yields to the group. The insistence of the German language in an Austro-Bavarian dialect is another dogmatic affirmation. They have the highest birth rate in North America. They have a simple Christian piety and teach nonresistance and abstinence from advanced education and the arts. But there are two crucial places where they disagree with the Amish: communal living and the embrace of advanced agricultural technology wherein the latest and best machinery is used on their huge farms.

Hostetler describes the sociology and biology of the Hutterites with great objectivity. He does not offer an evaluative opinion of this durable, inbred, successful communal society except to note its thriving record. At the end of his article he cites the mental health studies of Eaton, Weil, Kaplan and Plaut who have hinted that perhaps "genetic and social factors have reinforced each other to produce a highly unusual distribution of functional psychoses." Next step, then, should add the psychological to the sociological and the biological studies of North American Hutterites. It has been nearly 35 years since Joseph Eaton studied the mental health of the Hutterites.

LANG, HARTMUT and RUTH GOHLEN
"Completed Fertility of the Hutterites: A Revision"
Current Anthropology, 26, 3 (June 1985): 395

Estimates of completed fertility among Hutterite women have consistently relied on medians rather than means of distributions. An estimate of mean completed fertility from the data of J. W. Eaton and A. J. Mayer ("The Social Biology of Very High Fertility Among the Hutterites: The Demography of a Unique Population," Human Biology, 25 [1953], pp. 206-64) is lower than median fertility estimated from the same data, which is itself lower than the median computed by Eaton and Meyer. Here the experts disagree in methodology and hence in conclusions.

LEE, S. C. and AUDREY BRATTRUD
"Marriage Under a Monastic Mode of Life: A Preliminary Report on the Hutterite Family in South Dakota"
Journal of Marriage and the Family, 29, 3 (1967): 512-20

Despite claims by some family sociologists for the universality of the nuclear family, in Hutterite colonies a pattern of family life is found which defies classification. Though the husband is the recognized head of the household, each marriage forms an auxiliary unit of the colony, not a full-fledged conjugal family. The family, being subservient to the church, loses its economic functions and part of its authority, training and discipline over children, all of which weaken its influence. Through religious sanction, however, the family tends to have successful and stable relationships. This is postulated as the way to maintain the colony's cohesion and stability.

MACDONALD, ROBERT
"The Hutterites in Alberta"
*Peoples of Alberta: Portraits of Cultural Diversity*, ed. Howard and Tamara
Palmer. Saskatoon, Sask.: Western Producer Prairie Books, 1985, pp.
348-64
>In a straightforward historical style, Macdonald outlines the back-
>ground and development of the Hutterite community in Alberta. He
>touches on many aspects of Hutterite life, including agriculture, com-
>munal living, the place of women, education and gradual technological
>modernization.
>While at times somewhat dry and pedantic in style, this article does
>provide an interesting and informative view of Hutterite life in Alberta.

MANIS, JEROME G.
"The Sociology of Knowledge and Community Mental Health
Research"
*Social Problems*, 15, 4 (1968): 488-501
>The sociology of knowledge is concerned with the social genesis of
>ideas as well as extratheoretical influences upon their forms and con-
>tent. An attempt is made to assess some of these influences upon com-
>munity mental health research by comparing concepts, theories and
>methods with that of general sociology. Major referents of the compar-
>ison regarding the Detroit, Hutterite, Kalamazoo, Midtown Manhattan,
>New Haven, Nova Scotia, Philadelphia and Texas studies. Alternatives
>to current concepts, theories and methods in community mental health
>research are considered. Among the major influences are the value-free
>and attributive perspectives, and empiricist and inductive procedures.

MCCONNELL, GAIL
"Hutterites: An Interview with Micael Entz"
*Visions of the New Jerusalem: Religious Settlement on the Prairies*, ed.
Benjamin G. Smillie. Edmonton: NeWest Press, 1983, pp. 164-76
>This article attempts to portray the Hutterite vision of the New
>Jerusalem as lived by those in the many communes located in Canada's
>west. Based as it is on an interview with a contemporary Hutterite, it
>gives the reader a strong sense of what these people believe. The inter-
>view material is strengthened by historical background, setting the con-
>temporary Hutterite beliefs and experience in their four-hundred-and-
>fifty-year history. The article would have been stronger, however, if the
>Hutterite vision of the New Jerusalem had been analyzed in the con-
>text of the larger Canadian society.

MOL, HANS
"Mennonites and Hutterites"
*Faith and Fragility: Religion and Identity in Canada*. Burlington: Trinity Press,
1985, chap. 5, pp. 87-102
>In this chapter on Anabaptist identity, the author focuses on the Hut-
>terites as an "almost perfect example of a well-bounded group success-
>fully warding off the inroads of other forms of identity." Their theol-

ogy and commitment to pacifism, adult baptism and communism sacralize the community which regards itself as the elect remnant in an evil world, threatened not only by the sinful enveloping Canadian culture but also by individual sinfulness from within, against which only the working of Christ and the Holy Spirit in the community can preserve them. Hence, the Hutterites try to maximize the impact of the theological variable through a process of life-long socialization culminating in baptism and designed to subordinate individuality to community.

Mol examines the external threats to Hutterite identity—persecution in Germany, attempts to Russify them, conflicts with North American authorities during the World Wars on issues of military service and the use of the German language, and anglicization through the educational and cultural policies of the Canadian government. However, at least equally significant are internal threats, which can be countered by an effective leadership and intensive socialization of community members. Poor leadership and lack of opportunity for advancement periodically weaken communal identity to the benefit of family identity and nepotism. The Hutterites see individual identity as a graver threat to communal identity than family identity, however, since humans are naturally in a state of sin. Submission of self to the community is therefore emphasized and made a prerequisite for baptism.

The internal and external factors threatening Hutterite identity are shown very well. None of these threats are lethal.

NELSON, T. M.
## "Cultural Difference in the Use of Colour in Northwest Canada"
*International Journal of Psychology*, 6, 4 (1971): 283-92

In this study, 2,425 six- to sixteen-year-old students from different types of schools (Northwest Territory Indian, Alberta Indian, Hutterite, white secular and white Roman Catholic) registered coloured crayons, either in an unforgettable dream or real-life event. Colour preferences for all groups except the Hutterites (who avoided black, the dominant colour in their society) were, from most to least preferred: white, black, green, blue, yellow and red. A key revealing colour significance was needed.

PETER, KARL A.
## "Problems in the Family, Community and Culture of the Hutterites"
*Canadian Families: Ethnic Variations*, ed. K. Ishwaran. Toronto: McGraw-Hill Ryerson, 1980, pp. 221-36

The fact that divorce, crime and similar problems are almost nonexistent among Hutterites might suggest that they have succeeded in establishing a perfect society. However, the author shows in this article that the Hutterite family and community is not free from problems; these problems are merely hidden from outsiders and solved without resorting to the methods or institutions of the non-Hutterite society.

This is necessary for the maintenance of Hutterite cultural self-determination and social independence. In order to avoid misleading conclusions, the author bases his research on a combination of participant observation and individual biography, penetrating the "wall of secrecy" by establishing trust. He reproduces an autobiographical sketch written by a twenty-two-year-old Hutterite woman undergoing personal and family crisis at the time and analyzes it to illustrate some of the problems facing the Hutterites. The Hutterite conception of human nature is dualistic and emphasizes the need for both "love and lash" to build moral character. (Corporal punishment is used in their schools.) Due to their early isolation, what the Hutterites know as knowledge and reason is devoid of the enlightenment emphasis on human credibility and centres on codified situational norms. However, Hutterite religious scholarship has stood still for over 300 years, so that these norms have not, as in Judaism, been subject to continual adaptation and re-interpretation, resulting in some contradictions. Slowly encroaching modernization has produced a dilemma of not being able to justify these norms in modern terms; to avoid their dissolution, these norms are compartmentalized; Hutterites, the author says, do not require as much mental consensus as behaviourial adherence. This is re-inforced by intellectual self-limitation and the clear predominance of the community over the individual. Swimming against the stream for long periods is thus made impossible, and even leaving the community is rarely a solution. The study is valuable in illustrating some of the sacrifices the Hutterites must make to maintain their communal structure and identity, and in the ways in which they approach problems that arise.

PETER, KARL, EDWARD D. BOLDT, IAN WHITAKER and
LANCE W. ROBERTS
"The Dynamics of Religious Defection Among Hutterites"
*Journal for the Scientific Study of Religion*, 21, 4 (1982): 327-37

The Hutterites of North America have been remarkably successful in maintaining their austere communal existence and separation from "the world." The permanent loss of members through defection has been minimal, and largely restricted to unmarried young men in search of adventure. Recently, however, a new form of defection has emerged which involves a conscious repudiation of central Hutterite tenets. Increasingly, individuals and even families are abandoning their colonies as a direct result of their conversion to evangelical Protestantism. The authors attempt to account for this phenomenon in terms of the attraction that personalized, individualistic Protestantism holds for the colelctivistic Hutterites, and how conversion can ease the burdens of defection. Finally, the article suggests that the Hutterites' own attempts to win converts ultimately renders them vulnerable to the proselytization of others. The pessimistic tone of this article assumes that Hutterite belief in *Gelassenheit* is mechanical and not personally fulfilling; this is not adequately substantiated in the article.

PETER, KARL and IAN WHITAKER
## "Hutterite Perceptions of Psychophysiological Characteristics"
*Journal of Social and Biological Structures*, 7, 1 (January 1984): 1-8

This article describes the characteristics of a form of psychophysiological differentiation used by the Hutterites. This means of differentiation is crystallized in the Hutterite term *sabot*, which designates a group who bear common inherited physical and psychological characteristics, serving as a basis for identification. Distinguishing physical traits may include height, complexion, growth of hair, posture, body morphology, susceptibility to disease and voice patterns. Common personality characteristics are also attributed to different *sabots*. The basis of this understanding lies in the lifelong experience a Hutterite has with members of a particular *sabot*. The *sabot* serves functions of self-identification among the Hutterites and offers role models for behaviour.

PETER, KARL
## "The Changing Roles of Hutterian Women"
*Prairie Forum*, 7, 2 (1982): 267-77

In this article Peter explores the ways in which the roles of Hutterite women have changed, and the factors which have helped to precipitate these changes. He links the infiltration of the idea of a personal saviour into Hutterite theology (which traditionally emphasizes communal salvation) as a factor in changing the self-perception and self-awareness of women. Technological adaptation has reduced some of the menial tasks of women in the colony, and this has modified social patterns. Women have more autonomy than previously, particularly in terms of choosing a husband, organizing their lives and choosing activities and work within the colony. Peter emphasizes, however, that the formal decision-making structure, with its strong emphasis on male power, is still unchanged. Peter's consideration of changes within the theological, technological and social fields provides a holistic approach to the study of the roles of Hutterite women.

PETER, KARL A.
## "The Certainty of Salvation: Ritualization of Religion and Economic Rationality among Hutterites"
*Comparative Studies in Society and History*, 25, 2 (1983): 222-40

Borrowing its theoretical framework from Max Weber, this article explores whether religious sanctions influence the development of an economic spirit. Peter concludes that Hutterite economic strength resulted from a different rationale than that of the Calvinists. The difference lies in the co-operative nature of the Hutterite ethic, and (originally) their attempts to bestow economic benefits on their protectors in exchange for toleration. The article also explores the tension between *Gelassenheit* (psychological sanction) and *Guetergemeinschaft* (practical conduct). It concludes that the attainment of salvation among Hutterites changed from being a spiritual phenomenon speaking through the individual conscience to being a gift bestowed on the individual as a consequence of faithful participation in the group life. The section of

this article dealing with the certainty of salvation has significant implications in light of the increasing appeal of evangelical theology to Hutterites. Perhaps a renewed emphasis on *Gelassenheit* would fill the void
which evangelical theology is currently filling. *Gelassenheit* emphasizes
restraint of self for the common good through simple living.

PETER, KARL A.
## "The Decline of Hutterite Population Growth"
*Canadian Ethnic Studies*, 12, 3 (1980): 97-110

Hutterite population growth attained considerable attention during the
last few decades because it was one of the highest among the world
populations and it remained stable over a period of more than 80 years.
Peter presents a number of observations which seem to indicate that
the population growth rate has declined. This decline, which seems to
have started between 1965 and 1968, is traced to the structural changes
taking place in Hutterite society, particularly changes in the division of
labour. Responsible employment within the colony and marriage traditionally went hand in hand. Technology has resulted in a postpone-
ment of the age of marriage, and thus indirectly to a reduction of the
birth rate. The article contains several tables of population statistics, yet
the conclusions of the author are tentative because of the nature of the
data, which is based on Hutterite self-enumerations. These enumera-
tions may underestimate population by up to one-third. The author
admits this shortcoming, and assumes that any aberrations are in the
same direction and a comparison of Hutterite self-enumerations over
time should give a fairly accurate picture in regard to the population
trend even if the figures themselves are not entirely accurate. See
response to this article by Boldt and Roberts, *Canadian Ethnic Studies*,
12, 3 (1980): 111-17.

PETER, KARL A.
## "The Acquisition of Personal Property Among Hutterites and Its Social Dimension"
*Anthropologica*, 23, 2 (1981): 145-55

This article discusses the growing practice among Hutterites of setting
apart specific articles or products as private property belonging to the
individual or to the immediate family rather than to the community as
a whole. This practice may constitute the tangible modification of the
earlier Hutterite ideal of communal ownership. The role of informal
social control in the process of cultural change is illuminated.

For related articles, see Karl Peter and Ian Whitaker, "The Hutterite
Economy: Recent Changes and Their Social Correlates," *Anthropos*, 98,
3-4 (1983): 535-46, and Karl Peter, "The Certainty of Salvation: Ritualization of Religion and Economic Rationality among Hutterites," *Comparative Studies in Society and History*, 25, 2 (1983): 222-40.

PETER, KARL A.
## "Rejoinder to 'The Decline of Hutterite Population Growth: Cause and Consequences'"
*Canadian Ethnic Studies*, 12, 3 (1980): 118-123

In this article Peter continues the discussion with Boldt and Roberts found on page 123 of this volume. He takes issue with Boldt and Roberts' hypothesis that structural tightness of the Hutterite colonies is challenged when individuals make choices contrary to the community standard, as in the choice of birth control. He proposes instead that changes such as the widespread use of birth control methods will not have dire consequences but will be cushioned by the alteration of the Hutterite value system and will be absorbed into a new level of social existence. The three-part dialogue found in this issue of *Canadian Ethnic Studies* between Peter and Boldt/Roberts highlights the presuppositions different scholars bring to the study of the Hutterites.

PETER, KARL and IAN WHITAKER
## "The Hutterite Economy: Recent Changes and Their Social Correlates"
*Anthropos*, 78, 3-4 (1983): 535-46

This article begins with a brief explanation of the economic system and division of labour within a Hutterite colony. Change is now being experienced in three areas: (1) technological, (2) regulatory restrictions, primarily bureaucratic in nature (e.g., marketing boards for dairy products) and (3) limiting of expansion due to changes in the surrounding farm population. These three areas of change have resulted in a utilitarian transformation of Hutterian societal structure.

One significant transformation has been greater specialization in agriculture to get better economic returns, which are now necessary to survive and to purchase land for new colonies. The article closes by questioning how the new economic aggressiveness will affect their relationship to the outside world.

This article is written in the same straightforward and readable style which characterize other articles by Karl Peter.

PETERS, VICTOR
## "The Process of Colony Division Among the Hutterians: A Case Study"
*Communes Historical and Contemporary*, ed. Ruth Shonle Cavan and Man Sing Das. Delhi: Vikas Publishing House, 1979, pp. 61-69. See also *International Review of Modern Sociology*, 6 (Spring 1976)

Unlike the Oneida and New Harmony utopian communities, the Hutterites have a phenomenal natural increase in North American members. There have been few converts from the outside (except for the more liberal Society of Brothers). This high birth rate has led to overpopulated colonies, resulting in a series of mandatory equitable divisions which create new colonies with adequate population, leadership and economic assets.

Division takes place when a population of about 150 is reached. The parent colony provides land, buildings, and equipment and is then divided into two equal parts with a minister and farm managers in each. In the case cited, the daughter colony was established on a land-base much smaller than is needed for economic survival, which suggests that a trend may be developing toward semi-industrial and commercial diversification.

What appears to have been a perfect colonization mechanism is now confronting powerful social forces requiring changes in strategy. Karl Peter of Simon Fraser University believes that throughout their history the Hutterites have demonstrated a flexibility which will lead to new strategies in an era of declining farm land.

PICKERING, W. S. F.
"Hutterites and Problems of Persistence and Social Control in Religious Communities"
*Archives de Sciences Sociales Des Religions*, 44, 1 (1977): 75-92

This article begins by providing a brief history and description of the Hutterite religious community. The community, Pickering states, has persisted because of a high birth rate coupled with a background of economic success, and through social control. While the author mentions a case of division among the Hutterites, on the whole his emphasis is on the unchanging nature of the community. This article serves as an informative introduction to the Hutterites. However, its explanation of religious belief is sketchy, a serious fault considering that belief is the professed cohesive force of the colonies. Furthermore Pickering's emphasis on the unchanging nature of the community is somewhat simplistic in light of the work of sociologist Karl Peter.

REDEKOP, CALVIN
"Communal Organization and Secular Education: Hutterite and Hassidic Comparisons"
*Communal Life, An International Perspective*, ed. Yosef Gorni, Yaacov Oved and Idit Paz. Efal, Israel: Yad Tabenkin, 1985

The author examines the methods intentional communities use to resist assimilation with the larger society by comparing two hassidic and two Anabaptist communities. The Lubavitcher hassidim and the Reba Place Fellowship communities interact with an urban environment in order to influence it and propagate their values; the Tasher and Hutterite communities are more separatistic, cut off both geographically and, where possible, socially from the outside.

All four groups have a strong interest in maintaining a separate identity and to that end carefully supervise the education of the young. The Lubavitcher and Reba Place groups utilize secular education more than the Tasher and Hutterites, but all four communities monitor its influence closely and balance it by strictly controlling the religious education of the young.

Redekop's examination shows that in communities emphasizing the influencing of society, greater interaction results, while groups primarily interested in self-perfection reduce such contact to a minimum. Those who interact with the larger society are better equipped to resist its assimilating influence than those who do not. Redekop concludes that groups seeking cultural and social segregation may use ecological separations, and then an intentional community's approach to education depends directly on its desire to maintain a distinct identity. The article is valuable in that it bases this argument on an examination of communities from more than one religio-ethnic background, using well-chosen test cases. The dependence of educational control on the community's desire to resist assimilation is conclusive.

Another level of research is needed to compare and contrast the Jewish and Christian outgoing groups with each other; and the Jewish and Christian separatists with a similar comparison.

REDEKOP, CALVIN
## "The Social Ecology of Communal Socialization"
*Communes Historical and Contemporary*, ed. Ruth Shonle Cavan and Mau Singh Das. Delhi: Vikas Publishing House, 1979, pp. 125-38. See also *International Review of Modern Sociology*, 6 (Spring 1976)

An analysis of the socialization practices of contemporary communes reveals considerable differences, even among communes which are ideologically quite similar. Some communes stress the technical applied aspects of the social process, while others stress beliefs and attitudes while the formerly listed factors are relatively unattended. The variables that seem to explain the different emphasis appear to be the relative isolation of the commune (rural and urban in the study) and the intention of the commune (whether it is a retreatist-isolationist commune or a mission-evangelistic commune). Evidence from several Mennonite communes suggests that the paradigm proposed is indeed useful in explaining socialization differences.

Redekop utilized his well-known study of the Old Colony Mennonites from Mexico whose rural-agricultural isolation failed to protect them from a hostile and, at times, predatory environment. Hence, hundreds of them have returned to Canada.

SCHEER, HERFRIED
## "The Hutterian German Dialect: A Study in Sociolinguistic Assimilation and Differentiation"
*MQR*, 54, 3 (July 1980): 229-43

Beginning with an analysis of Hutterite loanwords borrowed from different cultural environments, Scheer turns to examine more carefully the linguistic differences among the three basic groups, as well as the role of both dialect differences and also socioethical distinctions which foster greater distance among those groups. Not all students of the Hutterites will agree with his conviction that as the Hutterites inevitably lose their distinctive linguistic patterns, so also will they inevitably lose their entire religious subculture.

SCHLUDERMAN, SHIRIN and EDUARD SCHLUDERMAN
## "Personality Development in Hutterite Communal Society"
*The Canadian Ethnic Mosaic. A Quest for Identity*, ed. Leo Driedger. Toronto: McClelland and Stewart, 1978, pp. 169-86

In this paper, Schluderman and Schluderman compiled the results of a number of systematic studies of socialization and personality development in Hutterite society which they had done previously. Based on studies of the adolescents in 15 Hutterite colonies in Manitoba, the authors concluded that Hutterites socialize and teach their young in a way that ensures the preservation of the Hutterian way of life.

SILVERMAN, RUTH and others
"Communal Education: The Society of Brothers"
*Young Children*, 35, 5 (July 1980): 15-20

This article describes the educational philosophy and practice of the progressive Hutterian Society of Brothers in Rifton, N.Y. The Society is a religious community which has assumed responsibility for educating its children from birth through eighth grade. They do not ban secondary or higher education outside the community. Educational objectives and values of the Society are identified.

For a related article, see W. S. F. Pickering, "Hutterites and Problems of Persistence and Social Control in Religious Communities," *Archives Sciences Sociales des Religions*, 44, 1 (1977), pp. 75-92.

SIMPSON-HOUSLEY, PAUL
"Hutterian Religious Ideology, Environmental Perception, and Attitudes Toward Agriculture"
*Journal of Geography*, 77, 4 (April/May 1978): 145-48

This study demonstrates how religious ideology influences Hutterian attitudes toward farming and the agricultural environment. The Hutterian Brethren are Anabaptist pacifists who live mostly on communal farms in Saskatchewan, Manitoba and Alberta, Canada. The responses of both Hutterian and non-Hutterian farmers to an attitudinal questionnaire were recorded and compared.

SIMPSON-HOUSLEY, PAUL and ROBERT J. MOORE
"Research Notes: An Initial Investigation of the Value of Work and Beliefs in Internal-External Reinforcement Responsibility in Hutterite Children"
*Prairie Forum*, 7, 2 (1982): 279-87

On the basis of the fundamental role of work and the strong pressures for conformity in the community, the authors hypothesize that Hutterite children would demonstrate more positive attitudes to work than would a group of non-Hutterite children. Results obtained through a Thematic Appreciation Test from fifteen Hutterite and twenty-eight non-Hutterite children tend to confirm this hypothesis. Since differences in labour attitudes manifested between the groups of children could have resulted from different generalized expectations for control of reinforcement, it was further hypothesized that children who see work as a solution to their problems would be more likely to see their own actions as instrumental in determining their destinies as opposed to factors beyond their control. Using the Intellectual Achievement Responsibility Questionnaire, Hutterite, rural white children, urban white and Metis children were used to test this hypothesis. While Hutterite and Metis children did not have significantly different scores from the scores of the white children, Hutterites scored slightly higher and Metis slightly lower, supporting the notion that the unique cultural experiences of Hutterite children in Saskatchewan promote positive attitudes to work and that underlying these attitudes is a belief in the internal control of reinforcement. The authors call for further research, extended beyond the confines of the area of intellectual-academic achievement situations as defined by the IAR scale.

STEPHENSON, PETER H. (ED.)
"Dying in Cross-Cultural Perspective"
*Omega: Journal of Death and Dying*, 14, 2 (1983/84): 101-99
This review researches and presents case studies discussing aspects of suicide, death, and grief among the people of New Guinea, Vanuatu (a Canadian Hutterite colony), rural Tennessee, Ireland and among American Indians. Rituals, myths, and legends are described in the eight articles of this special issue.

STEPHENSON, PETER H.
" 'He Died Too Quick!' The Process of Dying in a Hutterite Colony"
*Omega: Journal of Death and Dying*, 14, 2 (1983/84): 127-34
In contrast to the fast (and therefore supposedly "painless") "death ideal" of much of Western culture, Hutterites consider a slow and drawn-out period of dying to be desirable. This extended period allows the dying person to socialize other Hutterians into a joyous acceptance of death's promise of a better heavenly life. The atypical behaviour of members of a colony where a sudden death disrupted this pattern, described in this paper (1) illuminates the relationship between family members and other colonists and (2) suggests that the symbolic use of death in the rebirth rite of baptism is much more powerful than has heretofore been thought. The author provides some general recommendations with regard to treating both terminally ill Hutterians and surviving members of their families. The pragmatic conclusion to this article is very perceptive.

STEPHENSON, PETER H.
" 'Like a Violet Unseen' — The Apotheosis of Absence of Hutterite life"
*La Revue canadienne de sociologie et d'anthropologie/The Canadian Review of Sociology and Anthropology*, 15, 4 (1978): 433-42
This paper attempts to understand how Hutterians imbue unseen and unheard phenomena with meaning. The paper consists of three basic parts. The first section is a structural analysis which, while it demonstrates that the absence of designata is an important aspect of Hutterian symbology, fails to relate meaning to acts. The second section utilizes pragmatic communication theory to understand how absence functions within actual behaviour (in the call to church and singing). However, the pragmatic theory is also superficial in that it produces a paradox which is an artifact of analysis, and it fails to penetrate the psychological reality of Hutterite life in which the absence of worldly things serves to

signify the omnipresent Holy Spirit. The third section utilizes a literary device and a musical metaphor in an attempt to evoke the mystical sentiment of the Hutterian reality.

See an additional article by Stephenson spelling out a mystical, occult sense of Hutterite ritual: "Hutterite Belief in Evil Eye: Beyond Paranoia and Towards a General Theory of Invidia." *Culture, Medicine and Psychiatry*, 3: 247-65.

WIPF, JOSEPH A.
## "Hutterite Life: The Role of the German School"
*Unterricht Spraxis*, 9, 2, (1976): 30-35

The history and practices of the Hutterite communal society in America are outlined in this article. Every Hutterite child attends a German school for 10 1/2 hours per week. Major emphasis is on skills of reading and writing German, and the language serves to unite the group in its spiritual and cultural heritage.

For a related article, see Ruth Silverman (and others), "Communal Education: The Society of Brothers," *Young Children*, 35, 5 (July 1980): 15-20.

# IV. Amish

# A. Books and Pamphlets

BENDER, SUE
*Plain and Simple: A Woman's Journey to the Amish*
San Francisco: Harper & Row, 1989

With a sensitive unspoiled folk-art background that survived degrees from Harvard and Berkeley, Sue Bender was deeply moved by quilts made by Amish women whose way of stitching and choice of colours expressed their unique perspective on Christian faith and life. Nothing less than living with Amish people would satisfy the sudden empathy triggered by the quilts.

Bender, accepted by two Amish families in Ohio and Iowa for a brief stay, was impressed with the integration of their lives without the slightest attempt to preach or proselytize. They never said "our way is better" revealing a wonderful combination of certainty and humility. The candid conversation with the host families was remarkable even though an outsider from California was rather special.

When the time came for Bender to do her own art project in the first Amish home, she walked 10 miles to the nearest village to buy one-eighth of a yard of cloth from each of 25 bolts of multi-coloured cotton. The Amish women helped make the ninepatch quilt.

No theory of deprivation could survive the interesting and creative happenings in the Amish community: neighbourhood quiltings, buggy trips to auctions, unique patterns of child nurture (unlimited love until two years; love and discipline after two), teaching children chores and the dignity of work, the sacredness of the land, a restraint on machinery, the embrace of sound but simple farming methods (rotation, irrigation and natural fertilizer), and unique clothing, a profound but simple laicized Christian community, and time for courtship and marriage. Sociologically, the Amish have a non-governmental social security system. Psychologically, there was a self-effacing humility Bender found stifling.

Instead of noting obvious differences, this perceptive and sympathetic participant-observer was forced to examine her frantic life in New York City and Berkeley. The clear Amish identity, beautifully delineated life style and old-fashioned fun and games (a wonderful privilege of water fights engaging all of the children) reflected solid foundations. The story of Sarah, skilled mid-wife and amateur chiropractor is a fascinating study in an undercurrent of restrained professionalism among an intelligent group of semi-communal dissenters.

Analogies of Amish life-style? Our diarist recalled attending an Orthodox Jewish service which reminded her of the Amish. Both reminded her that she was a second-class citizen.

The central achievement of the Amish is selective social change. Sue Bender is concerned about the vulnerability to corrosive change in the new Amish communities away from the Amish mainstream. But corporate decisions regarding changes should sustain Amish values.

Trying to emulate Amish practices and tempted to go back to Ohio and Iowa, the author decides to describe her discoveries and experiences in a book. She stopped her therapy practice and her art. She applied some Amish practices in Berkeley: a lean, spare home; art focused on a mix of beauty and practicality, and the folk-art following a "path that has heart." The supreme artistic expression of her new crypto-Amish outlook was the ninepatch quilt. The ninepatch provides the key number to set forth nine parts of her new credo shaped by the experience with two Amish families in Iowa and Ohio.

No one from the outside has ever spelled out the Amish faith and life any better. It is a celebration of a rich discovery by a therapist, artist, wife and mother from very sophisticated backgrounds. Participant-observer is a superb method deeper than mere quantification.

COLEMAN, BILL
*Amish Odyssey*
New York: Van der Marck, 1988; Toronto: St. James Press, 1988

Declaring himself a photographer in the romantic realist tradition of Winslow Homer and Thomas Eakins, Bill Coleman has published a remarkable collection of Amish pictures taken over a ten-year span in Pennsylvania. In the introduction he thanked the Amish for tolerating him during the past decade.

Coleman says that he is not a scholar of Amish life but has discovered much about it "by little cameos here and there." His work was made urgent by the feeling that he wanted to document their way of life before it disappears as a victim of twentieth-century "omnivorous technology." His fear that the Amish may collapse under the impact of technology is not shared by many scholars of Amish life and culture. Perhaps his pessimism is explained by an epigram from an Amish woman who was photographed in her buggy as it passed by. She leaned out and said, "You have stolen my soul."

It is amazing how fascinating the Amish life and work are to the "outside" world: the Amish and the land, their religious practices, their families, their folkways, the focus on the farm and their sub-culture which can become a counter-culture under opposition. There are many pictures with contrasting lighting and focus. They include Amish walking on the road after a wedding, the buggies of various types, children at play, seasonal changes and the gathering at meeting house (church) and pre-industrial farming. Coleman has exhibited these photos in fifty galleries including a one-man show at the National Press gallery in Washington.

The romantic dimension of Coleman's work outshines the realistic perspective. It would have helped if he had read Hostetler, Huntington, Kraybill and Keim to strengthen the realist aspect of Amish life. Then he would better understand why he was tolerated but not welcomed.

EDIGER, MARLOW
*Vocabulary Development, Reading, and Old Order Amish Pupils*
Bloomington, Ill.: Mennonite College of Nursing, 1983

Old Order Amish are readily distinguishable from others in society by their dissociation from "modern" convenience and dress. Students in an Amish school in Iowa receive instruction in language arts from a secular basal language arts workbook, and a basal reader containing biblical stories. Comprehension is evaluated from completed exercises. Pupils in grades 3, 4, 6, 7 and 8 completed the Iowa Tests of Basic Skills. Since the Amish philosophy and culture emphasize hard work, self-reliance and practical situations, the Iowa Tests might not be a valid measure for these pupils. The high math results indicate its applicability in the practical day-to-day living of the Amish, while the vocabulary and reading tests evaluate concepts that may be culturally unfamiliar.

FISHER, SARA E. and RACHEL K. STAHL
*The Amish School*
Intercourse, Pa.: Good Books, 1986

This booklet describes Amish education from an informed and sympathetic point of view. It includes chapters on the origins of Amish schools after the Great Depression, when most states raised the age of compulsory school attendance from fourteen to fifteen or sixteen years and traditional one-room public schools were being replaced by larger schools with expanded curricula. The Amish continued to maintain the one-room schools, where basic skills important for the children's later life are taught. However, since Amish parents did not want to send their children to high school after grade eight, frequent conflict with state authorities seeking to enforce school attendance until the age of sixteen was inevitable. The Amish endured fines and even imprisonment. A landmark in this struggle to retain control over the education of their children occurred when in 1967, non-Amish people sympathizing with the Amish set up the National Committee for Amish Religious Freedom and pursued one case (*Wisconsin vs. Yoder*) to the Supreme Court, which ruled in favour of the Amish in 1972.

The pamphlet also describes how and what Amish children are taught; reading, writing and arithmetic are supplemented by learning the beliefs and practices and necessary skills of an Amish community. Competitiveness and "worldly" pursuits are discouraged; discipline and obedience are stressed. The curriculum is basic, but the standards are higher than in many public schools — 70 percent is a passing grade. Amish schools play a major part in socializing Amish children and maintaining the community's identity. One feels that valuable lessons, such as community and mutual aid, are taught at Amish schools which public schools might do well to imitate. However, this is bought at the cost of a limited education that discourages independent, critical thought.

GARDNER, ERIC F.
*Investigation and Measurement of the Social Values Governing Interpersonal Relations Among Adolescent Youth and Their Teachers*
Syracuse, N.Y.: Syracuse University Press, 1963

This study sought to measure the prescription or "ought-to" values within relationships among adolescents. Emphasizing measurement over values, tests for the study were in four categories: (1) "ought-to" values perceived necessary for the "good life"; (2) ethical-moral-social values; (3) social relationships; and (4) restraints on value violations. As a first step in this ongoing investigation, responses of several social and cultural groups were compared. Examples of these samples are delinquents, southern Black boys and girls, and Formosan and Amish adolescents. The validity is tentatively proven if test results measure up to theoretical expectations.

HIEBERT, CLARENCE
*The Holdeman People*
South Pasadena, Calif.: William Carey Library, 1973

This was, in its original form, a Ph.D. dissertation at Case Western Reserve University (1971). For annotation, see p. 199, Vol. 1, *Sociology of Canadian Mennonites, Hutterites and Amish*, (1977).

HOSTETLER, JOHN A.
*Amish Society*
Baltimore and London: Johns Hopkins University Press, 1980

This third edition of Hostetler's *Amish Society* has received wide acclaim as the work of "the major Amish scholar in sociology." Published first in 1968, and later in 1974, the latest edition has expanded and updated chapters in light of developments of the past decade. Many see Hostetler taking a more objective look at Amish society in the third edition. The scientific basis for *Amish Society* is that of ethnography, a descriptive study of an individual culture in the anthropological tradition. For example, Hostetler helps his readers to see social and religious meaning in such rituals as footwashing, dress, dialect, aloofness from government and mutual aid.

The significance of Hostetler's work is also enhanced by the fact that relatively little research on the Amish has been carried out by sociologists. One criticism has been some confusion between statements of the Amish ideal and examples of that ideal realized in Amish life. For example, as one reviewer states, claims such as "the Amish person will have no doubt about his basic convictions" (p. 8), and "wealth does not accrue to the individual for his enjoyment" (p. 146) might best be offered as elements of the ideal rather than real culture.

The book remains a landmark and will be a definitive work on Amish society for some time to come.

HOSTETLER, JOHN A.
*Amish Life*
Scottdale, Pa., and Kitchener, Ont.: Herald Press, 1983

Part of a three-booklet set, *Amish Life* deals in a clear and concise way with this group's particular origin, history and present lifestyle. The other two booklets discuss related groups, the Mennonites and Hutterites. While brief, the book is quite comprehensive and informative in speaking of Amish life. Topics include the argiculture-based community, marriage and family, education, rules and customs, and survival in

North America. While all of these are issues integral to Amish life, the central theme within Amish society, as expressed by Hostetler, is the belief that redemption is available through the community. The above-mentioned rules, or *ordnung*, are in large part responsible for regulating every aspect of Amish life.

*Amish Life*, as with its two counterparts, is complemented by colour-ful and artistic photographs, used very effectively. The book is a useful educational tool, although somewhat beyond the secondary school level. See also Hostetler, *Mennonite Life* and *Hutterite Life*.

HOSTETLER, JOHN A.
*Amish Roots: A Treasury of History, Wisdom and Lore*
Baltimore: Johns Hopkins University Press, 1989

For the first time in his career John Hostetler has set aside the main-stream method of researching and writing about the Amish in favour of an anthology in which the Amish write about themselves. John C. Wenger, Franklin H. Littell, Warren Burger, Arthur Kollmorgen, C. Henry Smith and Lord Snowdon contribute from non-Amish back-grounds. But it is primarily a collection of short pieces from Amish writers past and present, with David Luthy, a convert from Catholicism residing in Aylmer, Ontario, leading the contributors with eleven items. Letters, poems, stories, riddles, legends and bits of family lore sparkle with unspoiled freshness and insight.

Hostetler says in the introduction that he was inspired by Edwin S. Gaustad's two-volume work, *A Documentary History of Religion in America* (1982). He said that all these building blocks permitted the reader to construct his own history of the Amish as Gaustad evoked a similar idea for American religious history as a whole.

Anecdotal history and sociology have merged in this book. A solid work like Hostetler's classic, *Amish Society*, now in its third edition, is a recommended back-up.

HOSTETLER, JOHN A. and GERTRUDE ENDERS HUNTINGTON
*Children in Amish Society: Socialization and Community Education*
Case Studies in Education and Culture Series. New York: Holt, Rinehart & Winston, 1971

See annotation in Vol. 1, p. 194, *Sociology of Canadian Mennonites, Hutter-ites and Amish* (1977).

KEIM, ALBERT N.
*Compulsory Education and the Amish: The Right Not to Be Modern*
Boston: Beacon Press, 1975

A focal point of the Amish resistance to assimilation pressures has been compulsory public education; they believe this represents a serious threat to their survival as a people. In this book, Keim has compiled nine essays documenting the Amish conflict with school authorities, written from various perspectives. The focal point of the entire debate is the *Yoder vs. Wisconsin* case of 1972 (text included in the Appendix); this is seen as definitive because it was the first and only time the Supreme Court ruled in favour of the Amish on this issue.

The book is significant, as it represents an accessible compilation of material which has until now been scattered newspaper clippings and legal documents. The study raises the question not only of the Amish right to direct their children's education, but also of their long-term ability to resist assimilation into the mainstream of society.

KRAYBILL, DONALD B.
*The Riddle of Amish Culture*
Baltimore: Johns Hopkins University Press, 1989

John A. Hostetler's *Amish Society* (Johns Hopkins University Press, 1963) was quickly recognized as the definitive book on the Amish. A dozen reprints and a revised edition confirmed its status. Would any scholar attempt another basic sociological study of the Amish?

Donald Kraybill has done just that with his *Riddle of Amish Culture*. John Hostetler has left Temple University to become Kraybill's colleague in the Center for Anabaptist and Pietist Studies at Elizabethtown College in Lancaster County, Pennsylvania, the home of 16,400 Amish people and 94 Amish districts, and Kraybill's acknowledgements recognize Hostetler's assistance.

Kraybill's work is, however, not merely a revision or update of Hostetler's. Kraybill limits the scope of his analysis to Lancaster County. Instead of Hostetler's concentration on the social theories of Bronislaw Malinowski (charter), Robert Redfield (little community), and Ferdinand Tonnies and Talcott Parsons (*Gemeinschaft-Gesellschaft*), Kraybill selects a new set of social theories to interpret his data, among them Peter Berger and Thomas Luckman on modernization and their concept of self-conscious collective decisionmaking. Kraybill also draws upon Sarah Cronk and Robert Friedman for *Gelassenheit* (self-surrender), Thomas Gallagher on structural analysis of social change, and Werner Enniger on symbols. He likes Hostetler's work on socialization, family life, and symbol systems.

Closely linked with modernization as rational decisionmaking is negotiation. "The concept of negotiation," Kraybill notes, "captures the dynamic interaction between Amish society and the larger society and solves many of the baffling puzzles, which are often compromises hammered out on the bargaining table."

If the negotiation does not satisfy Amish progressive activists, the mainstream Amish face internal divisions. Three of such have happened in the modern era: in 1870, 1910 and 1966. The expulsion of the progressives is not a failure of Amish culture. It is, Kraybill argues, the ultimate strategy for the preservation of Amish culture.

Resistance to the automobile and the compromises regarding buggies illustrate Kraybill's central point on negotiation. In the 1920s Pennsylvania laws required electric lights on all vehicles, whether motorized or horse drawn. At first the Amish leaders said "no," yet in the 1930s they acquiesced to the electric lights. By the 1940s and 1950s the church permitted battery-operated lights and in the 1960s and the 1970s reflective triangles and flashing red lights were granted approval.

On the government side, the Pennsylvania legislature in 1987 conceded that the Amish might extinguish flashing lights in the daytime.

Nor did Amish buggies need to be licensed, inspected, or taxed and destructive steel horseshoes could be used on paved roads. Kraybill observes: "Representatives on either side of the bargaining table knew they had struck a good deal." Meanwhile the buggies underwent constant modernization: battery-operated windshield wipers, thermopane windows, and a choice of four colours for floor carpets. The cost of the updated buggy is $2,500. The crucial point in negotiated modernization is continued resistance on the issue of the automobile, with genuine give and take on buggy safety and buggy embellishments.

Kraybill outspokenly rejects any attempt to make the Amish a fossilized, traditional subculture. They have provided an excellent antidote for what Peter Berger calls homelessness as a byproduct of modernity. The Amish do not suffer from erosion of meaning or the loss of belonging. They are sophisticated enough to negotiate with a mainstream culture that threatens them with assimilation, creeping urbanism or the sociological zoo of tourism.

*The Riddle of Amish Culture* provides us with a clear picture of the Amish management of social change. In those terms it is an important supplement to Hostetler's work on Amish society. Kraybill's conceptualization and data reveal the dynamic interchange between Amish society and the "English" culture which surrounds it. It is reasonable to assume that the pattern of social change among the 16,400 Amish in Lancaster county is also a paradigm for the 94,000 Amish who live elsewhere in the USA and in Canada.

See also his chapter, "Marketing the Amish Soul" (with J. A. Hostetler), *Image Ethics*, ed. Jay Ruby and John Katz (Oxford University Press, 1989); also, "Suicide in a Religious Subculture: The Old Order Amish" (with J. A. Hostetler), *International Journal of Moral and Social Studies*, 1 (Autumn 1986): 249-64.

KUVLESKY, WILLIAM P.
*A Comparative Analysis of Life Situations of Rural Youth From Two Different Cultural Settings: Northern Taos County, New Mexico & Eastern Holmes County, Ohio*
College Station, Tex.: Texas A and M University Agricultural Experiment Station, 1978

A comparative, interpretive analysis of the social organization of contrasting groups of rural youth from New Mexico and Ohio, approached from an ethnomethodological perspective, relies on direct observation, intensive personal interviews and key informants to produce a broader understanding of particular youth coping with their social contexts. Subjects were six Spanish American youth of Taos County, New Mexico and five youth from predominantly Mennonite and Amish in eastern Holmes County, Ohio. Among various aspects of life situations, dramatic differences existed in religious orientations: Taos youth did not view themselves as religious and did not attend church regularly, while the opposite was true for the Holmes youth.

For a related study see Bernie Wiebe and Calvin W. Vraa, "Religious Values of Students in Religious and Public High Schools," *Psychological Reports*, 38, 3, Pt. 1 (June 1976): 709-10.

LEE, KAREN K.
*Amish Society — In Celebration of Rural Strengths and Diversity*
Paper presented at Annual National/Second International Institute on Social Work in Rural Areas, July 28-31, 1984

The Amish society has retained the essence of rural life and tells us how this preservation is possible. Originally associated with Swiss Anabaptists, Amish are often confused with Mennonites because of the early association with Menno Simons. Because the Amish do not make the "prideful" claim of salvation, they are non-evangelical. They maintain folk cohesion and social homogeneity through conscious isolation and the maintenance of a distinct lifestyle. Specific social rules, called the *Ordnung* are established by each congregation. The most important rules involve highly visible aspects of social life, making deviants obvious. Farming is the preferred occupation, and mutual aid such as barn raising is common.

LUTHY, DAVID
*The Amish in America: Settlements That Failed 1840-1960*
Aylmer, Ont.: Pathway Publishers, 1986

David Luthy, a graduate of Notre Dame University, South Bend, Indiana is a convert to Amish Christianity from the Catholic church. Although conforming to Amish life style in costume and agricultural vocation, Luthy has developed the excellent Amish Historical Library at Aylmer, Ontario, serves as an editor at Pathway Publishers, and travels indefatigably across North America doing research on the Amish.

This book on Amish settlements that failed is an enormous collection of data on the mobility of a house-church and kinship system of social organization which permits frequent moves of small groups to new communities. An odd fact emerges — Lancaster Amish have no daughter communities, while the recent settlements described by Luthy are mainly from four states: Indiana, Iowa, Michigan and Ohio.

The analysis of reasons for failure focuses on poor farming conditions, inability to attract new settlers and new ministers, the characteristic tension with the public school system, and defections to progressive Mennonites, Dunkards, Holdemans, new Amish settlements and Apostolic. Luthy does not acknowledge a conflict with the home congregation and community. The book includes a name and subject index of 5,000 entries. No researcher can ignore the work of this remarkable student of Amish life and culture.

NATIONAL ORGANIZATION ON LEGAL PROBLEMS
OF EDUCATION
*Frontiers of School Law*
Topeka, Kans.: Washburn University, n.d

This volume contains twenty conference speeches covering a wide spectrum of legal issues and professional problems, such as (1) the right of nontenured teachers to due processing nonrenewal cases; (2) the legal ramifications of the *Equal Employment Opportunity Act* of 1972; (3) the authority of Congress to limit the jurisdiction of federal courts; (4) the aftermath of the Amish case; (5) the school desegregation case; (6) women's rights in education; (7) the busing controversy; (8) special programming of children; (9) equal educational opportunity for handicapped children; (10) sex education; (11) student rights; (12) high school pregnancies; and (13) guidelines for police-school co-operation.

PELLMAN, RACHEL THOMAS, KENNETH PELLMAN
and JUDY SCHROEDER
*A Treasury of Amish Quilts*
Intercourse, Pa.: Good Books, 1990
*Amish Quilt Patterns*
Intercourse, Pa.: Good Books, 1985
*Amish Crib Quilts*
Intercourse, Pa.: Good Books, 1985
*The World of Amish Quilts*
Intercourse, Pa.: Good Books, 1985
*Mennonite Quilts and Pieces*
Intercourse, Pa.: Good Books, 1985
*Small Amish Quilt Patterns*
Intercourse, Pa.: Good Books, 1985

Folk art offers a living refutation of the dogma that only graduates of professional art schools can function with the visual arts. The Inuit, Grandma Moses, the Indians, the Appalachian whites and, in these books, the Amish and Mennonites are artistically creative. Beautiful quilts have become a central feature of Mennonite sales held coast to coast in North America. These sales are for support of Third World people suffering from famine and disasters.

Mennonite art critics, like Edna Shantz, have pointed out that two-thirds of the Amish quilt designs are not original with them but are borrowed from their neighbours. Like all authentic folk art, however, these books reveal quaint designs and patterns that originated in a pre-industrial rural, pastoral culture.

The publisher, Good Books, is a Mennonite house located in the heart of the Amish and Mennonite country in Lancaster County, Pennsylvania.

RUTH, JOHN
*A Quiet and Peaceable Life*
Rev. ed.; Intercourse, Pa.: Good Books, 1985

Author John Ruth asks us to understand the "plain people" of North America in terms of their own concerns, and to consider sympathetically their own expressions and the biblical cadences they echo (p. 4). This collection of poetry, prose and black and white photographs together forms an artistic and respectful tribute to the "Quiet in the Land." Ruth includes sub-titles such as "Not that Outward Adorning," "Simple, Substantial and Beautiful" and "Blessed are the Peacemakers."

While there is some information content in this booklet, it seems intended more as a meditative, reflective work.

SMUCKER, BARBARA
*Amish Adventure*
Toronto: Puffin-Penguin, 1987

A novel based on a cross-cultural plot in which a non-Amish youth circumstantially participates in an Amish family that almost wins his permanent allegiance.

# B. Graduate Theses

BEACHY, ALVIN J.
"The Amish of Somerset County, Pennsylvania: A Study of the Rise and Development of the Beachy Amish Mennonite Churches"
M.Th. thesis, Hartford Seminary, 1952

The author grew up with the Beachy Amish and then left to pursue an advanced education, including a Harvard doctorate. His life and this thesis suggest changes, even though limited in scope and number, do take place among the Amish.

BRESSON, REBECCA
"Inbreeding and the Old Order Amish"
M.A. thesis, California State University, Fullerton, 1978

This study's purpose is to test the hypothesis that if inbreeding is practised among members of a small, isolated population, high frequencies of rare genetic diseases appear. These frequencies are statistically measurable. The resulting inbred and rare diseases show some phenotypical as well as genotypical characteristics, thereby allowing for a selective study.

The Old Order Amish appear best suited, according to the author, to meet the requirements established by the hypothesis, and they are geographically accessible.

For a related study, see Muin Joseph Khory, "A Genealogic Study of Inbreeding and Prereproductive Morality in the Old Order Amish." Ph.D. dissertation, Johns Hopkins University, 1986. Annotated; 6 pp.

BUCHANAN, FREDERICK S.
"The Old Paths: A Study of the Amish Response to the Public School System"
Ph.D. dissertation, Ohio State University, Columbus, 1967

A doctoral study attempting to (1) describe the nature of the threat posed to the Ohio Amish by state-controlled schooling, (2) review the principal factors contributing to the open conflict between the Amish and the school authorities, and (3) analyze the Amish response to public schooling. The root of the Amish resistance to public schooling is their belief that as a community of Christians, they should maintain a boundary between themselves and the secular world. As a result of pressure they have established their own elementary schools using uncertified Amish teachers. The author concludes that since diversity of educational goals and methods is an essential fact of cultural pluralism, and in order to prevent the disruptive disintegration of the Amish value system, the Amish should be allowed to rear their children in conformity with their traditional pattern of life.

For related studies, see Albert E. Holliday, "The Amish and Compulsory Education," *Pennsylvania Education*, 3, 3 (January 1972): 6-10, and Thomas W. Foster, "Separation and Survival in Amish Society," *Sociological Focus*, 17, 1 (January 1984): 1-15.

CARTMEL, DARYL W.
## "An Ethnography of the Old Order Amish Settlement in Allen County, Indiana"
M.A. thesis, Ball State University, 1972

This brief ethnographic study concentrates on certain variables in Amish culture in order to isolate significant values expressed in Amish behaviour. The variables investigated have been the setting of the population within the territory, their social organization, religion and cultural dynamics. The borders of the territory and the topographical features found in it, along with residence patterns and economic occupations, are outlined. The social organization is described in terms of family, kin, school, church, and the settlement as a whole. Religion is presented through the belief pattern, the rituals of the church meeting, communion, wedding, funeral and the home. Points of tension in the development of the community are described.

The description of these variables leads to the conclusion that the Amish in Allen County find a rural bias of vital importance to close personal relations, and that these two aspects of their culture are an expression of their Christian faith.

For a related study, see Eugene P. Eriksen, Julia A. Eriksen and John A. Hostetler, "The Cultivation of the Soil as a Moral Directive: Population Growth, Family Ties, and the Maintenance of Community among the Old Order Amish," *Rural Society*, 45, 1 (Spring 1980): 49-68.

COYLE, JEAN M.
## "Attitudes Toward Provision of Services to the Elderly in Rural Communities: Two Case Studies"
M.A. thesis, Eastern Illinois University, 1982

Two Central Illinois farming communities (one Amish and one non-Amish) were selected for this study. Residents of Amish communities and some other small, traditional, non-Amish (English) rural communities often prefer to provide various types of services, such as hot meals for invalids, housekeeping, etc. for themselves and their neighbours rather than through outside programs such as Meals on Wheels. The study dealt with perception of need for services, use of outside services by the elderly, etc. Both communities felt that various kinds of services for/to the elderly "had been," "were being" and probably "always would be" most effectively provided by the community residents themselves.

CRONK, SANDRA LEE
"*Gelassenheit*: The Rites of the Redemptive Process in Old Order Amish and Old Order Mennonite Communities"
Ph.D. dissertation, University of Chicago, 1977

This dissertation examines the Old Order Amish and Old Order Mennonite style of Christian living based on principles distinct from those of the general culture. It explores the inherent meanings in this lifestyle through a study of traditional ritual, nineteenth-century challenges to that ritual and the resulting Old Order movement. This social ritual, based on the revelation of Christ — "yieldedness" to God, simple living and self-restraint — were embodied in the term *Gelassenheit*. Mainstream redemption processes (e.g., technology, court systems, Evangelical piety) brought many challenges to the traditional ritual process of *Gelassenheit*, and eventually divisions within the Mennonite Church between "progressives" and "conservatives" resulted in the Old Order withdrawal.

This dissertation is a significant examination of Old Order social ritual, and its value within the religious self-identity of this group to the present.

For an abstract of this dissertation, see *MQR*, 52, 1 (January 1978): 183-85.

FISHMAN, ANDREA R.
"Reading, Writing, and Meaning: A Literacy Study Among the Amish"
Ph.D. dissertation, University of Pennsylvania, 1984

The Amish have a written corpus of material: the Bible, *Martyr's Mirror*, magazines from Pathway Publishers, school books, the Sugarcreek *Budget* and other materials. The home is the primary conduit for reading, supported by a brief eight-year experience in elementary school. Although meaning is most often in the text, the Amish know that meaning actually resides in the community. Text has context.

The most fascinating argument in this dissertation is the suggestion that Amish literacy is fundamentally oral rather than literate. The author notes from Goody and Watt (1986) that literate cultures are inward and individualistic while oral cultures are homogeneous, coherent and mutual. "It's [sic] members participate spontaneously and uncritically in their world, nonplussed by contradictions between imagination and reality, myth and history. From this description the Amish are an oral culture" (p. 385). Moreover, in the oral cultures community decisions and literacy are almost identical without super-literate intellectuals. What is the central medium of writing? Not books, journals or scientific studies. Rather, the basic medium is the hand-written letter.

Fishman's work is a very original contribution to the mountain of theses on Amish topics. A next step would be to check the argument about the oral versus literate culture with David Luthy, a graduate of Notre Dame University, who is now the leading Amish archivist and historian of Canada; and to check with his brother-in-law, Joseph Stoll, who edits journals by Pathway Publishers in Aylmer, Ontario. Is this evidence of the rise of Amish intellectuals who belong to a literate culture?

GALLAGHER, THOMAS E., JR.
"Clinging to the Past or Preparing for the Future? The Structure of Selective Modernization Among Old Order Amish of Lancaster County, Pennsylvania"
Ph.D. dissertation, Temple University, 1981

Gallagher examines the process of "selective modernization" among the Amish of Pennsylvania. Casual and scholarly observers perceive the Amish as clinging to the past and rejecting the modern world, as seems to be indicated by dress, farm equipment and horse-drawn carriages. Scholars have observed, however, that changes do take place, and that they can be explained by a need to preserve the Amish lifestyle and as a requirement of external conditions.

Gallagher seeks to develop a more coherent Amish world view (through many in-depth research techniques), and further, a more consistent explanation of change. He cites the major component of Amish world views as obedience to God's will. Therefore, when the Amish reject something modern, it is not because it is modern, but because it is seen as encouraging movement away from the will of God. Rejecting modernity is not an end in itself, but a means to an end – obedience to God.

For a related study see Thomas J. Meyers, "Stress and the Amish Community in Transition," Ph.D. dissertation, Boston University Graduate School, 1983.

HURD, JAMES PARKER
"Mate Choice Among the Nebraska Amish of Central Pennsylvania"
Ph.D. dissertation, Pennsylvania State University, 1981

This thesis demonstrates the interrelationships among some demographic features of the Nebraska Amish population, particularly as they relate to marriage and mate choice. The central thesis is that forms or patterns of behaviour, particularly those related to marriage and kinship, can be fully understood only by including in the analysis two forces shaping cultural norms: sexual selection and biological relationships. Data are collected on all individuals and their known ancestors in the community's three Amish church affiliations, and include genealogies, church membership and marriage histories. The main conclusions of the analysis are that the Nebraska Amish church affiliations are closely-knit groups of interrelated kin who usually find their spouses within their own church. In summary, the results are consistent with predictions from sociobiological theory, and emphasize the importance of considering these biological variables in any analysis of human mating patterns.

For a related study, see James P. Hurd, "Kin Relatedness and Church Fissioning among the 'Nebraska' Amish of Pennsylvania," *Social Biology*, 30, 1 (Spring 1983): 59-66.

KHOURY, MUIN JOSEPH
"A Genealogic Study of Inbreeding and Prereproductive Mortality in the Old Order Amish"
Ph.D. dissertation, Johns Hopkins University, 1986

This study examines inbreeding patterns of the Old Order Amish of Lancaster County, Pennsylvania and the effects of inbreeding on prereproductive mortality (PRM, death below age twenty years) in the Amish, both in the historical genealogic population and in the present-day Amish population. Analysis of the genealogic registry revealed that inbreeding levels have risen significantly over time. The average intermarriage in the present generation is slightly less than the equivalent of a second cousin marriage, with 98 percent of all marriages related.

LAURENCE, HUGH GETTY
"Change in Religion, Economics, and Boundary Conditions among Amish Mennonites in Southwestern Ontario"
Ph.D. dissertation, McGill University, 1980

See annotation on p. 52 of Vol. I. *Sociology of Canadian Mennonite, Hutterites and Amish* (1977).

LEWIS, RUSSEL E.
"A Comparison of Old Order Amish and Hutterite Brethren Family Systems and Community Integration"
M.A. thesis, Michigan State University, 1972

This thesis is an attempt to compare in detail the form and function of the family systems of both groups in question, along with a detailed analysis of community integration among both groups. By doing so, it may be possible to decide if one society has a better chance for survival as a distinct cultural group in North American society than the other.

This study also takes a critical look at the relationships between technology and human values. The capability of a society to cope with new technologies, without altering its value structure to a major degree, is an important asset for small-group survival.

The comparative method is used throughout the thesis. Three aspects of each cultural group, Amish and Hutterites, are covered in depth: (1) the family system; (2) community integration; and (3) the uses of modern technology. The data are taken from the ethnographies and other studies which have been made of the two cultural groups.

Both the Amish and the Hutterites have obtained an extremely high level of integration among their communities, but the Hutterite communities have in fact reached a higher level. This fact, coupled with the fact that the Hutterian Brethren are capable of harnessing a greater amount of energy due to their acceptance of modern technology, leads to the hypothesis that the Hutterian Brethren will indeed have a better chance for survival as a distinct cultural group in North America.

For related studies, see Marlow Ediger, "Stability Versus Change in Society," *Trends in Social Education*, 24, 1 (February 1977): 43-45, and John W. Bennett, "Social Theory and the Social Order of the Hutterian Community," *MQR*, 51, 2 (October 1977): 292-307.

MEYERS, THOMAS JAY
## "Stress and the Amish Community in Transition"
Ph.D. dissertation, Boston University, 1983

This study examines occupational stress in a sample of farm and factory workers from two Amish settlements in Northern Indiana. Meyers does not use the "life events" methodology on the grounds that it assumes that any demand on the individual is necessarily bad and that it is the quantity of events that is critical. He argues, rather, that an individual must perceive a situation to be distressing, that the quality of events is critical. He argues that social support is an essential factor in coping with stress and hypothesizes that: "Amishmen in industry with high levels of social support are less susceptible to stress and its various consequences than Amish farmers with low levels of social support. Meyers identifies four categories of stressors: environmental, responsibility pressure, role conflict and work load. He finds that among factory workers, environmental stressors have the strongest relationship with psychological distress; among farmers, responsibility pressure, role conflict and work load are most potent for psychological distress. Underlying each of these demands is the farmer's insecure financial situation. Meyers describes the socio-emotional and instrumental aid provided by the Amish culture and community. Due to the structure of their work, Amish farmers tend to rely on their spouses, and Amish factory workers on their co-workers for social support. Meyer acknowledges that his study was not based on a random sample and had other limitations. More systematic research in this area would be fruitful.

SHANAFELT, ROBERT A.
## "The Amish and Their Germanic Background"
M.A. thesis, Kent State University, 1982

In contrast to the ethnographic studies of Amish done by Hostetler (1980) and Huntington (1965), Shanafelt approaches the study of this group as a Christian sectarian response to particular historical and cultural forces. He first examines the development of religion in Germany. Shanafelt looks at medieval popular religion and its impact on the Reformation as particularly helpful in understanding the religious focus of the Anabaptists, of which the Amish are a schismatic branch. The author then examines German values and concepts transformed by the Amish Anabaptists into a new social and symbolic system, and finally looks at the socio-religious system of Amish today in relation to this German history and these original values.

Shanafelt concludes that the dynamics of Amish culture can be understood as an elaboration of sectarian responses to predominating socio-religious questions in Switzerland and Germany during the Reformation period.

For a related study see John A. Hostetler, "The Plain People: Historical and Modern Perspectives," *America and the Germans*, ed. Frank Trommler and Joseph McVeigh, Vol. 1 (Philadelphia: University of Pennsylvania Press, 1985).

SMUCKER, MERVIN R.
## "Growing up Amish: A Comparison of the Socialization Process Between Amish and Non-Amish Children"
M.Sc. thesis, Millersville State College, Pennsylvania, 1978

The basic purpose of this study was to determine whether Amish and non-Amish children from the same geographical area differ in terms of how they view their families. Related issues examined are the influence (if any) of IQ scores, and the difference in homogeneity of responses.

The sample consisted of 102 Amish children and the same number of non-Amish children. Various IQ and other tests were administered to them, and the results compared.

Although no significant correlation was found between IQ and Family-Rating scores in either group, a salient trend was discovered among the Amish group scores: while the IQ-Family Rating correlation coefficients were positive and relatively constant for Amish children from grades four through six, they became increasingly negative from grades six to eight.

For related/similar studies, see Barbara E. Bernstein, "A Crosscultural Study of Sixth-graders' New Year's Resolutions: Middle Class vs. Mennonite and Amish Youth," *Social Behaviour and Personality*, 5, 2 (1977): 209-14, and Doris R. Entwisle, "Subcultural Differences in Children's Language Development," Centre for the Study of Social Organization of Schools, Johns Hopkins University, 1967.

WENGER, A. FRANCES
## "The Old Order Amish Concept of Care"
Ph.D. dissertation, School of Nursing, Wayne State University, 1988

Noting the paucity of research on health care among the Amish, Wenger spent three years in ethnographic research in the Old Order Amish settlement of Elkhart-LaGrange, Indiana, concentrating her work on a group of thirteen families whose children all attended the same Amish school. She selected an Amish school as her focal institution because schools are among the few institutions operated by the Amish.

She approached the community through the chairperson of the Indiana Amish school board and the chairperson of the individual school's board, and then attended a school parent-teacher meeting, where she presented her research proposal.

After a three-month period of visiting appropriate key persons, including the bishop and teachers, Wenger was able to begin ethnographic interviews and participant observation in the community. Although she did her research through interview, Wenger also attended Amish social events such as quilting parties and funerals to understand their culture better. She found that the persons she interviewed could express their concept of care better if they spoke in Pennsylvania Dutch.

Caring about other people is considered a central part of being Amish and a way that Amish society holds itself together. The Amish use four different words to express their concept of care, Wenger found. One word that expresses caring means to think about another person. Another word means to do everything possible to help someone. A third word means actually waiting on or serving someone, while a fourth means to protect or watch over someone. The Amish also emphasize what Wenger calls "anticipatory care," seeing people often so that one can easily tell when others are not well or are in need of care.

The Amish do not believe that automobiles, telephones or electricity are evil; however, they do not like the effect such technology has on families and communities. What they reject is the effect of technology, not technology itself. By not driving automobiles or having telephones in their homes, the Amish can use technology selectively, controlling the technology rather than allowing the technology to control them.

The seeming contradiction between Amish rejection of modern devices and their acceptance of modern medicine is not a contradiction at all, according to the author. The Amish do use modern medicine, but they also accept many other kinds of health care. For instance, they will use the services of Amish folk healers, reflexologists and other unconventional practitioners. "They can talk about going to Mayo Clinic and about going to sit in a uranium mine in the same breath," the author noted.

They prefer to take an active role in their health care, but they believe that conventional health-care professionals don't want to hear about other health-care alternatives.

The rising cost of health care has affected the Amish. Every person interviewed mentioned the high cost of modern medical treatment. An Amish family may discuss a particularly expensive treatment with their bishop if they believe they may have to ask the church for help.

Although there is a kind of health insurance administered by the Amish called Amish Aid, the Amish interviewed by Wenger do not use the service. However, many Amish men work in local factories and will sometimes accept workers' compensation for a job-related injury.

Wenger has researched a new dimension of Amish life. It would be useful to know more concerning the interaction of modern medicine and alternative health care. Also, research could probe the total absence of health-care professionals among the Amish because of their limited educational strategy. A final appendix would be useful on Amish folk healers.

YODER, KAREN KAY
"Influence of Cognitive Style of an American Subculture's Health Seeking Behaviour and View of Nurses"
Ph.D. dissertation, University of Michigan, 1984

Because the Old Order Amish follow an unusual lifestyle, nurses may be unsure how to meet their health needs. To provide information enabling nurses to offer client-centred services, this study compared twenty-three Old Order Amish and twenty-three rural non-Amish, all sixty years of age or older, and living in close proximity. Four major variables were examined: (1) ethnicity; (2) cognitive style; (3) health seeking behaviour; and (4) characteristics desired in a nurse. One of Yoder's findings was that ethnicity — that of the Amish — had a significant bearing on these variables, providing guidelines for practitioners dealing with "specialized clientele."

# C. Articles

ALLEN, GORDON
## "Random Genetic Drift Inferred from Surnames in Old Colony Mennonites"
*Human Biology*, 60, 4 (August 1988): 639-53

A population of German-speaking Mennonites in Mexico has accumulated a random inbreeding coefficient estimated as 0.0091 in four centuries, despite numbering in thousands even at times of migration. The availability of two parental surnames per index adult permitted a more precise analysis than is usually possible except in Iberoamerican populations. Maternal names were more diverse than paternal names. This and some other phenomena were better described and quantified by chi-square and the sign test than by the inbreeding coefficient. In particular, the analysis by chi-square showed the importance of extended families recruited for migration. Use of both maternal and paternal surnames to estimate random inbreeding corrects an upward bias that results from using paternal names only, especially when female names are more diverse.

Although this population is unusual in many respects, the analysis of surnames illustrates some general principles.

(1) In any small monogamous population with some large surviving sib-ships as in invertebrates, the array of maternal alleles in polyallelic systems should differ greatly from that of paternal alleles because paired, different alleles have been multiplied by the same progeny numbers.

(2) The common use of fathers' surnames alone in estimating random inbreeding overestimates the coefficient by omitting some names (hence some alleles), especially when mothers have a larger array of names than fathers.

(3) When reduced effective population number results from large groups or blocks of close relatives, random genetic drift between generations in multiallelic systems can be very effectively measured by use of contingency chi-square. In a parallel analysis, the unweighted sign test can demonstrate the excess of decreases over increases in allele frequencies. The inbreeding coefficient is relatively insensitive to these changes.

(4) The estimates of total genetic drift since founding of the Dutch Mennonite population are probably inflated by multiple origin of some names and would also fail to register illegitimate unions with host populations. To measure these errors would require true bioassay methods, including comparison of gene frequencies with those of source and host populations.

Genetic research among Mennonite, Hutterite and Amish people is a striking new development based on the inbreeding among the plain people but less characteristic of progressive Mennonites. Moreover, defectors from one of the conservative Mennonite, Hutterite or Amish groups usually join a more progressive Mennonite group with polyallelic possibilities.

BERNSTEIN, BARBARA E.
## "A Cross-cultural Study of Sixth-Graders' New Year's Resolutions: Middle-class versus Mennonite and Amish Youth"
*Social Behaviour and Personality*, 5, 2 (1977): 209-14

Bernstein compares the New Year's resolutions of middle-class sixth-graders and Mennonite and Amish sixth-graders. She discovers that the New Year's resolutions of Mennonite and Amish children generally revolved around everyday activities and the process of doing them better (e.g., "Do my lessons more carefully"). The resolutions of middle-class children were more goal-oriented (e.g., "Raise school grades by one step") and also tended to be more exotic and dramatic, dealing with activities outside their ordinary experience.

As might be expected, Amish and Mennonite children showed greater concern over religious responsibilities and less concern over sports and hobbies than did middle-class youngsters, but these and other minor cross-cultural differences were not significant.

However, some interesting sex differences were found. In both cultures, boys were more concerned about religion, personal relationships and sports and hobbies, whereas girls were more concerned about home responsibilities and personal health habits. The only cultural difference in this regard had to do with schoolwork. Middle-class boys wrote more than girls about schoolwork, while the reverse was true among the Amish and Mennonites. It is noteworthy that these sex differences did not achieve significance among the middle-class youth, but they did achieve significance among the Amish and Mennonite youth ($p < 0.05$). Significance was also achieved with the two cultures pooled ($p < 0.025$).

Another interesting finding was that girls consistently listed more resolutions than boys. Amish and Mennonite males wrote an average of 2.18 resolutions, while girls averaged 6.22. The gap was narrower among middle-class subjects, with male and female averages 4.12 and 6.00 resolutions, respectively. Though this sex difference was more pronounced among the Mennonites and Amish, it was highly significant in both cultures ($p < 0.005$).

Taking the two sections of the control group, a question can be raised over Bernstein's class designation of middle-class students, and religious-ethnic label for the Mennonites and Amish. Were the middle-class students Jewish, Catholic, Protestant, Buddhist or secular? Were origins from Israel, Italy, Ireland or China? Were the Mennonites from affluent professional families? Were the Amish families land-rich, cash-poor with children within two years of terminating their education?

BRYER, KATHLEEN B.
**"The Amish Way of Death: A Study of Family Support System"**
*American Psychologist*, 34, 3 (March 1979): 255-61

Bryer interviews twenty-four Amish families to inquire about their attitudes towards death: their funeral customs and rituals of mourning, their personal experience with death, and the social support for the dying person and the bereaved family. She discovers that the tightly knit Amish family and community provides a network of support which leads to healthy attitudes towards death and dying. The article presents implications for contemporary society in terms of improving the quality of life and death for the dying, their families and the professionals involved in their care. This article is a sensitive probe into an important aspect of the Amish community.

COLLUM, DANNY
**"Clouds in Witness—Where America Meets the Amish"**
*Sojourners*, 14, 4 (April 1985): 44-45

This article reviews the film "Witness," made by Australian filmmaker Peter Weir. The setting is an Amish community in Lancaster County, Pennsylvania, and the plot revolves around the dramatic intrusion of "the world" into their midst, in the form of homicide investigator John Book. Collum points out some merits of the film, but also states that, "in his attraction to the purity of the Amish, Peter Weir (director) romantically glosses over some hard questions about the relevance or viability of their kind of absolutism" (p. 45).

CRONK, SANDRA
**"*Gelassenheit*: The Rites of the Redemptive Process in Old Order Amish and Old Order Mennonite Communities"**
*MQR*, 55, 1 (January 1981): 5-44

The Old Order Mennonite and Old Order Amish communities began in North America with the goal of creating a loving brotherhood. The basis of this brotherhood was the concept *gelassenheit* or "yielding," which structured one's internal relationship with God as well as one's external relationships. The Amish and Mennonite social rites of working, worshipping and communal organization were challenged in the nineteenth century by the larger North American society's technology, politics, and legal system, as well as its pietism and evangelical thought. The Old Order divisions in the second half of the nineteenth century came as a result of dissension on how to combat these social forces. There came to be a focus on conflict and power struggles rather than on personal surrender and communal harmony. This article is comprehensive and well written, containing a significant amount of primary evidence to support the author's arguments. It provides an excellent treatment of the influence of pietism and evangelical thought on Old Order Amish and Mennonite worship and religious self-identity.

DEVRIES, GEORGE
"Lessons from an Alternative Culture: The Old Order Amish"
*Christian School Review*, 10, 3 (1981): 218-28

This article suggests lessons that other Christians can learn from the Old Order Amish. DeVries suggests we are learning rapidly that our own consumer technology is wasteful with undesirable social and economic effects. The Amish, who live simply but well within a solid, close-knit community, teach us much about the role of technology in society, simpler life styles, conservation, mutual responsibility and the values of family and community. DeVries states, "Although there are negative aspects to Amish life, their adjustment to modern culture deserves re-examination." There remains some room for question, however, about whether withdrawal from society and self-seclusion is "adjustment to modern culture."

DRIEDGER, LEO
"The Anabaptist Identification Ladder: Plain-Urbane Continuity"
*MQR*, 51, 4 (October 1977): 278-91

Driedger observes that plain people have been studied largely from a structural perspective and the focus has been upon the maintenance of a rural ethnic community. Driedger suggests that a focus on change has been neglected. He proposes that change takes place along a continuum (ladder) between a more structured, tradition-directed community pole, and a more open, less structured urban community pole. Despite a range of diverse communities there is continuity by individuals of more traditional groups joining more liberal Anabaptist groups with assimilation into the larger society. Driedger looks specifically at the Hutterites, the Old Order Amish, the Old Colony Mennonites and urban Mennonites. This article examines modern Anabaptist groups from the perspective of change as a slow, continuous and controlled process which does not result in assimilation. Driedger applies his findings by commenting on how they relate to the trend of increasing amalgamation of Anabaptist and Mennonite groups into larger conferences. He hypothesizes that this trend may lead to a destruction of the Anabaptist identification ladder.

DRIEDGER, LEO
"Individual Freedom vs. Community Control: An Adaptation of Erikson's Ontogeny of Ritualization"
*Journal for the Scientific Study of Religion*, 21, 3 (1982): 226-42

Driedger presents a convincing analysis of a Saskatchewan Old Colony Mennonite community on the basis of Erik Erikson's ontogeny of ritualization. The six stages, moving from the *numinous* trust and mutual recognition to the *nomatic* integrity, are discerned within the life of Driedger's grandfather Johann in his interaction with, and excommunication from, his rigid Mennonite community. The colony resisted initiative and industry on the part of its members, and because Johann Driedger tested and pushed beyond these boundaries, he was banned. The author sees this model as very useful in examining the interaction of such a community, and carries it further in postulating a later outcome beyond Driedger's death, according to the pattern of stages.

EDIGER, MARLOW
## "Other Minorities: Old Order Amish and Hutterites"
*Social Studies*, 68, 4 (July/August 1977): 172-73

Ediger states that social studies curricula should include units on the Old Order Amish and the Hutterites. The author outlines the lifestyles and beliefs of each group, stressing their independence from the national society and their interdependence within their own communities.

For a related article, see Marlow Ediger, "Stability Versus Change in Society," *Trends in Social Education*, 24, 1 (February 1977): 43-45.

EDIGER, MARLOW
## "The Old Order Amish in American Society"
*Education*, 101, 1 (Fall 1980): 29-31

This article contains generalizations about the Old Order Amish which can be translated into general and specific objectives for a social studies unit on minority groups in the United States.

For related studies, see John W. Friesen, "Concepts of Mennonites in School Curricula," unpublished paper, August 1984, and Priscilla Perisho (ed.), *Interfaith Relations in Children's Books: A Bibliography*, New York: Friendship Press, 1976.

EDIGER, MARLOW
## *Old Order Amish and the Philosophy of Education.*
Research Report, Mennonite College of Nursing, Bloomington, Ill., 1985

The Old Order Amish are a religious sect representing both a traditional and a changing culture. Conservatism is evident in their rural life, large families, use of horses, non-use of electricity and uniformity of dress. The Amish also present a rapidly changing culture due to the scarcity of farmland available to younger families and to competing modern ideas. The majority buy health services but do not carry insurance on property or personal life. They insist on strict separation of church and state and do not participate in the social security system. School, up to grade eight, consists of basic curricula such as reading, writing, arithmetic and religion.

EDIGER, MARLOW
## *Old Order Amish, Culture, and the Language Arts.*
Research Report, Mennonite College of Nursing, Bloomington, Ill., 1983

During the 1979-1980 school year, twenty-three Old Order Amish pupils in the Pleasant Hill School near Bloomfield, Iowa took the Iowa Test of Basic Skills. Despite variation among themselves and among grades, students were strongest in spelling and weakest in capitalization. Fifteen ranked over 50 percent on the total language arts subjects.

EDIGER, MARLOW
*Old Order Amish Pupil Achievement in Work Study Skills*
Research Report, Mennonite College of Nursing, Bloomington, Ill., 1982

Following a brief discussion of some characteristics of the Amish culture, data on work study skills are reported for twenty-three pupils in grades three, four, six, seven and eight in Pleasant Hill School near Bloomfield, Iowa. Percentile ranks ranged from five to eighty-three. Eleven pupils scored above the fifteenth percentile on map skills and on use of reference materials, while twelve were above the fifteenth percentile on the total score for the Work Study Skills subtest.

Also see Marlow Ediger, "Old Order Amish, Culture, and the Language Arts," 1983.

EDIGER, MARLOW
*Old Order Amish Pupils, Culture and Mathematics Achievement*
Research Report, Mennonite College of Nursing, Bloomington, Ill., 1982

Following a brief discussion of some characteristics of the Amish culture and schools, data from the Iowa Test of Basic Skills are reported for twenty-three pupils in grades three, four, six, seven and eight in Pleasant Hill School near Bloomfield, Iowa. Thirteen pupils scored at or above the fifteenth percentile in mathematics concepts; seventeen were at or above that level in problem solving; and all twenty-three were above the fifteenth percentile in computation. For the composite score, nineteen pupils scored at or above the fifteenth percentile.

See also Marlow Ediger, "Vocabulary Development, Reading and Old Order Amish pupils," Mennonite College of Nursing, Bloomington, 1983.

EDIGER, MARLOW
"Stability Versus Change in Society"
*Trends in Social Education*, 24, 1 (February 1977): 43-45

The author uses lifestyles of three cultural groups (Amish, Hutterites, Bedouins) to illustrate social stability isolated from change. He says that students should study stable cultures in order to understand the role of tradition, minority group contributions and different ways people achieve common goals of food production, housing and personal satisfaction

For a related article, see Marlow Ediger, "Other Minorities: Old Order Amish and Hutterites," *Social Studies*, 68, 4 (July/August 1977): 172-73.

ENTWISLE, DORIS R.
"Subcultural Differences in Children's Language Development"
Johns Hopkins University, Center for the Study of Social Organization of Schools, Baltimore, 1967

Patterns of the linguistic development of children of different socio-economic environments were determined by a study of word associations. The relation of residential area, social class or subcultural group membership to linguistic development was the main concern of the study. Groups were compared by holding constant age and IQ. The word associations were obtained by response to a list of ninety-six stimulus words. Of particular interest (for this bibliography) is the finding that Amish children develop even more slowly than rural Maryland children.

ERIKSEN, EUGENE P., JULIA A. ERICKSEN and JOHN A. HOSTETLER
"The Cultivation of the Soil as a Moral Directive: Population Growth, Family Ties, and the Maintenance of Community Among the Old Order Amish"
*Rural Sociology*, 45, 1 (1980): 49-68

The authors take the position that the Old Order Amish culture is largely maintained by the ability of individual Amish families to establish their children on farms. In the past, the norms of family farming, hard work and high fertility have been in balance with the ecological environment of Lancaster County, Pennsylvania. Recently the scarcity of land and the high prices required for the land that is available have made farming less of an option for young Amish families. The hypothesis of this article is that Amish who are unable to farm are more likely to leave the religious community. By examining demographic records, kinship ties and economic data the authors conclude that their hypothesis is correct. This article is thorough in its approach, giving detailed information on the research methods used and avoiding a simplistic approach to a very complex question.

ERIKSEN, JULIA and GARY KLEIN
"Women's Roles and Family Production Among the Old Order Amish"
*Rural Sociology*, 46, 2 (1981): 282-96

This paper examines the ways in which the productive role of Amish women helps maintain Old Order Amish society and the way these roles vary with woman's position in the life cycle. Three areas are examined: (1) women's role in production, (2) public and private spheres of women's influence, (3) childbearing. The authors conclude that while Amish men predominate in the public sphere, women's contributions are seen as equally important due to Amish religious beliefs that prize domestic values. Amish society is patriarchal but the division of labour is more equal than in the rest of American society. The research is based on a small sample and therefore the author's conclusions are limited.

FOSTER, THOMAS W.
"Amish Society"
*The Futurist*, 15, 6 (December 1981): 33-40

In this article, Foster describes the Amish as a "frugal community," to use the concept of E. F. Schumacher. In a comparative study of Schumacher's ideal of an ecologically balanced conserver society and the lifestyle of the Amish, Foster looks at ideas of work, the agricultural community and redeeming of wastefulness. The Amish conform in many ways to Schumacher's ideal conserver society; in Foster's words, "The Amish agree wholeheartedly with [his] belief in the 'therapeutic value of real work'" (p. 34). While the Amish society is not an immediate sociological blueprint, it may perhaps inspire the development of small, conservation-centred communities within the larger industrialized nations.

Foster speaks of the Amish using sociological and economic terminology; unfortunately he does not emphasize the integral convictions of faith which underlie and motivate the Amish lifestyle.

FOSTER, THOMAS W.
"Separation and Survival in Amish Society"
Sociological Focus, 17, 1 (January 1984): 1-15

This paper describes a number of threats to the cultural values and traditions of Old Order Amish society. The influences upon the Amish of government legislation, high fertility rates and rising rural land prices are specifically considered, as is the phenomenon of increasing factory employment in many Old Order communities. This paper further explores the manner in which the Amish are adapting to external threats to their traditional beliefs and lifestyles. The occupational structure of the Geauga County (Ohio) Amish is analyzed as a case in point and an assessment is made of the impact that widespread factory employment and modernization are having upon that settlement. Finally, several cultural survival strategies being widely employed by the Amish throughout the United States, are described and briefly evaluated including: (1) non-violent resistance to government authority, (2) partial accommodation to factory work, (3) psycho-social techniques of cultural boundary maintenance and (4) cottage industry employment. The thorough nature of this study of the American Amish highlights the need for similar Canadian studies and comparisons in this field.

FRANK, MARY (ED.)
"Children in Contemporary Society, IYC Series: Part IV. Rural Children and Rural Families"
Children in Contemporary Society, 13, 2 (January 1980)

The rural population, comprising one quarter of the nation's total, is diverse. Hence no single label can be applied to its inhabitants, its families, or its children. This collection of articles, highlighted with drawings by five-year-old rural residents, describes adaptations to modern American life made by three types of rural families: the Amish, the migrants and the Appalachians. It discusses the educational, health, housing and religious influences in rural life that shape the family and its children, emphasizes the need for accurate 1980 census reporting to reveal demographic change in the rural population, and takes a broad look at changes experienced by the rural community.

FREEMAN, LARRY
## "The Impact of Legal Decisions on the Future of Education"
National Institute of Education (DHEW), Washington, D.C., November 1974

After setting out some statements on ideologies which have contributed to the melting pot theory of education, the author examines the rationale for teacher-licensing procedures. Recent court opinions are discussed, in relation to the declared need for a principle of neutrality in respect to language, by which the language or dialect of any student should not be disparaged or denied. The Treaty of Guadalupe Hidalgo between the U.S. and Mexico in 1848 recognized the differences in customs, traditions and language of the people of New Mexico, and the 9th Amendment to the federal Constitution provides grounds for claiming the right to such differences by all U.S. citizens.

GINGERICH, JAMES NELSON
## "Ordinance or Ordering: 'Ordnung' and Amish Ministers Meetings, 1862-1898"
MQR, 60, 2 (1986): 180-99

This article traces the background and development of the Amish *Ordnung*, or ordering. Basically, these are rules dealing with matters of congregational life, ministerial service and church discipline. Gingerich discusses these rules particularly in terms of the *Diener-Versammlungen*, the ministers' meetings where such issues were addressed. By the 1870s, the issue of *Ordnung* had precipitated a split in the Amish-Mennonite church in America; the progressives ordered their church on the organic process of *Diener-Versammlungen*, while the Old Order had structured its life around a codex of fixed regulations.

GOLDFINE, JUDITH
## "The Defense of Leroy Barber: An Interview with Marvin Karpatkin"
School Review, 79, 1 (November 1969): 91-103

The legal right of the Amish to educate their own children is analyzed.

GRUTER, MARGARET
## "Ostracism on Trial: The Limits of Individual Rights"
Social Science Information, 24, 1 (1985): 101-11

In this article, Gruter deals with rejection and its implications for societal interaction. She explores such questions as a person's rights to social participation, and under what condition these rights can be abrogated. She points out that the legal system confronts rejection in all areas, and that groups will "use ostracism, a social form of rejection, to protect their continuity or cohesiveness." As a sample case, Gruter uses the banning of Andy Yoder from an Ohio Old Order Amish community. She describes this as a "defense mechanism" of the group against any further "contamination" of individual decisions. While Gruter makes some interesting points concerning the process of rejection within a social and religious group, her "argument" remains somewhat unclear and perhaps unfocused.

HARROFF, STEPHEN B.
"Plain People at Worship"
*Brethren Life*, 23 (August 1978): 210-24

The preaching services of two groups of plain people are used to compare and contrast salient features of these "set apart" societies. Following a detailed description of each group's meeting is a discussion of similar features such as physical arrangements, order of service, etc. These differences are then considered as determinants for the relative speed by which cultural assimilation affects each group. Tentative conclusions indicate that the Old Order Amish, who meet in homes, preserve a distinctive home language, and regularly recall the martyrdom of their ancestors, thereby establish more striking "boundaries" for their community and accordingly might be expected to assimilate more slowly.

HOLLIDAY, ALBERT E.
"The Amish and Compulsory Education"
*Pennsylvania Education*, 3, 3 (January 1972): 6-10

This article describes how the Amish resist modern education for a religious reason. They also fear the loss of their cohesive spiritual tradition. The government, however, wishes to impose compulsory high school education upon them.

HOSTETLER, JOHN A.
"The Plain People: Historical and Modern Perspectives"
Offprint from *America and the Germans: An Assessment of a Three-Hundred-Year History*, ed. Frank Trommler and Joseph McVeigh. Vol. 1. Philadelphia: University of Pennsylvania Press, 1985, pp. 106-17

In this introduction to the plain people, the various Anabaptist groups of German descent, Hostetler commends the "folk society" model as useful, but not sufficient. He describes the religious basis for the life style and organization of the plain people, who attempt to live according to the Sermon on the Mount, "in the world, but not of it," and stress obedience to God, which expresses itself in humility, nonresistance, and submission to the community of believers on the one hand, and separation from a "carnal" and "sinful" surrounding world on the other. Their lifestyle emphasizes honesty, hard work and prudence, yet is averse to consumerism, status symbols and other manifestations of the capitalistic ethic. The plain people also have to cope with problems, both because of tension with the host society and because of internal fragmentation into numerous sub-groups. Hostetler argues that the maintenance of the plain people's ethnicity is a positive fact, and that they can function as mediating structures within the larger society, counter-balancing the alienating tendencies of large-scale industrialization and bureaucratization and emphasizing "traditional" values which are incompatible with totalitarian societies. Yet he acknowledges the danger of excessive ethnocentrism. Hostetler's article is interesting and his vision of ethnic pluralism is appealing, provided it is based on mutual toleration, not on segregation.

HOSTETLER, JOHN A.
"Old Order Amish Survival"
*MQR*, 51, 4 (October 1977): 252-61

The article begins with a brief history and demographic description of the Amish population. The thesis of this article is that Amish survival cannot be accounted for by revitalization and revivalistic theory. The basic pattern of persistence is reflected in the Amish undramatic, quiet ways of coping. Hostetler looks at how the Amish have dealt with technology, schooling and government. The survival of the Amish community is linked with the divisions among the Amish and the variation in their responses to perceived threats.

HOSTETLER, JOHN A.
"Amish Schooling: A Study in Alternatives"
*Council on Anthropology Newsletter*, 3, 2; paper presented at symposium "Consequences of Implementing Alternative Schools," Quebec, 1972

This paper summarizes issues of Amish conflicts with public school consolidation and enforcement of extended compulsory school-age limits. It cites a long-standing strategy for community control in which schools maintain a culturally divergent minority-group tradition. The arguments in favour of consolidation are unacceptable to the author; Amish society is localized, formal and familistic, and opposed to separating school from life. Outlining four points, Hostetler explains the Amish desire for school on a human rather than an organizational scale. He concludes that, "The Amish have, thus, been able through community discipline and support and protection of their children to remain a discreet minority, steadfast to their own vision of the good life."

HURD, JAMES P.
"Sex Differences in Mate Choice Among the 'Nebraska' Amish of Central Pennsylvania"
*Ethnology and Sociobiology*, 6, 1 (1985): 49-57

This analysis of 190 marriages (in 1980) in the "Nebraska" Amish population of central Pennsylvania demonstrates systematic differences between male and female marriage patterns. Exogamous females marry three to four years later than endogamous females, perhaps because they must search farther afield for a mate. Patrilocal residence is twice as frequent as matrilocal. When churches fission, males tend to regroup with their male relatives at the expense of females regrouping with female relatives. These male biases in residence patterns and church affiliation are presumably due to preferential male farm inheritance and the importance of reciprocal male labour. Mate choice is seen as a strategy for consolidating resources and ultimately for increasing reproductive success.

HURD, JAMES P.
"Kin Relatedness and Church Fissioning Among the
'Nebraska' Amish of Pennsylvania"
*Social Biology*, 30, 1 (Spring 1983): 59-66
This study hypothesized that when a kin-oriented society fissions, individuals tend to regroup with close relatives and separate from more dis-
tant ones. A study of members of the Nebraska Amish church in Mif-
flin, Centre, Snyder and Union counties in Pennsylvania shows that as
a result of a fission in 1978, the 288 married individuals who left
regrouped at increased levels of relatedness, especially male-to-male
relatedness.

JESPEN, DAVID A. and PAUL M. RETSH
"Cross-disciplinary Approach to Teaching Career Guidance"
*Exceptional Children*, 40, 7 (April 1974): 514-16
This article describes a course in career guidance in which the student
teachers worked with a variety of study clients (e.g., Amish elementary
students, handicapped students in special education classes and potential dropouts), instead of being partitioned according to their preferred
roles. The advantages of this approach are discussed, and preliminary
evaluation data are presented.

KATZ, MICHAEL S.
"A History of Compulsory Education Laws"
(Bi-centennial Series) Phi Delta Kappa, Bloomington, Ind., 1976
Although some critics of public education are now questioning the
value of compulsory schooling for all children, this concept is deeply
ingrained in American history and social values. The Puritan notion of
education as a moral, social obligation was thus given the sanction of
law. By 1918, all states had passed school attendance legislation. However, as the population increased, and as the demand for labour grew,
enforcement began. Not all have supported this; court cases dealing
with opposition to mandatory schooling have arisen. For example, the
1972 *Wisconsin v. Yoder* ruling by the Supreme Court granted Amish
parents exemption for their children from laws compelling public
school attendance past the eighth grade.

KLIMES, RUDOLF E.
"Selected Legal Cases on State Control Over Private Home
Education"
Andrews University, Berrien Springs, Mich. Center for Studies &
Services in Education. Alexandria, Va.: ERIC Clearing House, 13254
(1975)
This paper examines five court cases concerning state control over pri-
vate home education. According to the author, the cases were selected
on the basis of their relevancy to the subject, but no attempt was made
to ascertain their representativeness. The cases discussed include *State
v. Peterman*, *Wright v. State*, *People v. Turner*, and *Meyer North v. State*.
The author concludes that private home schools may operate where

state regulations permit, if they employ a qualified teacher and use an educational program and schedule that conforms with acceptable educational practice.

LEVY, JOANNE
## "In Search of Isolation: The Holdeman Mennonites of Linden, Alberta and Their School"
*Canadian Ethnic Studies*, 11, 1 (1979)

> After describing briefly the history of the Holdeman Mennonites, this article recounts how the Linden, Alberta congregation, which had enjoyed fairly good relations with non-Holdeman neighbours, became dissatisfied with the education their children received at the public school. They considered it too liberal and found that it conflicted with their moral and religious beliefs. In the course of a new phase of self-examination and increased isolation from the influence of larger society, the Holdeman Mennonites of Linden decided to withdraw their children from the public school and set up their own school, Kneehill Christian School. After negotiations with the Board of Trustees failed, Holdeman parents found themselves charged with violation of the compulsory attendance provisions of the *School Act*. The Holdeman Mennonites' refusal to employ certified teachers had resulted in Kneehill not being recognized as a private school. Nevertheless, Assistant Chief Provincial Court Judge Olivier ruled that the Bill of Rights which guarantees religious freedom rendered the *School Act* inoperative in this particular case, since the defendant's right to religious freedom would be violated if the *School Act* were enforced. As a result, the Holdeman Mennonites were allowed to retain a school unauthorized by provincial legislation. It was a key development in the history of a unique ethnic group in Alberta. However, the question is whether this legally aided boundary maintenance may result in a decreasing quality of education and a discouragement to seek further education for Holdeman children.

LINES, PATRICIA M.
## "Curriculum & the Constitution"
Issuegram 34, Education Commission of the States, Denver, Colorado, 1983

> The U.S. Supreme Court has to date decided four major cases dealing with curricula or the rights of students. Two decisions accommodated conscience-based objections by students: the Court held that a compulsory school attendance law should not apply to Amish children beyond the eighth grade and exempted children from flag salute requirements. Lower court decisions in 1982 upheld the prohibition of one school play, stated that another play was improperly prohibited, ruled against the banning of two books and one film, made two decisions against mandatory instruction of the creationist theory, and approved sex education courses in New Jersey. The educational implications of these decisions are noted.

LOVEJOY, STEPHEN B. and DALE F. PARENT
## "Conservation Behaviour: A Look at the Explanatory Power of

The Traditional Adoption-diffusion Model"
Paper presented to Annual Meeting of Rural Sociological Society,
September 1982

This study focuses on the Environmental Protection Agency's Black
Creek Watershed project in Northeastern Indiana in relation to the
farmers' attitudes toward environmental innovations, as well as their
continued use of such innovations two and a half years after the project's completion. One variable was the questioning of Amish and non-
Amish. Although the research indicated a lack of knowledge concerning
factors of conservation behaviour, it suggested greater emphasis on identifying social, economic and seasonal factors into a single model which
could explain and predict the use of conservation practices. In addition,
research indicated more contacts should be made with small farmers, and
emphasized the need for formal communication links and education.

LUDWIG, DAVID J. and CAROL BEILHARZ
"Symbolic Features of Amish Youth"
*International Journal of Symbology*, 5, 3 (November 1974): 28-33

In this study, thirty-five Amish and thirty-seven non-Amish sixth,
seventh and eighth graders drew pictures of a Christmas scene, their
mother and father and three coins, and responded to five pictures from
the thematic apperception test. Results indicate that the Amish youth
experience a closed environment in their personality development,
characterized by a family unity with a dominant, authoritarian father
and by a de-emphasis on competition and achievement. Findings also
suggest that Amish youth use more family and religious symbols and
fewer aggressive and achievement themes. The relationship between
perception and developmental environment is also discussed.

MARKLE, GERALD E. and SHARON PASCO
"Family Limitation Among the Old Order Amish"
*Population Studies*, 31 (1977): 267-80

In the context of the demographic assumption that human fertility
adjusts to the environment, this article sets out to demonstrate that the
Old Order Amish of Indiana deliberately control their marital fertility
in accordance with their family finances. The Indiana Amish Directory,
originally compiled for research in medical genetics, is the source of all
the demographic data for this study. Two Amish ministers and their
wives were interviewed; it was during these interviews that the authors
of this article gained evidence that birth control in the form of self-
control was practised. The findings of this article conflict with the findings of Ericksen, *et al.*, "Fertility Patterns and Trends Among the Old
Order Amish," *Population Studies*, 33, 2.

MARTINEAU, WILLIAM H. and RHONDA S. MACQUEEN
"Occupational Differentiation Among the Old Order Amish"
*Rural Sociology*, 42, 3 (Fall 1977): 383-97

This study examines the patterns and consequences of non-farm
employment in the Amish of Lancaster County. Non-farm employ-

ment has become more common because of the expense of purchasing
a farm and the scarcity of available land, even though the preference of
most Amish people is to farm. At the community level, non-traditional
employment presents a serious threat to community integration and
continuity since the agricultural occupation and its lifestyle is founded
in religious doctrine. This article stresses the seriousness of this occupational trend for the Amish community, yet the tone of the article is
optimistic. The authors emphasize the creativity with which the Amish
have faced other threats. It concludes that the Amish community is too
complex to split over the nonfarming issue. Kinship ties, a more flexible
ideological climate, and recognition of the many values in the lifestyle
will continue to hold the community together for some time to come.
The extent to which it can remain the same, however, may well depend
on the continuing success the Amish have in preserving community
autonomy and in maintaining cultural substitutes for the protection and
insulation which spatial distance and isolation once provided.

MCDERMOTT, R. P.
"Social Relations as Contexts for Learning"
*Harvard Educational Review*, 47, 2 (1977): 198-213
  This article examines the importance of understanding the way relations between teachers and children affect the development of learning
  environments, and how classroom interaction may promote or retard
  learning. It describes how teaching styles depend on cultural contexts
  and examines successful and unsuccessful classrooms with examples
  from a variety of school systems, including Amish and inner-city
  Americans.

MILLER, JEROME K. and WILLIAM AUGILAR
"Public Library Use by Members of the Old Order Amish
Faith"
*MQR*, 23, 3 (Spring 1984): 322-26
  This study of public library use in Arthur, Illinois reveals that 14 per-
  cent of the nearby Amish population have purchased nonresident, fam-
  ily library cards. Comparison with rural populations in downstate Illi-
  nois and library use in Ohio Amish settlements suggests change in
  Amish culture and an important role of public libraries near Amish set-
  tlements.

MILLER, J. VIRGIL
"Amish-Mennonites in Northern Alsace and the Palatinate in
the Eighteenth Century and Their Connection with
Immigrants to Pennsylvania"
*MQR*, 50, 4 (1976): 272-80
  The Mennonites of the Amish branch began to move to Alsace and
  southern Germany around 1700 from their original homes in Switzerland. By 1750 they had a series of congregations between Montbeliard
  and the Palatinate. Their movements can be traced by studying the
  family names and the places where they were located during that

period. Some of the same family names that appeared in Pennsylvania after 1750 were found in northern Alsace and the Palatinate.

MORRIS, WAYNE D.
"One State's Struggle with *Wisconsin vs. Yoder*: The Kansas Compulsory School Attendance Statute and the Free Exercise of Religion"
*Washburn Law Journal*, 17, 3 (1978): 574-94

This article reviews the *Wisconsin vs. Yoder* case, where the United States Supreme Court held that the first and fourteenth Amendments prevent states from compelling Amish children to attend formal high school to age sixteen, and examines the actions of various state officials attempting to follow that case. It is available from School of Law, Washburn University, Topeka, Kansas 66621 ($3.00/copy).

NETHERS, JOHN
"A Study of the Oliveburg Amish Community of Ashland, Richland County, Ohio"
*Mansfield News Journal*, March 5, 1989

Since his master's thesis at Ohio State University thirty years ago on the Holmes County, Ohio Amish (the largest concentration of Amish of any county in North America), Nethers has been researching the Amish. This article was one of twelve scheduled in the *Mansfield News Journal* Sunday magazine. It is a characteristically descriptive study of the economic, social, technological and religious life of this community.

During his sabbatical from Ashland College, Ohio in 1987-88, Nethers visited sixty Amish communities while travelling 11,000 miles in sixteen states and provinces of the United States and Canada. A major book is forthcoming from this extensive field study.

For an article reflecting Nether's early concentration on Holmes County, see his "Occupational Changes Among the Old Order Amish in the Holmes County Vicinity of Ohio," *Communal Societies Quarterly* (Fall 1983), 122-39.

OLSHAN, MARC A.
"Modernity, the Folk Society, and the Old Order Amish: An Alternative Interpretation"
*Rural Sociology*, 46, 2 (1981): 297-309

Social scientists have frequently invoked the concept of the folk society as an analytical device to describe the Old Order Amish. The Amish use of buggies, kerosene lamps and one-room schools is presumably evidence of the folk-like character of Amish society. Such an evaluation is consistent with a conception of modernity based on technological sophistication. Modernity, however, may be defined alternatively as the perception of choice between different paths of social development. A society is modern to the extent that it self-consciously attempts to control and direct it own education. The quality of modernity is independent of technological sophistication, since technology may be self-consciously eschewed as well as embraced. Amish self-consciousness is evidenced by the selective manner in which agricultural and organizational innovations are adopted. By self-consciously manipulating their path of social development the Amish actually exemplify the antithesis of passive, folk-like behaviour. They thus arguably become a model for other modern societies. This is an excellent article, written in a straightforward manner, which challenges the reader to examine his/her own evaluation of the Amish way of life.

OLSHAN, MARC A.
"Should We Live Like the Amish?"
*Christianity Today*, 27, 3 (February 1983): 68

It is true that the simple lifestyle of the Amish has attracted much attention. Yet, as this article points out, it is ironic that the Amish faith, which is the basis of their culture, has been usually ignored.

ROLL, BETH
"Ethnic Cultures and Values"
*Media and Methods*, 14, 4 (December 1977): 28-29

This article describes films about American ethnic groups: the Eskimos, Cree Indians, the Shinnecock Indians, Italian-Americans and the Amish. Additional films about foreign and American culture are also annotated.

ROZEN, FRIEDA SHOENBERG
"The Permanent First Floor Tenant: Women and Gemeinschaft"
*MQR*, 51, 4 (October 1977): 319-28

Rozen examines the role of women in four groups: two "plain people" groups, the Old Order Amish and the Hutterites, and two Jewish groups, the Chassidim of Brooklyn and the rural kibbutzim of Israel. Rozen laments the lack of data of the real role of women in these groups, and the fact that the data which is available was collected by men in cultures in which communication barriers exist between women and men other than their husbands. Rozen finds that in all four societies women are a subordinate group. In her discussion, Rozen contrasts terms such as *gemeinschaft/gesellschaft*, nature/culture and non-achieving intimate group/achieving bureaucracy as possible frameworks to understand the role of women. At the end of the article, Rozen observes that connections to the outside world are dominated by men in these societies and she suggests that blocking women in this way has protected the *gemeinschaft* world. Although this is a brief article, and it is based on scanty available data, Rozen has raised many valuable questions which demand further study by sociologists.

SAVELLS, JERRY
"Social Change Among the Amish in Eight Communities"
*Pennsylvania Mennonite Heritage*, 13, 1 (1990)

Travelling 6,500 miles during thirty months, Savells visited eight communities and conducted 130 interviews to provide a cross-section of North American Amish groups.

Using an operational definition of change Savells looked at five major social institutions — family, religion, economics, education and politics — to discover the pressures that indicate modernization.

His data make very clear that within the common ethos of the Amish there are variations. For example, Plain City, Ohio and Intercourse, Pennsylvania Amish permit diesel generators to supply electricity to the barn while continuing the ban on electrified homes.

In a striking conclusion Savells observes: "Acculturation ... of Old Order Amish communities is neither rampant or whimsical. Rather, special change has consistently been scrutinized carefully and accepted gradually — where the results could be monitored for any possible unwanted side effects. The Old Order Amish enclave is not so much a model of 'paradise lost' as it is a model of 'evasive innovation' to save and protect a small but significant religious minority who wish to be 'in the world but not of the world.'"

Other articles on the Amish by Jerry Savells are: "Social Life Among the Amish in Eight Communities," *Alpha Kappa Delta National Symposium Proceedings*, 17 (February 1989): 82-86, and "Economics and Social Acculturation Among the Old Order Amish in Eight Communities," *Journal of Family Studies*, 19 (Spring 1988): 124-26.

SCHWEIDER, DOROTHY and ELMER SCHWEIDER
## "The Beachy Amish in Iowa, A Case Study"
*MQR*, 51, 1 (January 1977): 41-51

The authors examine the origin, economic and religious ideas and practices, and social relations of the Beachys. Because the Old Order are the dominant group within Amish society, their lifestyle has come to epitomize the Amish way of life. Although the Beachy embrace many of the same religious and social customs, they nevertheless deviate in several significant ways. Overall, they are more liberal in their economic practices and less concerned about maintaining separation from the world. The article concludes by observing that the acculturation of the Beachy Amish means that it has less of an appeal to potential converts from the Old Order. There is a relative paucity of printed materials on the Beachy Amish, and although this significant article is written in an American context, it pertains to the Canadian situation as well.

SILVERMAN, WILLIAM (ED.)
## "Legal Developments in Urban Education"
*Education and Urban Society*, 3, 3 (May 1971): 373-78

This article discusses Amish parents who, because of religious tenets, refused to enroll their children in high school, and so violated the Wisconsin *Compulsory School Attendance Law*. The court ruled the law unconstitutional as it applied to these parents, opening issues for current community control. For a related book, see Albert N. Keim, *Compulsory Education and the Amish: The Right Not to be Modern* (Boston: Beacon Press, 1975).

STOLTZFUS, VICTOR
"Reward and Sanction: The Adaptive Continuity of Amish Life"
MQR, 51, 4 (October 1977): 308-18

Stoltzfus examines a number of rewards and sanctions of Amish life to see how they contribute to its continuity and adaptation within the larger social system of contemporary American society. Rewards include religion, mutual aid, pleasure, family and work, and focused identity. Sanctions include admonishment, accusation in church, and temporary and total excommunication. This article is quite general in nature as it seeks to explain the continuity of Amish society. The section entitled "Rewards and their Impact on the Life Cycle" is perceptive. Here Stoltzfus shows that during early adulthood there is a high "cost" compared to rewards, as opposed to later adulthood where "cost" is lower than the cumulative rewards.

THOMPSON, WILLIAM E.
"The Oklahoma Amish: Survival of an Ethnic Subculture"
Ethnicity, 8, 4 (December 1981): 476-87

This article focuses on ways that an Oklahoma Amish community creates, defines, maintains and manipulates various symbols in an effort to deal with five problems threatening the survival of Amish life: disenchanted youth, inroads of modernity, tourism, vanishing farmland and governmental intervention.

WITTMER, JOE
"Cultural Violence and Twentieth Century Progress"
Practical Anthropology, 18 (1971): 146-55

This article describes the cultural, economic and social pressures facing the Old Order Amish, focusing on conditions in the late 1960s. The distinctive, traditional and agricultural lifestyle of the Amish contrasts and conflicts in several respects with the lifestyle of the surrounding majoring culture. Since the Amish oppose the kind of education children receive in secular public schools, they may refuse to send their children there and face conflicts with the authorities on that matter. The pacifism of the Amish also makes them victims of harassment, especially in wartime, an experience reinforced by the refusal of many Amish to fight in the Vietnam war. Amish conscientious objectors often perform alternative services, but such tasks expose them to societal influences which many cannot handle and which many seek to avoid, preferring imprisonment to any kind of service. The Amish also suffer from economic and social pressures, as their beliefs do not permit them to accept government assistance or to take full advantage of modern technology. In some cases, resentment by non-Amish translates into artificial economic pressures on the Amish. However, since this article was written, some of the advantages of the labour-intensive way of farming of the Amish have become apparent; greater continuity in their methods and a system of mutual aid helps them weather economic storms. Non-Amish resentments and cultural hostility often express themselves in violence and harassment. These factors have contributed to a growing migration of Amish to South American countries that offer them opportunities they lack in the USA.

WITTMER, JOE
"Be Ye a Peculiar People"
*Contemporary Education*, 54, 3 (1983): 179-83

The author discusses his experience of attending school as an Amish child during the time when America was at war with Germany. Offered are five suggestions for the public school teacher who has Amish children in the classroom.

WITTMER, JOE and ARNOLD MOSER
"Counseling the Older Amish Child"
*Elementary School Guidance and Counseling*, 8, 4 (May 1974): 263-70

The author describes the cultural heritage of the Amish and the resulting difficulties that Amish children have in public schools. Wittmer also discusses implications for counsellors.

WITTMER, JOE
"Perceived Parent-child Relationships: A Comparison Between Amish and Non-Amish Young Adults"
*Journal of Cross-Cultural Psychology*, 2, 1 (March 1971): 87-94

The parent-child relations questionnaire was administered to twenty-five Amish and twenty-five non-Amish late teenagers. Amish parents were seen as "less rejecting, less neglecting, less casual, less likely to reward directly, and less likely to use symbolic methods of punishment." Amish fathers were seen as more loving than non-Amish fathers. Results are discussed in light of the Amish culture.

YODER, PATON (ED.)
"Baptism as an Issue in the Amish Division of the Nineteenth Century: Deacon John Stoltzfus"
*MQR*, 53 (1979): 306-23

Baptism, its meaning, but also increasingly its mode, has always been a topic of significance to descendants of the Anabaptists even when they have denied it a theological primacy commensurate with the opprobrious nickname. The author finds it one of several issues which helped to propel nineteenth-century Amish toward their painful division of the 1870s. Yoder has recovered Deacon John Stoltzfus' short treatise on baptism, read at one of the *diener Versammlungen* (meeting of ministers) and published in their protocol in 1868. Stoltzfus tried to use his formulations on the disputed issue to mediate between the two groups that were drifting apart — to no avail.

# Appendices

# Appendix A

## Church Member Profile II

Mennonites and Brethren in Christ now know more about what has happened to their people in the last eighteen years, 1972-1990.

"Church Member Profile II" follows up a similar survey done in 1972, and published in *Anabaptists Four Centuries Later* by J. Howard Kauffman and Leland D. Harder (Herald Press, 1975). All five denominations that cooperated in the 1972 survey participated in the current one: the Brethren in Christ Church, Evangelical Mennonite Church, General Conference Mennonite Church, Mennonite Brethren Church and the Mennonite Church.

Project co-ordination was carried by an administrative committee functioning under the auspices of the Institute of Mennonite Studies of Associated Mennonite Biblical Seminaries, Elkhart, Indiana. Committee chairman is Leo Driedger, University of Manitoba, Winnipeg.

A primary purpose of the current survey, says the project director J. Howard Kauffman, "is to identify trends in the beliefs, attitudes and behaviour of Mennonite and Brethren in Christ church members."

Compared with 1972, Kauffman says, the new data show that:

Farm residence among Mennonites declined from 34 to 23 percent; urban residence increased from 35 to 48 percent.

Farmers as a percentage of all males were 23 percent in 1972, 14 percent in 1989.

The number of married women employed full or part time increased from 38 to 52 percent.

The number of persons per household decreased from 4.5 to 3.2.

Scores have eroded slightly on items measuring adherence to pacifism, and there is a somewhat greater acceptance of non-combatant service in the military.

Scores on the race relations scale have improved.

Acceptance has increased for divorce, remarriage of divorcees, moderate drinking and social dancing.

Attitudes opposing abortion, homosexual acts and smoking have strengthened.

The proportion of respondents favouring the ordination of women rose from seventeen to 44 percent. Church members are polarized as to how extensively women should enter church leadership roles.

Howard Kauffman and Leo Driedger are recording and interpreting the principal findings of the survey. Chapters will include findings on modernization, secularization and assimilation among Mennonites. The project's associate director, Leland D. Harder, North Newton, Kansas, is using the data to write a study book for use in church or school groups. Driedger, Harder and Kauffman will write articles for journals.

"I hope that congregations and church leaders will study the results as one way to see what is happening in our faith family and to reflect on what Christian faithfulness means for us in today's world," says Richard A. Kauffman, director of the Institute of Mennonite Studies and a member of the administrative committee.

The survey findings are drawn from a data base of 3,083 or 70 percent of the eligible sample, in 153 congregations. Howard Kauffman noted that the 1989 survey included some topics not covered in 1972 and about two-thirds of the original questions.

The project has been made possible by funding from the five co-operating denominations plus grants from Mennonite Mutual Aid Association, Goshen, Indiana; Mennonite Central Committee, Akron, Pennsylvania; Brotherhood Mutual Insurance Company of Fort Wayne, Indiana; and the Schowalter Foundation, Newton, Kansas.

The "Church Member Profile II" will be published under the title, *The Mennonite Mosaic, Identity and Modernization*, by J. Howard Kauffman and Leo Driedger (Scottdale, Pa., and Waterloo, Ont.: Herald Press, 1991).

# Appendix B

## The Major Mennonite and Amish Research Libraries and Archives: Canada and the United States

The Mennonite libraries have shifted from their early focus on Reformation history to North American church and commuity life and, more recently, the collections received sociological data and documents. The largest library is the collection at Goshen College (Indiana), with special emphasis on the Mennonites and Amish of Swiss origins. The Bethel College (Kansas) is also a major collection, with specialization on Mennonites of Russian origin. At Conrad Grebel College, Waterloo, Ontario, two sociologists, J. W. Fretz and C. Redekop, have built up the sociological materials and both have given their extensive papers on the colonies in Paraguay and Mexico to form the definitive collection on these unique communities.

All of these libraries have full-time staff and considerable space, regularly expanded:

Bethel College Mennonite Library and Archives, North Newton, Kansas 67117

Canadian Mennonite Bible College Library, 600 Shaftsbury Blvd., Winnipeg, Manitoba R3P 0M4

Conrad Grebel College Historical Library, Waterloo, Ontario N2L 3G6

Eastern Mennonite College, Menno Simons Library, Harrisonburg, Virginia 22801

Associated Mennonite Biblical Seminaries' Library, Elkhart, Indiana 46514

Mennonite Brethren Historical Library, Tabor College, Hillsboro, Kansas 67063

Mennonite Brethren Historical Library, Fresno Pacific College, Fresno, California 93702

Lancaster Mennonite Historical Society, 2215 Millstream Road, Lancaster, Pennsylvania 17602

Mennonite Brethren Historical Library, 1-169 Riverton Avenue, Winnipeg, Manitoba R2G 2E5

Mennonite Historical Library, Bluffton College, Bluffton, Ohio 45817

Mennonite Historical Library, Goshen College, Goshen, Indiana 46526

Amish Historical Library, R.R. 4, Aylmer, Ontario N5H 2R3

## The Main Mennonite, Hutterite and Amish Bookstores in North America

Fellowship Bookcentre, 302 Kennedy, Winnipeg, Manitoba R3B 2M6

Provident Bookstore, Campus Court, 150 University Avenue, Waterloo, Ontario N2L 3E4

Provident Bookstore, 165 Pittsburgh Street, Scottdale, Pennsylvania 15683

Mennonite Brethren Bookstore, Hillsboro, Kansas 67063

Faith and Life Bookstore, 724 Main Street, Newton, Kansas 47114

The Amish Historical Society Bookstore, R.R. 4, Aylmer, Ontario N5H 2R3

Plough Publishing House, Woodcrest Bruderhof, Hutterian Brethren, Rifton, New York 12471

# Mennonite Yearbooks and Handbooks with Detailed Names of Leaders, Names of Congregations and Organizations Throughout North America and the World

Mennonite World Handbook. Mennonites in Global Witness, 1990. 465 Gundersen Drive, Suite 200, Carol Stream, Illinois 60188.

The most detailed compendium of information available on Mennonites in every continent.

Mennonite Yearbook, 1990. Mennonite Publishing House, Scottdale, Pennsylvania 15683-1999.

Handbook of Information. General Conference Mennonite Church, 1990. 718 Main Street, Newton, Kansas 67114-0347.

# Appendix C

## Special Collections of Amish Materials

1 *The Nancy Gaines Collection*
1655 Mannheim Pike
Lancaster, Pa., 17601
A large collection of books, dissertations and theses written in English and dealing with Amish faith and life.

2 *Heritage Historical Library*
Route 4,
Aylmer, Ontario N5H 2R3
The Library, filing and displaying Amish materials in seventy-three categories, is now the definitive collection in North America. The eleven principal categories are: Fraktur art, genealogies, Anabaptist testaments, Martyrs Mirror, hymnals, Froschauer (1524-89) Bibles, prayerbooks, tourism, education (the largest category in the library), documents and Old Order Mennonites.

There are sixty-two additional parts of the collection, with one covering sociological textbooks treatment of the Amish:

12 Admonitory Writings
13 Agriculture and Farm Machinery
14 Almanacs and Yearbooks
15 Amish Aid Plans
16 Amish Christian Church (Berne, Indiana)
17 Amish Division of 1693
18 Amish in Court (Social Security, lawsuits, Canada Pension Plan, etc.)
19 Amish-Mennonite Conferences
20 Amish Ministers' Meetings
21 Artistic Portrayals of the Amish
22 Autobiographies and Biographies
23 Beachy Amish Church
24 Bibles and Bible Storybooks
25 Buggies (licensing, SMV emblems, etc.)
26 Childhood and Young Adulthood
27 Christmas, History and Celebration of
28 Civilian Public Service in World War II
29 Conservative Amish Mennonite Church
30 Cookbooks
31 Courtship and Marriage
32 Devotional Materials
33 Doctrinal Works (Menno Simons, etc.)
34 Dolls and Crafts
35 Egly Amish (Defenseless Mennonites)
36 Excommunication and Shunning
37 Fictional Accounts (novels, plays, etc.)
38 Foreign Articles and Books

39 Fuel and Energy Studies
40 Funeral Handkerchiefs
41 General Amish Studies
42 General Mennonite Studies
43 German Language Studies
44 Health Practices and Medical Studies
45 Horses, Problems Related to Travel with
46 Immigration to North America
47 Iron Curtain Ministries
48 I-W Services in the 1950s and 1960s
49 Menno Sauder Collection
50 Milk Production and Shipping Problems
51 Music Studies
52 "New Amish" (Apostolic Christian Church)
53 Non-Conformity in Christian Living
54 "One True Church" Individuals and Groups
55 Peace and Non-Resistance
56 Pennsylvania German Dialect
57 Pennsylvania Germans
58 Periodicals
59 Publishers (Raber, Pathway, Kinsinger, etc.)
60 Quilting
61 Religious Fiction by Amish Authors
62 Settlement Directories and Maps
63 Settlement Histories (current and extinct)
64 Shops and Manufacturers
65 Show Towels and Samplers
66 "Sleeping Preachers"
67 Sociology Textbooks Treating the Amish
68 Somewhat Related Groups
69 Stove Manufacturers
70 Surnames (current and extinct)
71 Tobacco, Attitudes Toward and Cultivation
72 Travel by Amish
73 Voting, Attitudes Toward

# Indexes

# Name Index

Adams, James Luther, xiii
Aherne, Consuelo Maria, 7
Ainlay, Stephen, 54
Allen, Gordon, 157
Anderson, Alan, 2, 33, 54
Anderson, Bengt, 118
Appavoo, David, 38, 55
Arnett, Ronald, 55
Arnold, Eberhard and Emmy, xi, 115
Aronson, Lisa, 56
Asheton-Smith, Marilyn, 12, 53, 56
Augilar, William, 171

Baar, Ellen, 56
Barker, Richard, 56
Baum, Ruth, 116
Beachy, Alvin, 149
Bechford, James, 3
Beilharz, Carol, 170
Bender, Sue, 140
Bender, Titus, 39
Bender, Urie, 30
Bennett, John, 119, 120
Berger, Peter, 145
Bernstein, Barbara, 158
Bibby, Reginald, 2
Bird, Michael, 12, 57
Boldt, Edward, 7, 57, 115, 120, 121, 122, 123, 129
Boynton, Linda, 12
Brattrue, Audrey, 126
Brednach, Rolf, 13
Bresson, Rebecca, 149
Brown, Dale, 57
Brown, Peggy, 58
Brubacher, Paul, 40
Brunk, Conrad, 58
Brunk, George III, 31
Bryer, Kathleen, 159
Buchman, Frederick, 149
Burkholder, J. Lawrence, 13
Burnet, Jean, 13
Burns, Joan, 71

Cain, Seymour, 3
Carlisle, W. J. 46, 59
Cartmel, Daryl, 150
Cavan, Ruth Shoule, 123
Chesebro, Scott, 40

Christiansen, Howard, 59
Claassen, Constance, 49
Cohen, Paul, 59
Coleman, Bill, 141
Collum, Danny, 159
Conyers, Claudie, 3
Cooney, Donald, 41
Corbett, Bill, 60, 139
Coyle, Jean, 150
Cressman, Arnold, 26
Cronk, Sandra, 151, 159
Currie, Raymond, 60, 81

Dalzell, Timothy, 42
Das, Man Singh, 118
Davis, Kenneth, xiv, 41
Davis, Winston, 3
De Lisle, David, 42
Denlinger, Martha, 13
De Vries, George, 160
Dickey, Dale, 43
Dill, Vicki, 60
Driedger, Leo, 2, 9, 14, 15, 54, 56, 62, 63, 64, 93, 160, 161, 178
Dyck, Cornelius, 3, 10, 15
Dyck, E. F., 65
Dueck, Abe, 35
Deuck, Al, 65, 98
Dueck, Kathryn, 103
Durkheim, Emile, xix, 13

Ediger, Elmer, 65
Ediger, Marlow, 66, 141, 154, 161-62
Eliade, Mircea, ix, xvi
Engbrecht, Dennis, 43
Enniger, Werner, 145
Ens, Gerhard, 114
Entwhistle, Doris, 162
Epp, Frank, 4, 16, 17, 66
Epp-Tiessen, Esther, 16, 44
Ericksen, Eugene, 163
Ericksen, Julia, 163

Fast, Darrell, 44
Felstead, Alan, 45
Fisher, Sara, 46, 142
Fishman, Andrea, 157
Flint, Joanne, 17
Foster, Thomas, 163-64

# Subject Index

acculturation, xvii, 20, 29
adaptive community, 52, 88, 175
adolescents, 95, 97, 158
adoption-diffusion model, 170
agriculture, 4, 42, 58, 135, 163
Alberta, 13, 60, 68, 80, 87
alcohol, 60, 81
aligning actions, 122
alternative culture, 160
alternative service, 27, 49
Altona, 17
altruism, 77, 109
America, 43, 66, 153, 155
Amish, xvii, 10, 13, 29, 103, 137-71
Amish photography, 141
Amish school, 142
Amish socialization, 144
Amish society, 143
Anabaptists, x, 36, 38, 42, 48, 58
anthropology, 18, 28
art, 12, 28, 56
Ascuncion Centre for
    Anthropological Study, 90
assimilation, 74, 93
authority, 37

baptism, 176
bargaining and opposition models,
    145
Beachy Amish, 149, 174
belief-orthodoxy, 69-70
believers church, xiii
bipolar mosaic, 104
Bolivia, 80
bookstores, 180
boundaries, 53, 54, 61, 74, 75, 123,
    153
Brethren in Christ, 75
Bruderhof, 114
business, 24

Canada, 4, 9, 16, 17, 22, 68, 86
Canadian Encyclopedia, 4
Canadian House of Commons, 47
Canadian laws, 6, 47
Canadian religion, 2
care, 155
census, 102
change, 18, 71, 157

charter, 145
Chassidim and Kibbutzim, 173
Chicago and Winnipeg, 62
child socialization, 144
children, 44, 56, 71, 155
church and state, 6, 47, 66, 84
church history method, 109
church member profile, 178, 179
church organization and polity
class, social, xiv, 99
colonization, 28-29, 88
colony division, 132
communal education, 135
communal sect, 119
communal studies centre, 6
communes, 40, 68, 120, 123, 125
community, 66
compulsory education, 145, 166
confessions, 83
conflict, 45, 48, 55, 56
conformity, 148
Conrad Grebel College, v
conscientious objector, 45, 48, 78, 84,
    96
conserver, frugal society, 164
continuity, 18, 51
controlled acculturation, xviii
cooperative movement, 43
costume, 12
counter culture, xv
creeds, 7
*Crestview Heights*, 18
critical identity frame, 26
cult, xvi
culture, 18, 32
cultural identity, 23
cultural transmission, 19
cultural violence, 175

death and dying, 118, 136, 159
defection, 116, 117, 129
demography, 107, 123, 125, 165
denomination, 23
dialect, 64, 104, 134
discipleship, 33
displacement of indigenous people,
    89
dissent and deviance, 45, 48, 49
divorce, 64

191